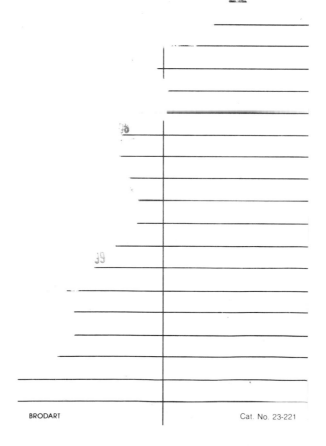

This timely collection of essays offers one of the first serious efforts to examine the end of the Cold War, its meaning and implications. The book presents the thinking of leading historians, political scientists, policy analysts, and commentators from the United States, Great Britain, Germany, France, Norway, and the former Soviet Union. Together they discuss such important issues as the origins of the Cold War, its ideological and geopolitical sources, the cost of that epic conflict, its influence on American life and institutions, its winners and losers.

The End of the Cold War

The End of the Cold War
Its Meaning and Implications

Edited by
MICHAEL J. HOGAN
The Ohio State University

CAMBRIDGE
UNIVERSITY PRESS

Published by the Press Syndicate of the University of Cambridge
The Pitt Building, Trumpington Street, Cambridge CB2 1RP
40 West 20th Street, New York, NY 10011-4211, USA
10 Stamford Road, Oakleigh, Victoria 3166, Australia

© Cambridge University Press 1992

First published 1992

Printed in the United States of America

Library of Congress Cataloging-in-Publication Data
The End of the Cold War : its meaning and implications / Michael J. Hogan, editor.
p.   cm.
Includes bibliographical references (p.   ) and index.
ISBN 0-521-43128-X (hardback). – ISBN 0-521-43731-8 (paperback)
1. World politics – 1989–   2. Cold War.   I. Hogan, Michael J., 1943–   .
D860.E56   1992
327'.09'045 – dc20   92-4603
                                                                              CIP

A catalog record for this book is available from the British Library

ISBN 0-521-43128-X hardback
ISBN 0-521-43731-8 paperback

To
Friends and Colleagues
in the
Society for Historians of American Foreign Relations

Contents

Preface

Although the end of the Cold War is widely regarded as a development of enormous importance, its significance has yet to be the subject of serious commentary among scholars with an interest in modern diplomacy. I reached this conclusion in my capacity as editor of *Diplomatic History,* the journal of record for specialists in the field, and following conversations with a number of colleagues here and abroad. All agreed that the journal should turn its attention to the subject as an aid to scholars, teachers, and general readers with an interest in diplomatic and national security affairs. With this idea in mind, I began to solicit the essays that follow, almost all of which first appeared in *Diplomatic History.*

My goal was to recruit contributions from distinguished specialists who represented different fields of study, different points of view, and in some cases different countries. I gave all of the contributors the same general instructions. I asked each of them to write a "think-piece" on the end of the Cold War, its meaning and implications. I described the piece I had in mind as a longer, more historically informed version of the kind of essay that appears on the editorial pages of the best newspapers. Although I suggested certain topics that might be taken up, I basically gave the contributors carte blanche to discuss whatever they considered important.

These instructions ran the risk of producing a smorgasbord of unconnected contributions—and, in fact, each of the essays has unique features. Taken as a whole, however, they tend to cluster around issues of undeniable importance, most of which I have tried to underscore in the introduction to this volume. Because the authors were not required to burden their essays with footnotes, except to cite sources of quotes in their texts, I have appended a brief, selective bibliography to the volume. Readers should look to this bibliography rather than to the essays for additional literature on the Cold War.

The authors prepared their essays in late 1991, and few changes were possible when I read the page proofs in February of the next year. As a result, the authors could not take account of the most recent literature or the most recent developments. Nevertheless, their essays help us to wrestle in a serious way with what the end of the Cold War means not only for the future but also for the way we view the past. In this sense, they aid us as citizens and scholars alike, for which I extend my sincere appreciation to the authors who have collaborated with me in this project.

Thanks are due as well to the Society for Historians of American Foreign Relations (SHAFR), which sponsors *Diplomatic History* and which granted permission to reprint the essays first published in that journal. I also wish to thank The Ohio State University for its support of *Diplomatic History,* and the journal's staff, notably Dr. Mary Ann Heiss, T. Darryl Fox, and Jozef Ostyn, for their aid in this project. Earnings from the sale of this book are being contributed to SHAFR in support of *Diplomatic History.* SHAFR has established a fund for this purpose in the name of Armin Rappaport, the first editor of the journal. Naturally, I invite others to contribute to the Rappaport Fund. I especially want to thank the authors in this volume who made their own contribution by waiving the usual republication fees.

This volume is dedicated to friends and colleagues in the Society for Historians of American Foreign Relations, and to the readers of *Diplomatic History.* Their loyal support and helpful advice have made my job as editor very rewarding.

MJH
Columbus, Ohio

The Authors

GAR ALPEROVITZ, author of *Atomic Diplomacy: Hiroshima and Potsdam* (1965), is a fellow at the Institute for Policy Studies and president of the National Center for Economic Alternatives. His collaborator, KAI BIRD, is a research associate at the Institute for Policy Studies and author of *The Chairman: John J. McCloy and the Making of the American Establishment* (forthcoming).

DENISE ARTAUD is a senior research fellow at the National Center of Scientific Research in France and also teaches at the Institut d'Etudes Politiques de Paris. She is the author of several books, including *La Fin de l'Innocence, les Etats-Unis de Wilson à Reagan* (1985); and is coeditor with Lawrence S. Kaplan and Mark R. Rubin of *Dien Bien Phu and the Crisis of Franco-American Relations* (1990). She is presently finishing a book on the United States and Nicaragua and will be conducting a seminar at the Military School of Coetquidan.

RICHARD J. BARNET is a senior fellow at the Institute for Policy Studies. He received his A.B. and J.D. from Harvard University, and is the author of twelve books on American foreign policy and the international economy, including *The Roots of War* (1972); *Global Reach* (1974); and *The Rockets' Red Glare* (1990). He is currently working on a new book on the impact of globalization.

NOAM CHOMSKY is Institute Professor in the Department of Linguistics and Philosophy at MIT. He has written and lectured widely on international affairs and U.S. foreign policy, with a particular focus on U.S.-Third World relations. His recent books on these topics include *Manufacturing Consent* (with Edward S. Herman, 1988); *Necessary Illusions* (1989); and *Deterring Democracy* (1991).

BRUCE CUMINGS, professor of East Asian and international history at the University of Chicago, is the author of a two-volume study entitled *The Origins of the Korean War* (1981 and 1990). The first volume won the John K. Fairbank Prize of the American Historical Association and the Harry S. Truman Book Award. The second volume received the Quincy Wright Prize of the International Studies Association. He served as the principal historical consultant to Thames Television/PBS for a six-hour documentary entitled *Korea: The Unknown War*. His latest book is *War and Television* (1992).

ALEXEI FILITOV serves at the Institute of World History in Moscow, where he is currently editing a monograph on the historiography of the Cold War. A graduate of the history faculty of Moscow State University in 1960, he defended his dissertation on the historiography of the Potsdam agreement in 1974. He is the author of a series of works on the postwar peace settlement, especially the German settlement.

JOHN LEWIS GADDIS, Distinguished Professor of History and director of the Contemporary History Institute at Ohio University, has served as Visiting Professor of Strategy at the Naval War College, Bicentennial Professor of American Studies at the University of Helsinki, and Visiting Professor of War and Peace at Princeton University. He is currently president of the Society for Historians of American Foreign Relations. His first book, *The United States and the Origins of the Cold War* (1972), won the Bancroft Prize. His other works include *Russia, the Soviet Union, and the United States* (1978; 2d ed., 1990); *Strategies of Containment* (1982); *The Long Peace* (1987); and *The United States and the End of the Cold War* (1992).

RAYMOND L. GARTHOFF, a retired diplomat, is a senior fellow at the Brookings Institution. A specialist in international relations, especially U.S.-Soviet relations, he has been a lecturer at George Washington University and Johns Hopkins University School of Advanced International Studies. He is the author of *Détente and Confrontation: American-Soviet Relations from Nixon to Reagan* (1985) as well as many other studies, and is now writing *The Great Transition: American-Soviet Relations and the End of the Cold War*.

MICHAEL J. HOGAN is professor of history at The Ohio State University and editor of *Diplomatic History*. He is also the author of *Informal Entente: The Private Structure of Cooperation in Anglo-American Eco-*

nomic Diplomacy, 1918–1928 (1977) and *The Marshall Plan: America, Britain, and the Reconstruction of Western Europe, 1947–1952* (1987). He is the recipient of the Stuart L. Bernath Lecture and Book Prizes of the Society for Historians of American Foreign Relations, the Quincy Wright Book Prize of the International Studies Association, and the George Louis Beer Prize of the American Historical Association.

ROBERT JERVIS is Adlai Stevenson Professor of International Relations and a member of the Institute of War and Peace Studies at Columbia University. His books include *The Logic of Images in International Relations* (1970, 2d ed., 1989); *Perception and Misperception in International Politics* (1978); and *The Meaning of Nuclear Weapons* (1989), which won the Gravemeyer Prize for Contributions to World Order.

NIKKI R. KEDDIE is professor of history at the University of California, Los Angeles, and editor of the journal *Contention*. A specialist in the history of the Near East, she is the recipient of numerous awards and fellowships. Her recent publications include *The Iranian Revolution and the Islamic Republic* (1986) and the coedited volume *Neither East Nor West* (1990).

BRUCE R. KUNIHOLM is professor of public policy studies and history, chair of the Department of Public Policy Studies, and director of the Institute of Policy Sciences and Public Affairs at Duke University. A former member of the Department of State's Policy Planning Staff, he has written about Great Power politics and diplomacy in the Near East, U.S. policy toward the Palestine question, and U.S. policy in the Persian Gulf. He is currently working on a history of U.S.-Turkish relations in the post-World War II era.

WALTER LAFEBER is Noll Professor of American History at Cornell University. He is the author of numerous books and articles, including *The New Empire: An Interpretation of American Expansion, 1860–1898* (1963), which won the Albert J. Beveridge Prize of the American Historical Association. His recent publications include *The American Age: U.S. Foreign Policy at Home and Abroad since 1750* (1989); and *America, Russia, and the Cold War*, 6th ed. (1990).

GEIR LUNDESTAD is director of the Norwegian Nobel Institute and secretary of the Nobel peace prize committee. Educated in Norway, he has been a fellow at Harvard University and at the Woodrow Wilson

International Center for Scholars. He is the author, most recently, of *The American "Empire" and Other Studies of U.S. Foreign Policy in a Comparative Perspective* (1990) and *East, West, North, South: Major Developments in International Relations, 1945–1990* (rev. ed., 1991).

ERNEST R. MAY is Charles Warren Professor of History at Harvard University. He is past president of the Society for Historians of American Foreign Relations and currently American chairperson for the multilateral Nuclear History Program. The author of numerous books and articles, his most recent work (with Richard E. Neustadt), *Thinking in Time: The Uses of History for Decisionmakers* (1986), received the Gravemeyer Prize for Contributions to World Order.

JOHN MUELLER, professor of political science at the University of Rochester, is an op-ed columnist for the *Wall Street Journal* and the *Los Angeles Times*. The author of *War, Presidents, and Public Opinion* (1973) and *Retreat from Doomsday: The Obsolescence of Major War* (1989), he is currently working on projects dealing with the rise of liberalism and with American public opinion during the Gulf war.

DAVID REYNOLDS is a fellow of Christ's College, Cambridge University. He was awarded the Stuart L. Bernath Book Prize for *The Creation of the Anglo-American Alliance, 1937–1941: A Study in Competitive Co-operation* (1981). His other books are *An Ocean Apart: The Relationship between Britain and America in the Twentieth Century* (1988); *Britannia Overruled: British Policy and World Power in the Twentieth Century* (1991); and, as editor and contributor, *The Origins of the Cold War in Europe: International Perspectives* (1992).

HERMANN-JOSEF RUPIEPER is professor of modern history at Marburg University (Germany). He is the author of *The Cuno Government and Reparations, 1922–23* (1979); *Arbeiter und Angestellte im Industrialisierungsprozess, 1837–1914* (1981); and *Der besetzte Verbundete: Die amerikanische Deutschlandpolitik, 1949–1955* (1991).

ARTHUR SCHLESINGER, JR., former special assistant to President John F. Kennedy, is Schweitzer Professor of the Humanities at the City University of New York. He is the author of many books and articles touching upon American political, intellectual, and diplomatic history and the recipient of numerous awards and prizes, including the Pulitzer Prize for history (1946) and for biography (1966).

RONALD STEEL, professor of international relations at the University of Southern California, is a regular contributor to the *New York Review of Books* and contributing editor of the *New Republic*. The recipient of numerous awards, including the Bancroft Prize, the National Book Critics Circle Award, and the American Book Award, he is the author of *Pax Americana* (1967); *Imperialists and Other Heroes* (1971); *Walter Lippmann and the American Century* (1980); and other works.

SAMUEL F. WELLS, JR., is deputy director of the Woodrow Wilson International Center for Scholars in Washington, DC. He has written articles on NSC 68 and the origins of massive retaliation, as well as numerous essays on contemporary issues of European security.

"... and it came to pass, when the people heard the sound of the trumpet, and the people shouted with a great shout, that the wall fell down flat."

Joshua 6:20

1

Introduction

MICHAEL J. HOGAN

The destruction of the Berlin Wall in late 1989 marked, in a symbolic way, the beginning of the end of the Cold War, at least insofar as that era in modern history is defined as an ideological and geopolitical struggle between the Soviet Union and the United States, between Russia and the West. That great event, which set the stage for the reunification of Germany and the end of the Soviet empire in Eastern Europe, had earlier been preceded by the reforms of *glasnost* and *perestroika* that Premier Mikhail S. Gorbachev had begun to engineer in the Soviet Union. Taken together, these astonishing developments became a cause for great celebration, especially in Europe and the United States. But history happens quickly these days. What most would consider the news of a lifetime now travels from the headlines to the backpage before we can fully appreciate its significance.

After the events of 1989, the focus of media attention and public policy shifted dramatically to developments in the Middle East, notably the Gulf war, to the demise of the Soviet Union, and to the "New World" that President George Bush and others hope to build on the ashes of the old order. There has not been a lot of time for careful reflection on what the end of the Cold War means to governments and people around the world. To be sure, editorial writers continue to fill the press with commentary on different aspects of the subject, much of it very incisive. Most seem to agree that the eclipse of the Soviet empire marks a decisive shift in the global balance of power, particularly an end to the era of bipolarity. Some have predicted a new era of unipolarity; others have

Michael J. Hogan

envisioned a multipolar world; still others have addressed any one
of a number of issues also taken up in this volume.

The period since 1989, however, has not seen the publication of
much scholarly commentary on the end of the Cold War, its meaning and implications for the way we view the past and foresee the
future. There has not been an outpouring of scholarly monographs
and articles on the subject, nor the convening of even a fair number of professional conferences.[1] This is not for lack of interest.
The end of the Cold War invariably emerges as a subject of great
interest and concern in less formal settings. Historians, political
scientists, and policy analysts, particularly those who teach the
Cold War or whose research deals with aspects of this era, feel a
special compulsion to come to grips with how the events since
1989 might influence their views of the past and predictions for
the future. This became clear to me when I began planning for the
publication of this volume. Originally intended as a symposium in
a professional journal, and first published in that forum, I initially
expected essays from seven or so scholars interested in the topic.
My experience as a journal editor told me to solicit pieces from
more than twice that number, however, on the assumption that
most would be unable to contribute. Imagine my surprise when
almost all of them agreed to participate, and a couple of others,
who learned of the enterprise indirectly, asked to join the list as
well! These were very busy scholars, among the most distinguished
people in their fields. Yet they clearly felt a strong need to address
what we all consider to be an important subject.

This common need did not translate into shared opinions, as
readers who turn the following pages will discover. The scholars
whose essays appear in this volume include historians as well as
political scientists and policy analysts. They include Americans and
non-Americans, conservatives and liberals, experts in American
history and diplomacy as well as area specialists. They were free
to pursue their own interests, of course, and their essays naturally
reveal different concerns—some with the superpowers of the Cold
War, some with Europe, some with the Third World. Even though
most of the authors share an interest in certain issues of obvious

---

1   Some of the recent works available on the subject are noted in the brief bibliography to
    this volume.

importance, they often interpret these issues differently and reach conflicting conclusions. The purpose of this introduction is to briefly outline the main topics of concern and the differences involved.

One issue of importance, especially to historians, has to do with the origins and sources of the Soviet-American confrontation. On this issue, the contributors split. Some of them see the conflict rooted in efforts by both countries to fill the power vacuums left by the Second World War. This is the view of Arthur Schlesinger and of John Lewis Gaddis, who argues that initiatives such as the Marshall Plan and NATO saved Western Europe from Stalinism in the years after 1947. Walter LaFeber, on the other hand, traces aspects of the struggle back to an earlier pattern of anticommunism and interventionism in American foreign policy. There are similar differences over the sources of the confrontation. John Mueller interprets the Cold War as essentially an ideological battle that ended with the collapse of communism in the Soviet Union and elsewhere. This part of Mueller's contribution parallels the argument of Francis Fukuyama in his celebrated essay "The End of History?"[2] The same can be said of the contributions by Schlesinger and Gaddis. Gaddis echoes the Truman Doctrine in concluding that the Cold War in Europe was really a battle between alternative ways of life, between freedom and autocracy. Schlesinger sees it as a "fundamental debate" between liberalism and communism. This debate gave the Cold War its moral intensity, both he and Gaddis agree, and was finally resolved with the defeat of authoritarianism and the triumph of liberalism.

Other contributors take a different point of view. According to Ronald Steel, ideology had a greater influence on American than on Soviet foreign policy, particularly the ideology of anticommunism, which tended to globalize the Cold War when linked to the strategy of containment in the Third World. Raymond Garthoff, while conceding an ideological dimension, also sees the Cold War in traditional, geostrategic terms. Samuel Wells takes a somewhat similar view in an essay that surveys the role of nuclear weapons in the Cold War. Much the same is true of Alexei Filitov, our contributor from the former Soviet Union. He sees the Cold War

2   Francis Fukuyama, "The End of History?" *National Interest* 16 (Summer 1989): 3–18.

not as an ideological battle primarily but as a military and geopolitical struggle that actually stifled honest debate over the benefits
of rival political and economic systems. Like Richard Barnet, Filitov believes that the Cold War strengthened the hand of Kremlin
hard-liners and legitimated Communist control. To Barnet, the result was a prolonged struggle between East and West that could
have ended sooner had the United States been less confrontational
and more inclined to negotiate. To Filitov, the struggle actually
slowed a historic trend toward political democracy and market
economies, both in the Soviet Union and elsewhere. It is fair to say
that Filitov, and to some extent LaFeber, sees the end of the Cold
War marking a return to history, not its end: With that great struggle
in the background, it is possible for the Russians and others to
resume the march toward political and economic liberties that the
Cold War interrupted.

LaFeber and Bruce Cumings also make the point that international relations over the last half-century involved more than a
confrontation between the United States and the Soviet Union. The
period witnessed important struggles between the United States
and Europe, for example, and between the developed and developing worlds. These and other struggles began before the Cold
War, LaFeber notes, and will to some extent continue in its aftermath. His point is obvious: The end of the Cold War does not
constitute a complete break with the past; nor does it mark
the end of international competition, perhaps not even the end of
Russian-American differences and ideological conflict.

Denise Artaud drives home a similar point. Although not dis-
counting the ideological aspects of the Cold War, she also sees it
as a clash of interests that centered primarily on Europe and that
might continue after the collapse of communism. Communism is
dying, she concedes, but it is not yet clear that liberal capitalism
will take its place, especially in Eastern Europe and the former
Soviet Union. Regional, religious, and ethnic strife in these areas,
together with persistent and severe economic difficulties, could lead
instead to the emergence of authoritarian regimes, and thus to a
resumption of the age-old struggle between democracy and totalitarianism. In this sense, Artaud clearly considers it too soon to
celebrate the end of history, meaning the end of fundamental ideo-

logical debate. She prefers to see the Cold War not as a unique ideological battle between communism and liberalism, but as one episode in a longer and perhaps continuing struggle between freedom and enslavement, democracy and totalitarianism.

If the contributors do not see eye-to-eye regarding the origins and sources of the Cold War, neither do they agree when it comes to answering two of the leading questions of the day: Who won the Cold War and how? In his essay on nuclear weapons in the Cold War, Wells goes beyond the familiar contention that American military power helped to deter a Soviet threat. He comes closer than any of the contributors to arguing that the defense buildup under President Ronald Reagan finally led the Soviets to cry "uncle." It forced them to acknowledge the failure of their economic system and particularly their inability to compete with the United States in the production of such modern military systems as the Strategic Defense Initiative. Steel, Garthoff, and Barnet assert a different point of view. Steel argues that American leaders exaggerated the Soviet Union's military capabilities all along, in effect creating the enemy they needed in order to justify the policies they pursued. Garthoff and Barnet echo George Kennan's earlier conclusion that the Soviet Union contained the seeds of its own destruction. The pressures of containment and the arms race, they argue, hastened but did not cause the Soviet collapse and the economic and political reforms engineered by Mikhail Gorbachev. To the extent that these reforms brought the Cold War to an end, Garthoff gives the credit primarily to Soviet, not American, leaders. John Gaddis, on the other hand, comes much closer to Wells in crediting containment, including the nuclear deterrent, with the "Long Peace" after 1945 and the collapse of the Soviet empire after 1989.

When it comes to winners and losers, Geir Lundestad, David Reynolds, Hermann-Josef Rupieper, and Alexei Filitov are convinced that Germany has emerged from the Cold War as a big winner, destined to become the key European leader as American (and Soviet) influence on the Continent declines. In addition, all of the authors in this volume agree that communism as an economic system, and perhaps as an ideology, was a big loser, as was the Soviet Union. At the same time, however, many of the contribu-

tors stress the tremendous toll that the Cold War has taken on the
United States. Although Gaddis sees the cost of the Cold War,
financial and otherwise, as a price that had to be paid to guarantee
a favorable outcome, others are more skeptical and more critical.
During the course of that struggle, Garthoff complains, the United
States too often abandoned traditional diplomacy, relied excessively on military instruments, supported dictators, and turned its
back on basic human rights. Gar Alperovitz and Kai Bird note
how the Cold War destroyed the Left in American politics,
preempted the discussion of domestic problems, and encouraged
political leaders to divert resources from fundamental economic
and social needs to national security programs. LaFeber points to
the dangerous growth of executive power since the Second World
War, to McCarthyism and the general decline of civil liberties, and
to abuses like Irangate. Filitov makes some of the same points by
way of concluding that neither of the superpowers won the Cold
War. The Soviet Union may have lost the most, he argues, but the
United States was a loser as well, especially in the decline of its
economic power relative to the power of its major competitors.

Alperovitz and Bird, along with Lundestad, Reynolds, and Barnet, elaborate Filitov's argument in essays that echo the verdict
reached by Paul Kennedy in his study of *The Rise and Fall of the
Great Powers*.[3] According to these contributors, the global system
of national security commitments, the arms race, and the military-
industrial complex that grew out of it fundamentally distorted the
American economy. They weakened the free market and led to
burgeoning budget deficits, a reduced level of investment, and the
decay of basic infrastructure. These developments, as my essay
suggests, may set the stage for a resurgence of partisan conflict in
the years ahead. At the very least they render any prediction of a
unipolar world premature, because the United States will increasingly lack the economic resources to capitalize on its military superiority. Garthoff and Steel make this last point. They believe
that a multipolar world is emerging in which economic power will
be more important than military might. In the new world, Steel
concludes, the economic dependency of the United States, espe-

---

3   Paul Kennedy, *The Rise and Fall of the Great Powers: Economic Change and Military
    Conflict from 1500 to 2000* (New York, 1987).

cially its need for foreign financing of the national debt, will deprive the country of its freedom to maneuver and render its military power increasingly meaningless. Alperovitz and Bird, together with Ernest May and Arthur Schlesinger, reach somewhat similar conclusions about the influence of the Cold War on the American economy and government. Alperovitz and Bird argue that defense spending was a constant prop to the American economy throughout the Cold War, masking such structural problems as unemployment, low productivity, and the inequitable division of income that are bound to become more obvious and more serious as national security expenditures decline. Schlesinger counts the institutionalization of the Cold War as a serious mistake and one of the great lessons to be learned from that conflict. May also notes how the Cold War altered the shape of the American government, institutionalizing a national security apparatus that is more or less unsuited to the foreign policy challenges of the future.

If the Cold War is viewed as a confrontation between the superpowers, then it does not follow for many of the contributors that Russia's defeat is America's victory. Nor does it follow that communism's collapse leaves capitalism triumphant. For Denise Artaud, as noted earlier, the future of capitalism and democracy in Eastern Europe and the former Soviet Union is still very much in doubt. Others draw the same conclusion about the Third World. Moreover, if Artaud is right to see the Cold War not simply as a struggle between communism and liberalism but as one episode in an ongoing battle between totalitarianism and democracy, then surely the verdict is still out on which side won and which side lost. LaFeber gets at the same point when he begins his essay by noting the millions of people who died over the last forty-five years in struggles that stopped short of a global battle between the United States and the Soviet Union. Are these not the most important losses of the era? And if so, does it make sense to frame a balance sheet for the period merely in terms of the Great Powers, their rival ideologies and competing systems?

The contributors to this volume also disagree on what the future holds. My essay asks if the end of the Cold War means an end to the Cold War political consensus in the United States and a revival of bitter regional, economic, party, and ideological battles over the

shape of domestic and foreign policies. Alperovitz and Bird speculate on how reduced defense expenditures will affect the American economy. Most of the other contributors are more concerned
with global politics. Gaddis foresees a future marked by tension
between the forces of integration encouraged by the Cold War, in
Western Europe, for example, and the forces of disintegration that
have become so obvious since 1989, in Eastern Europe and the
former Soviet Union, to cite two illustrations. The task as he sees
it is to forge a new balance of power—one that balances the forces
of integration and fragmentation against each other.

Other contributors make a clear distinction between the developed and developing worlds. Concerning the developed world, John
Mueller offers a generally rosy forecast. The end of ideological
struggle means to him that a major war is now unlikely, a global
war virtually impossible. Robert Jervis agrees with this assessment. Given the collapse of communism, he argues, the prospect
for a major war between the European, American, and Japanese
blocs appears remote at best. War is simply too costly and too
deadly, he concludes, and increasingly irrational at a time when
developed and developing countries alike are becoming more interdependent economically and more inclined to support market
values and political democracy. Bruce Cumings reaches a similar
conclusion. He envisions continued "accommodation and envelopment" of the old Socialist states by the victorious capitalist
countries as well as continued collaboration among the industrial
powers, who have everything to lose and nothing to gain from
destabilizing competition. Short of a global depression, Cumings
argues, the prospects are bright for a trilateral system of cooperation and free trade that will promote multilateralism, encourage
interdependence, and stimulate growth.

Many of the other contributors see no reason to assume a kinder,
gentler world. Lundestad and LaFeber, to name just two, seem
convinced that relations between the United States and its allies
are likely to become more strained in the years ahead, in part because the allies will be less dependent on the United States for
military protection against the Soviets, in part because they will
no longer be compelled by the Cold War to submerge their interests in common programs to contain communism. On the con-

trary, as these contributors see it, the end of the Cold War may mark the start of a new era of global economic competition between the United States, Japan, and the European Community. They foresee a world, once divided into rival Communist and capitalist groups, potentially divided into competitive currency blocs locked in an economic combat that is increasingly sharp and dangerous.

LaFeber is also reluctant to blow the whistle on rivalry between East and West. Although politically restructured and economically weakened, the former Soviet Union, or even the Russian republic alone, is still a military superpower with security goals that are unrelated to Communist ideology, cast largely in a tsarist pattern, and potentially at odds with U.S. interests. Artaud makes a similar point. Of all of the contributors to this volume, she is the one most reluctant to proclaim an end to the Cold War, so far as that struggle involved a clash of real and enduring interests. On the contrary, she believes that over the long term, Europe might well remain the focal point of tension between the United States and whatever takes the place of the former Soviet Union, especially if European unification fails and Eastern Europe dissolves in an orgy of national and ethnic conflict. In addition to European unity and to containing local conflicts, Artaud, Lundestad, Rupieper, and Reynolds all agree that European stability ultimately depends on defining a new role for a united Germany, rebuilding Eastern Europe, and forging European security arrangements that continue to include the United States.

The future of the Third World, and relations between the First and Third worlds, figures prominently in many of the essays that follow, several of which focus almost entirely on this subject. Again, opinions differ. While all of the contributors assume that regional conflicts are inevitable, particularly in the Third World, John Mueller at least sounds an optimistic note. During the Cold War, Mueller points out, superpower competition tended to exacerbate regional struggles, even if it did not cause them. With the end of the Cold War, however, the major powers are less likely to take a great interest in every local conflict and may actually cooperate, as they did in the Gulf war, to contain regional aggression in both the Third World and Eastern Europe. Nikki Keddie and Bruce Kuniholm, as well as Artaud, Lundestad, and Reynolds, agree that regional conflicts are invariably rooted in indigenous sources that have little or nothing to do with relations between the major powers. For this reason, according to Keddie, the end of the Cold War is likely to bring fewer changes to the Middle East than many have expected. Keddie and Kuniholm agree with Mueller that local aggression might be contained through cooperation among the Great Powers, similar to their recent collaboration against Iraq. But they also remind us that in the Middle East, as throughout the Third World, local conflicts will be difficult to predict, let alone to control, precisely because they are rooted in the history of the region.

Keddie makes another point that reverberates in the essays by Noam Chomsky, Bruce Cumings, and Walter LaFeber: After 1946, U.S. policy in the Middle East, Latin America, Africa, and East Asia was less a reaction to Soviet expansion than an effort to dominate these regions and control their resources. According to these authors, the collapse of communism and the end of the Cold War will not reduce America's dependence on these resources and thus its efforts to exercise hegemony over the Third World. The policy of interventionism, which predates the Cold War, will continue even as communism declines. To Cumings, the invasion of Panama and the Gulf war both illustrate how little will change with the end of the Cold War and the collapse of the Soviet Union. Indeed, Keddie and Chomsky seem to worry that intervention will actually increase now that the Soviet Union is unable to operate as a brake on American policy.

If the contributors disagree on what the future holds, they do see eye-to-eye on the value of history. My essay puts the connection between partisanship and foreign policy in a historical context. Schlesinger surveys the history of the Cold War to discover six errors from which current and future policymakers can benefit. Jervis doubts that historians will be useful guides to the future, but only because they have not mined the past for a history that is appropriate. Needed, he says, are new historical studies of the core values and traditions that might shape U.S. diplomacy in the years ahead, and of those eras in which the Great Powers collaborated and the prospects for major war appeared remote. For Mueller, who sees the Cold War as the equivalent of World War III, a fresh look at the first and second postwar periods will help us to appreciate the new era that is dawning. To his way of thinking, history can also aid our understanding of the nature and causes of regional conflicts. LaFeber, Cumings, and Reynolds make the point that 1945 was not year zero. They think that the end of the Cold War will bring into bold relief some of the other conflicts it has helped to obscure, conflicts between key countries at the center of the world economy or between the center and the periphery. Because these long-term conflicts predate the Cold War, the need to understand them will increase the importance of historical studies to policymakers here and abroad. For Reynolds, the past has other utilities as well. A review of the interwar period might help us to understand the problems now posed by Germany and Japan, for example, just as the decline of colonialism and the dissolution of the Austro-Hungarian Empire can aid our understanding of the problems currently emerging from the collapse of the Soviet Union and its sphere of influence in Eastern Europe.

Although themes and topics often overlap in the following essays, the authors also represent such a wide variety of views that it was difficult to arrange their contributions in a logical fashion. Nevertheless, the volume does break down into two broad categories, with approximately half of the essays in each category. Those in the first category deal generally with the nature of the Cold War, with how that struggle was waged, and with the price that each side paid. This group includes the contributions by LaFeber, Gaddis, Mueller, Schlesinger, Wells, Filitov, Cumings, Steel, Barnet, and Garthoff. The essays in the second category focus largely, though not entirely, on regional and national issues. They include the contributions by Chomsky, Keddie, Kuniholm, Rupieper, Artaud, Lundestad, Alperovitz and Bird, May, and Hogan. The volume concludes with the essays by Reynolds and Jervis, which focus particular attention on what the future holds and how history might help us to grapple with it.

The diversity of views expressed in the following pages constitutes one of the volume's principal strengths, as does the variety of approaches, disciplines, and nationalities represented. Nor is the diversity of opinion surprising. After all, whatever its shortcomings may be, the volume seeks to cover a range of important topics, themes, areas, and events. The causes and consequences of the Cold War, in addition, are matters of enormous complexity, which historians have analyzed for many years without reaching a consensus. What is more, however difficult it is to set straight the historical record, it is even more challenging to foretell the future, particularly when the time and space permitted for both endeavors is necessarily limited. To their credit, the contributors to this volume accepted this challenge, not, I am sure, with absolute confidence that their views would always prove correct, let alone square with the conclusions of their collaborators. On the contrary, they did so knowing full well that in writing contemporary history scholars always run the risk of being undone by unfolding events—proved wrong by history, as it were, if not by historians. They accepted this risk because as teachers and scholars, and as citizens of the planet, we must try to understand what the end of the Cold War means both to our view of the past and our expectations of the future. The road to understanding is a long one, to be sure, but it must start somewhere. This is our beginning. Our claim is not to be definitive, only suggestive.

2

An End to Which Cold War?

WALTER LaFEBER

Before we conclude that the Cold War era has ended, it might be well to decide which Cold War is under discussion. To telescope the past forty-five years into only a U.S.-Soviet confrontation might be convenient, but it is also ahistorical. While Americans and Russians, thankfully, did not kill each other in large numbers on battlefields, twenty-one million people did die in wars between the end of World War II and the Communist empire's collapse. Four million of these died in the Vietnam conflict of 1945 to 1975, and there were other casualties of that conflict in the realms of democratic and constitutional values that should not go unnoticed.

The Cold Wars, then, were of various intensities, not a single conflict, and many of the most important (and often most lethal) events of the post-1945 era occurred in those confrontations that were at times only faintly, if at all, related to the U.S.-Soviet struggle. The point deserves emphasis, not least because the policies that led to American involvement in these other, sometimes lethal, Cold Wars are continuing, even though the rationale that often shaped and drove those policies—anticommunism—has lost most of its validity and political appeal. There are historical continuities in U.S. foreign policy that need to be identified and closely examined, and those continuities can be missed, or, more often, dismissed amid the triumphalism that has multiplied like yellow ribbons since the tearing down of the Berlin Wall in November 1989 and the defeat of Iraqi forces in early 1991.

Four different but related Cold Wars can be identified. All have deep historical roots; that is, all have their origins well before 1945, but reached a maturity, and in some instances brought about state-

13

sponsored violence, in the half-century after 1945. All four remain alive, to a greater or lesser extent, despite the end-of-Cold-War talk, and they promise to be powerful forces in shaping both American society and world affairs in the future.

The first Cold War involves the ongoing struggle, dating back at least to World War I and the Paris Peace Conference, between the United States and the European countries to determine the kind of Europe that should evolve, and to decide how great a role Americans will have in that determination. The success of the Marshall Plan (although that success was a dangerously close-run thing as late as 1950), of the North Atlantic Treaty Organization (NATO), and of U.S. multinational corporations helped to mute the historic differences between the old and new worlds. But NATO, to take one example, was designed not merely to meet a possible (if improbable) Soviet invasion. It was also designed, as the well-known saying had it, to keep the Russians out, the Germans down, and the Americans in. In early 1950, Secretary of State Dean Acheson told a closed-door session of the Senate Foreign Relations Committee that "even if there were no Russia, if there were no communism, we would have grave problems in trying to exist [*sic*] and strengthen those parts of the free world" nearly destroyed by two world wars.[1] As Frank Costigliola points out in his book on U.S.-French relations since 1945, Gaullism, the bitter arguments over Germany's role in Europe, and condemnation of the so-called invasion of the American multinationals all indicated that the historic problems had not disappeared. They had only become subordinated to common anti-Communist policies.[2] The U.S. economic and military presence in Europe evolved out of this common commitment to contain communism and Soviet power in the late 1940s. With those threats rapidly disappearing, however, old animosities have resurfaced. They can be seen in U.S. efforts to use NATO as leverage on European affairs, and in the determination of some Europeans (especially the French) to develop military security independently of U.S. influence and interests.

---

1   U.S. Congress, Senate Foreign Relations Committee, *Review of the World Situation, 1949–1950*, 81st Cong., 1st and 2nd sess., 108.
2   Frank Costigliola, *France and the United States: The Cold Alliance Since World War II* (New York, 1992).

Economically, moreover, the industrialized world seems to be dividing along the lines of a mark bloc, a dollar bloc, and a yen bloc, as former British Prime Minister Margaret Thatcher suggested. Given the power of international finance and multinationals that easily move $1 trillion per day through the world's financial markets and across national boundaries, these three blocs possess a greater political than economic significance. In this context the three blocs bear an eerie resemblance to the three-bloc world that emerged from the Washington conference treaties of 1922, although at least in that instance the blocs were to be cemented by a common allegiance to the dollar. Within a decade after the conference, the dollar could not command that allegiance; all-out political warfare erupted. The present distinction between the political and economic significance of the blocs hardly decreases the danger of conflict. Economist Fred Bergsten has suggested that the ultimate irony of Marxism might be that just as its appeal collapsed, the predictions of its founder about destructive struggles between capitalists might come true.

The conflicting interests between Americans and West Europeans were apparent throughout the Cold War—during Korea; over the question of recognizing China; in the Suez, Cuban missile, 1973 Middle East, and 1986 Libyan bombing crises; and over the relationship between domestic subsidies and the professed U.S. quest for a more open trading world. The growing differences between the United States and Japan over trade policy, China, and military security issues are well known. Bruce Cumings rightly observes that the 1960 U.S.-Japan security treaty and its corollary arrangements were designed by U.S. officials to ensure that Japan remained number two. With the world's third largest navy, the region's largest air force, domination of large parts of Southeast Asia's economy, and multiplying investments inside the United States and the European Economic Community that are turning Tokyo into the world's central banker, Japan—in both American and Japanese eyes—may more closely resemble the signator of the 1922 treaties than the cosigner of the 1960 pact.

All of these developing conflicts formed important chapters in U.S. diplomatic history during the Cold War, and they will probably sharpen as the blocs develop, as economic issues more often supersede military questions, and as the cry of anticommunism becomes archaic rather than cohesive. A central strand of U.S. policy since 1945 has been the need to control and coopt Germany and Japan. Given the continued assumptions of U.S. foreign policy, that need will sharpen, not lessen.

When the world is defined in terms of three blocs, several problems stand out: the revived nationalisms (often actually ethnic differences) that are fracturing, or threatening to fracture, parts of the former Soviet Union, southern Europe, parts of Africa, and Canada; and the exclusion from the blocs of a majority of the world's people. The republics of what used to be the Soviet Union and large parts of South Asia, the Middle East, and Latin America have little or no relationship as yet to the blocs, although these less-industrialized regions need systematic economic help. These regions instead become more unpredictable and violent; Iraqi policies, the tragically contradictory U.S. policy toward Iraq (contradictions that continued well after the collapse of East European communism), and the resulting war form one example.

This leads to a second part of the historic Cold War: the ongoing struggle between the world's commercial centers and the outlying countries that provide markets and raw materials. Thomas J. McCormick's *America's Half-Century* defines U.S. Cold War policy as in large part a forty-five-year attempt to stabilize and organize that "periphery."[3] The best known example of this attempt is the long struggle in Vietnam. U.S. policy originally aimed to keep Vietnam a productive part of a war-ravaged French colonial empire, and then, after 1949, as both a support for French anti-Communist policy and an open market and raw-material source for a new Japan. Along the way, U.S. officials somehow read history as proving that the Chinese Communists could dominate a Vietnam ruled by Ho Chi Minh; interests along the Asian periphery would be endangered until the falling dominoes (in Dwight Eisenhower's famous phrase of 1954) might fall on Japan itself. The contradictions in this set of assumptions about Vietnam were so great that while from 1949–50 U.S. officials had a policy in search of a commitment, by 1967 and 1968 they had a commit-

3 Thomas J. McCormick, *America's Half-Century: United States Foreign Policy in the Cold War* (Baltimore, 1989).

ment in search of a policy; and while presidents, especially John F. Kennedy, sent troops into Vietnam to block Chinese influence (which Kennedy carefully distinguished from Soviet influence), President Richard M. Nixon sought Chinese help so he could pull U.S. troops out of Vietnam. Meanwhile, the war was lost, but Japan soon turned the supposed dominoes into cornerstones of an economic coprosperity sphere.

The U.S.-Vietnam conflict continues to merit close examination because in many respects it can reveal as much as the U.S.-Soviet conflict about the motivations of American global policies, the importance of broad economic as well as military interests, the limits of Washington's power, and the fragility of American society and its political consensus when confronted with the demand for substantial, long-term sacrifices. As Marilyn Young observed in 1990, "The struggle over [the Vietnam War's] interpretation is central to contemporary American politics, foreign and domestic, and to American culture as well."[4] The war also merits close study because as the Iraqi conflict and its aftershocks demonstrate, the U.S. need to stabilize peripheral areas did not end in Saigon in 1975 or with the Nicaraguan elections of 1990. President Bush's post-Iraqi-war declaration that "By God, we have kicked the Vietnam syndrome once and for all" might ring truer if both he and his military advisers did not continually use the Vietnam War as the benchmark for their own policies. In any case, the thirty-year American experience in Vietnam cannot be kicked down an Orwellian memory hole; that experience was anticipated by U.S. policies well before 1945 (for example, in Central America, the Caribbean, and even China) and was followed by similar experiences, even as the Cold War was being declared over.

The third integral part of the post-1945 Cold War has been fought within the United States. It is now a truism to note that U.S. officials could not have conducted their global military and economic policies without solving the central problem that Locke, Madison, and Tocqueville, among others, anticipated more than 150 years ago: the problem of turning an individualistic, open, commercial, and domestic-oriented society into a consensual, secret, militaris-

---

4   Marilyn B. Young, *The Vietnam Wars, 1945–1990* (New York, 1990), 313–14.

tic, international force. Harry S. Truman and Dean Acheson went far in solving this problem in 1947 with the Truman Doctrine, which ingeniously divided the world into two parts, the free peoples and the totalitarian powers, and demanded that Americans and their representatives in Congress choose which part of this simplified globe they wished to support. With this stroke, Truman and his successors (each of whom until George Bush tried to use the Truman Doctrine to quiet domestic dissent) strengthened executive domination over U.S. foreign policy. This Manichean division of the world and the apotheosis of executive power led not unnaturally to the crises of Watergate and the much greater danger of the Iran-contra subversion.

Again, this dimension of the Cold War extends back beyond 1945. As early as the century's turn, Woodrow Wilson wrote about, and William McKinley and Theodore Roosevelt exemplified, the new "republican king," as Clinton Rossiter called the president in 1960. Judging by Bush's invasion of Panama (about which Congress refused to hold hearings even to create a historical record) and the war against Saddam Hussein (in which the president used his powers as commander in chief to move four hundred thousand troops to the Middle East and present Congress with a fait accompli), executive power has not diminished even though Truman's original enemy—communism—no longer can be used so effectively to mobilize consensus and neutralize dissent. If conflict sharpens among the economic blocs, and if U.S. interests focus on economic policies (which according to the Constitution, at least, are largely under congressional jurisdiction), then executive-legislative differences can intensify.

Even if these three historic struggles continue, the fourth part of the Cold War, the long conflict between the United States and the former Soviet Union, seems to have changed fundamentally. Again, however, a larger historical framework raises questions. Animosity between Russia and the West, on both the ideological and national security levels, began in the 1890s, not in 1917 or 1945. As the republics of the former Soviet Union move away from Communist economic practices and toward new relationships with Japan and Europe, their policies will perhaps bear little resemblance to Stalin's, but could have considerable resemblance to the tsar's.

What is more, ethnic and economic problems in the republics could lead us back to study more closely the European crises of 1910–1914.

The end of the Cold War is carrying Americans back to history. The 1945 to late 1980s era now appears as an American Augustan Age when the problems of the old republic and the threats abroad were disciplined by consensus at home and overwhelming power overseas. Vietnam, Korea, the Middle East wars, and Iran-contra are among the reasons why such appearances deceive. With the collapse of the Communist empire, both foreign and domestic affairs could become more interesting, and, of peculiar importance, the need for diplomatic historians could grow.

3

The Cold War, the Long Peace, and the Future

JOHN LEWIS GADDIS

When the fictional dictator Big Brother proclaimed the propaganda slogan "War Is Peace" in George Orwell's novel *1984*, first published in 1948, he turned out to be a better prophet than anyone, including his creator, could ever have imagined. For we can now see that the Cold War, the most dangerous, bitter, and protracted rivalry between Great Powers in modern history, did in time become the most protracted period of freedom from Great Power war in modern history. Whether or not one approves of the *means* by which this happened, whether or not one even agrees on the *way* in which it happened, the simple fact is that the Cold War did evolve into a Long Peace.[1] Whether the Long Peace can survive the end of the Cold War is, however, quite another matter.

The Cold War was many things to many people. It was a division of the world into two hostile camps. It was a polarization of Europe in general, and of Germany in particular, into antagonistic spheres of influence. It was an ideological contest, some said be tween capitalism and communism, others said between democracy and authoritarianism. It was a competition for the allegiance of, and for influence over, the so-called Third World. It was a game of wits played out by massive intelligence organizations behind the

This essay was originally prepared for presentation at the 90th Anniversary Nobel Jubilee Symposium "Beyond the Cold War: Future Dimensions in International Relations," held in Oslo, Norway, 6–8 December 1991.

1 Among the Great Powers. The qualification—which seems to me redundant—has become necessary because certain critics of the Long Peace thesis persist in suggesting that it was meant to apply to *all* of international relations since World War II. For evidence that it was not see John Lewis Gaddis, *The Long Peace: Inquiries into the History of the Cold War* (New York, 1987), 216, 230–31, 233–34, 239–41, 243–45.

scenes. It was a struggle that took place within each of its major adversaries as supporters and opponents of confrontation confronted one another. It was a contest that shaped culture, the social and natural sciences, and the writing of history. It was an arms race that held out the possibility—because it generated the capability—of ending civilization altogether. And it was a rivalry that even extended, at one point, beyond the bounds of earth itself, as human beings for the first time left their planet, but for a set of reasons that are likely to seem as parochial to future generations as those that impelled Ferdinand and Isabella to finance Columbus when he first set out for the New World five hundred years ago.

The new world of the post-Cold War era is likely to have few, if any, of these characteristics: that is an indication of how much things have already changed since the Cold War ended. We are at one of those rare points of "punctuation" in history at which old patterns of stability have broken up and new ones have not yet emerged to take their place.[2] Historians will certainly regard the years 1989–1991 as a turning point comparable in importance to the years 1789–1794, or 1917–1918, or 1945–1947; precisely what has "turned," however, is much less certain. We know that a series of geopolitical earthquakes have taken place, but it is not yet clear how these upheavals have rearranged the landscape that lies before us.

Paleontologists tell us that the survival of species depends, not so much on the sturdiness of their genes or the efficiency of their metabolisms, as on their ability to adapt to sudden changes in environment: on how well they can cope, for example, when volcanic eruptions or collisions with asteroids blot out the sun for months at a time, or when rainfall patterns shift, or when glaciers advance and retreat.[3] The Long Peace evolved out of the particular conditions of the Cold War; but if the post-Cold War environment does in fact turn out to be a very different one, then the Long Peace may not survive within it. Early indicators are not encouraging, what with an international war in the Persian Gulf, a civil war in

---

2 See Niles Eldredge, *Time Frames: The Evolution of Punctuated Equilibria* (Princeton, 1985).

3 Stephen Jay Gould, *Wonderful Life: The Burgess Shale and the Nature of History* (New York, 1989).

Yugoslavia, and a potentially violent breakup of the Soviet Union, all within the past year. These disruptions may merely be the birth pains of a new and more peaceful international system; but they could also reflect the character of that system itself. It would be a perverse twist of Orwellian logic if the slogan for our new era should turn out to be: "Peace Is War."

No one can foretell, with any assurance, whether that is going to happen. But now that we can at last view the Cold War from beginning to end, it ought to be possible to get a clearer sense than we have had of what that conflict was all about, and to use that knowledge as a basis for attempting to anticipate what is to follow it. Projecting patterns from the past is, to be sure, an imperfect way of seeing into the future. But barring prophecy—whether of divine, ideological, or astrological inspiration—it is the only such means we have: history has always been a less than perfect teacher. This essay deals, therefore, with patterns and probabilities. It makes no assumptions about "laws" of history or the alleged certainties that flow from them. It should, as a consequence, be read with all the caution the phrase *caveat emptor* has always implied. But one has to start somewhere.

When President Harry S. Truman told the Congress of the United States on 12 March 1947 that the world faced a struggle between two ways of life, one based on the will of the majority and the other based on the will of a minority forcibly imposed upon the majority, he had more than one purpose in mind.[1] The immediate aim, of course, was to prod parsimonious legislators into approving economic and military assistance to Greece and Turkey, and a certain amount of rhetorical dramatization served that end. But President Truman also probably believed what he said, and most Americans and Europeans, at the time, probably agreed with him. Otherwise, the United States would hardly have been able to abandon its historic policy of peacetime isolationism and commit itself, not only to the Truman Doctrine, but to the much more ambitious Marshall Plan and eventually the North Atlantic Treaty Organi-

---

4   The Truman Doctrine speech is in *Public Papers of the Presidents of the United States: Harry S. Truman, 1947* (Washington, 1963), 178–79.

zation as well. Those plans worked, in turn, because most Europeans wanted them to. The danger at the time seemed to be real, and few people at the time had any difficulty in explaining what it was: freedom was under attack, and authoritarianism was threatening it.

In the years that followed, though, it became fashionable in academic circles to discount this argument. The Cold War, for many scholars, was not about ideology at all, but rather balances of power and spheres of influence; hence it differed little from other Great Power rivalries in modern and even ancient history.[5] Others saw the Cold War as reflecting the demands of an unprecedentedly powerful American military-industrial complex that had set out to impose its hegemony over the rest of the earth.[6] Students of Cold War origins never entirely neglected issues of ideology and principle, but few of them were prepared to say, as Truman had, that that conflict was *primarily* about the difference between freedom and its absence.[7] Such a view seemed too naïve, too simplistic, and, above all, too self-righteous: politicians might say that kind of thing from public platforms, but professors in the classroom and in their scholarly monographs should not.

As a result, it was left to the people of Eastern Europe and now the Soviet Union itself—through their own spontaneous but collective actions over the past three years—to remind us of a fact that many of us had become too sophisticated to see, which is that the Cold War really was about the imposition of autocracy and the denial of freedom. That conflict came to an end only when it became clear that authoritarianism could no longer be imposed and freedom could no longer be denied. That fact ought to make us look more seriously at how ideology contributed to the coming of the Cold War in the first place.

Much of twentieth-century history has revolved around the testing of a single idea: that one could transform the conduct of politics, government, and even human behavior itself into a "science"

---

5 See, for example, Louis J. Halle, *The Cold War as History* (New York, 1967).
6 A recent version of this argument is Thomas J. McCormick, *America's Half-Century: United States Foreign Policy in the Cold War* (Baltimore, 1989).
7 This generalization definitely applies to my own previous work on this subject. See, for a recent example, John Lewis Gaddis, *The United States and the End of the Cold War: Implications, Reconsiderations, Provocations* (New York, 1992), 50–51.

which would allow not only predicting the future but even, within certain limits, determining it. This search for a "science" of politics grew out of the revolution that had long since occurred in physics and biology: if scientific laws worked so well in predicting motions of the planets, the argument ran, why should similar laws not govern history, economics, and politics? Karl Marx certainly had such an approach in mind in the 1840s when he worked out his theory of dialectical materialism, which explicitly linked political and social consciousness to irreversible processes of economic development; his collaborator Friedrich Engels insisted in 1880 that the progression from feudalism through capitalism to socialism and ultimately communism was as certain as was the Darwinian process of natural selection.[8]

This movement to transform politics into a science began, it is important to emphasize, with the best of intentions: its goal was to improve the human condition by making human behavior rational, enlightened, and predictable. And it arose as a direct response to abuses, excesses, and inequities that had grown out of the concept of freedom itself, as manifested in the mid-nineteenth century *laissez faire* capitalism Marx had so strongly condemned.

But the idea of a "science" of politics was flawed from the beginning for the simple reason that human beings do not behave like the objects science studies. People are not laboratory mice; it is impossible to isolate them from the environment that surrounds them. They make judgments, whether rational or irrational, about the probable consequences of their actions, and they can change those actions accordingly. They learn from experience: the inheritance of acquired characteristics may not work in biology, the historian E. H. Carr once pointed out, but it does in history.[9] As a result, people rarely act with the predictability of molecules combining in test tubes, or ball bearings rolling down inclined planes, or even the "dependent variables" that figure so prominently in the writings—and, increasingly, the equations—of our contemporary social scientists.

It was precisely frustration with this irritating unpredictability

8   See Robert C. Tucker, ed., *The Marx-Engels Reader,* 2d ed. (New York, 1976), xix–xxvii, 696–97, 712.
9   Edward Hallett Carr, *What Is History?* (New York, 1961), 151.

of human beings that led Lenin at the beginning of this century to invert Marx and make the state the instrument that was supposed to secure human freedom, rather than the obstacle that stood in the way of it. But that same problem of human intractability in turn caused Stalin to invert Lenin and make the state, its survival, and its total control of all its surroundings an end in itself, with a consequent denial of freedom that was as absolute as any autocrat has ever managed to achieve. A movement that had set out in 1848 to free the workers of the world from their chains had wound up, by 1948 and through the logic of its "scientific" approach to politics, insisting that the condition of being in chains was one of perfect freedom.

Anyone contemplating the situation in Europe at the end of World War II would have had good reason, therefore, to regard the very nature of Stalin's regime as a threat, and to fear its possible expansion. That expansion had already taken place in Eastern Europe and the Balkans, not so much because of Stalinism's accomplishments in and of themselves, but rather because of the opportunity created for it by the foolish behavior of the Europeans in allowing another flight from freedom—fascism—to take root among them. In one of history's many paradoxes, a successful, necessary, and wholly legitimate war against fascism created conditions more favorable to the spread of communism than that ideology could ever have managed on its own.

The dangers Truman warned against in 1947, hence, were real enough. There is such a thing as bending before what one mistakenly believes to be the "wave of the future": fascism had gained its foothold in Europe by just these means. Many Europeans saw communism as such a wave following Hitler's defeat, not because they approved of that ideology, and not because they really expected the Red Army to drive all the way to the English Channel and the Pyrenees; the problem rather was that Europe had fallen into a demoralization so deep and so pervasive that Communists might have found paths to power there by constitutional means, much as the Nazis had done in Germany in 1933. Had that happened there is little reason to believe that constitutional procedures would have survived, any more than they did under Hitler; certainly the experiences of Poland, Romania, Hungary, and, after

February 1948, Czechoslovakia do not suggest otherwise. Stalin's system could have spread throughout Europe without Stalin having to lift a finger: that was the threat. The actions the United States took, through the Truman Doctrine, the Marshall Plan, and NATO, were seen at the time and I think will be seen by future historians as having restored self-confidence among the Europeans, as having preserved the idea of freedom in Europe by a narrow and precarious margin at a time when Europeans themselves, reeling from the effects of two world wars, had almost given up on it.

To be sure, some historians have claimed that Europe might have saved itself even if the Americans had done nothing.[10] There is no way now to prove that they are wrong. But few Europeans saw things this way at the time, and that brings us to one of the most important distinctions that has to be made if we are to understand the origins, evolution, and subsequent end of the Cold War: it is that the expansion of American and Soviet influence into Europe—the processes that really began that conflict—did not take place in the same way and with the same results. The Soviet Union, acting from primarily defensive motives, imposed its sphere of influence directly on Eastern Europe and the Balkans, against the will of the people who lived there. The United States, also acting for defensive reasons, responded to invitations from desperate governments in Western Europe, the Mediterranean, and even the Middle East to create countervailing spheres of influence in those regions.[11] Compared to the alternative, American hegemony—for there is no denying that such a thing did develop—definitely seemed the lesser of two evils.

This distinction between imposition and invitation—too easily lost sight of in too much of the writing that has been done about Cold War history—proved to be critical in determining not only the shape but also the ultimate outcome of the Cold War. The system the United States built in Western Europe quickly won legitimacy in the form of widespread popular support. The Warsaw

10   See, for example, Alan S. Milward, "Was the Marshall Plan Necessary?" *Diplomatic History* 12 (Spring 1989): 231–53.
11   Geir Lundestad, "Empire by Invitation? The United States and Western Europe, 1945–1952," *Journal of Peace Research* 23 (1986): 263–77.

Pact and the other instruments of Soviet control in Eastern Europe never did. This happened because Europeans at the time understood the difference between authoritarianism and its absence, just as more recent Europeans and now citizens of the former Soviet Union itself have come to understand it. Survivors of World War II had no more desire to embrace the Stalinist model of "scientific" politics than their children and grandchildren have had to remain under it. Moscow's authority in Eastern Europe turned out to be a hollow shell, kept in place only by the sheer weight of Soviet military power. Once it became apparent, in the late 1980s, that Mikhail Gorbachev's government was no longer willing (or able) to prop it up, the system Stalin had imposed upon half of Europe almost half a century earlier collapsed like a house of cards.

The way the Cold War ended, therefore, was directly related to the way in which it had begun. Perhaps Harry Truman had it right after all: the struggle really was, ultimately, about two ways of life, one that abandoned freedom in its effort to rationalize politics, and another that was content to leave politics as the irrational process that it normally is, thereby preserving freedom. The idea of freedom proved more durable than the practice of authoritarianism, and as a consequence, the Cold War ended.

The Cold War did, however, go on for an extraordinarily long period of time, during which the world confronted extraordinary perils. Historians will have to account for this odd coupling of danger with duration, together with the fact that we have, rather like the Abbé Sieyès during the French Revolution, somehow survived. How close we came to not surviving we will probably never know; but few people who lived through the Cold War took survival for granted during most of its history. The vision of a future filled with smoking, radiating ruins was hardly confined to writers of science fiction and makers of doomsday films; it was a constant presence in the consciousness of several generations after 1945, and the fact that that vision has now receded is of the utmost importance.

I do not mean to imply by this that the nuclear threat itself has gone away. With the proliferation of lethal technology to more and more nations possessing less and less wisdom, the probability that someone may actually use a nuclear weapon someday against someone else could well be increasing. But although horrible enough, such an event would be far from what most people feared during most of the Cold War, which was the prospect of thousands of Soviet and American nuclear warheads raining down upon the territories of the United States, the USSR, and much of the rest of the world. The use of one or two nuclear weapons, in the post-Cold War world, would not end the world as we have known it. During the Cold War, it might have.

Nuclear weapons have evolved from their initial status in our minds as the ultimate instrument of the Apocalypse to, first, a means of deterrence, and then a method of reassurance, and then an object for negotiation, and then an inconvenience to be circumvented, and finally an embarrassment of such magnitude that old Cold War antagonists now race to divest themselves of what they once raced each other so avidly to possess. From having worried about how nuclear weapons could destroy us we have progressed to worrying about how we can safely destroy them, and that is undeniably progress.

How, though, did this happen? How did we get from the world of Dr. Strangelove and "The Day After" to what would have seemed—not so long ago—an even more improbable world in which the leaders of former Soviet republics, including Russia itself, report dutifully to a peripatetic American secretary of state on how they propose to spend funds allocated by the United States Congress for the purpose of dismantling and disposing of the once formidable Soviet nuclear arsenal?

Nuclear weapons have for so long been the subject of our nightmares—but sometimes also of our delusions of power—that it is difficult to answer this question dispassionately. We have tended to want to see these devices either as a Good Thing or a Bad Thing, and hence we have talked past one another most of the time. But the role of nuclear weapons in Cold War history was neither wholly good nor bad, which is to say, it was more interesting than either the supporters or the critics of these weapons have made it out to be.

Nuclear weapons were, of course, a very bad thing for the people of Hiroshima and Nagasaki; but those Americans and Japanese spared the necessity of additional killing as a result of their use might be pardoned for seeing some good in them. Nuclear weapons were a bad thing in that they greatly intensified the fears the principal Cold War adversaries had of one another, and that much of the rest of the world had of both of them. But they were a good thing in that they induced caution on the part of these two Great Powers, discouraging irresponsible behavior of the kind that almost all Great Powers in the past have sooner or later engaged in. Nuclear weapons were a bad thing in that they held the world hostage to what now seems the absurd concept of mutual assured destruction, but they were a good thing in that they probably perpetuated the reputations of the United States and the Soviet Union as superpowers, thereby allowing them to "manage" a world that might have been less predictable and more dangerous had Washington and Moscow not performed that function. Nuclear weapons were a bad thing in that they stretched out the length of the Cold War by making the costs of being a superpower bearable on both sides and for both alliances: if the contest had had to be conducted only with more expensive conventional forces, it might have ended long ago. But nuclear weapons were a good thing in that they allowed for the passage of time, and hence for the education of two competitors who eventually came to see that they did not have all that much to compete about in the first place.

It is important to remember, though, that the peaceful end to the Cold War we have just witnessed is not the *only* conceivable way the Cold War could have ended. In adding up that conflict's costs, we would do well to recognize that the time it took to conclude the struggle was not time entirely wasted. That time—and those costs—appear to us excessive in retrospect, but future historians may see those expenditures as long-term investments in ensuring that the Cold War ended peacefully. For what we wound up doing with nuclear weapons was buying time—the time necessary for the authoritarian approach to politics to defeat itself by nonmilitary means. And the passage of time, even if purchased at an exorbitant price, has at last begun to pay dividends.

One of those dividends is that, now that the Cold War has finally ended, we can see just how useless nuclear weapons really are for most purposes most of the time. President Bush, in his television address of 27 September 1991,[12] wiped out more nuclear warheads in a single unilateral gesture than decades of negotiations over arms control have managed to remove, and President Gorbachev quickly offered to go even further. But these decisions do not necessarily mean that the weapons whose numbers both leaders have promised to reduce, and in some categories to eliminate altogether, never had any useful purpose. It could be that their purpose—ensuring a peaceful end to the Cold War—simply took a long time to achieve.

Now that we know that there will indeed be a post-Cold War era, what can we say about its character? International relations theorists have long argued that the Cold War itself would be an analogue for things to come. "Realists" and their latter-day successors, the "neo-realists," assume a drive for power among states that is supposed to transcend particularities of time and place, and therefore to yield general if not detailed forecasts about their future behavior.[13] But the "realist" view of "power" grew out of a particular time and place, which was the high Cold War: it defined "power" almost entirely in political-military terms, and insisted that no state would ever willingly give it up. That is precisely what the Soviet Union did, though, with respect to Eastern Europe in 1989, and—even more dramatically—with respect to itself in 1991. "Realism" has no way of accounting for the peaceful relinquishment, by a great state, of its own instruments of authority and legitimacy, and that fact has to call into question the predictive potential of Cold War theory for a post-Cold War age.

My own guess is that we will come to see the Cold War more as an anomaly than as an analogue. It will, I think, turn out to be one of those atypical periods in history that historians have to work overtime to explain—like the rule of the regicide Protector, Oliver Cromwell, in seventeenth-century England, or the Reign of Terror in revolutionary France, or the Stolypin reforms in pre-

12 *New York Times,* 28 September 1991.
13 A good introduction to this literature is Robert O. Keohane, ed., *Neorealism and Its Critics* (New York, 1986).

World War I Russia, or the advent of Prohibition in the United States, or the existence of Marxism-Leninism as an ideology that some people, once upon a time, actually believed in.

If this is the case—if the post-Cold War world is not going to resemble the Cold War world—then what will it resemble? We can answer this question with no greater precision than we can specify when the next earthquakes will hit California, the Caucasus, China, and Japan. But we know that there are going to be earthquakes in these parts of the world, and we know approximately where the fault lines run along which they will occur. It might be a useful thing, therefore, if we could locate historical fault lines: long-term patterns that—because they are long term—are not apt to disappear in the foreseeable future. These could help us to identify history's equivalent of those tectonic processes that produce earthquakes in the first place, and although that would tell us little about when future upheavals will strike and what their exact consequences are going to be, it would at least give us some idea of what to expect.

The historical fault line most likely to affect the post-Cold War era, I believe, is one that dates back at least to the eighteenth century, and that has in many ways dominated the history of the nineteenth and the twentieth: it is the tension that exists between forces of integration and fragmentation in the modern world.[14]

The forces of integration have to do, for the most part, with securing freedom from want: with satisfying the economic needs of individuals, societies, and nations. As Adam Smith pointed out in *The Wealth of Nations* in 1776 and as subsequent experience has generally confirmed, improvements in the material conditions of life require breaking down barriers to trade, investment, the exchange of technology, labor flows, and the transmission of ideas. The reason for this is that the techniques that produce material satisfaction—free markets, new products, improved means of communication—tend to work in much the same way everywhere. Whether one is talking about tractors, tea kettles, or television

14 I have developed this idea more extensively in Gaddis, *The United States and the End of the Cold War*, 193–216. For an excellent analysis of future world problems written from a similar perspective see Robin Wright and Doyle McManus, *Flashpoints: Promise and Peril in a New World* (New York, 1991).

sets, the procedures required to produce them and to benefit from them do not vary throughout the world. To use a word much favored by international political economists, these products are "fungible," which is to say that they can be usefully employed, without significant modification, in many different states and cultures. Indeed, according to economic theory, the more transfers of this type that take place across international and intercultural boundaries, the better off everyone is. States unwilling to allow such transfers—as those states that tried to practice autarchy during the Cold War painfully discovered—tend to suffer as a result.

But common sense, which often differs from economic theory—ought to tell us that the satisfaction of material needs is not the only thing people care about. There are also immaterial or intangible needs that have to be satisfied: these can be boiled down to the concept of freedom from fear. The difficulty here is that the procedures necessary to secure freedom from fear are not the same all over the world. They may well involve political democracy in most places; but people have also been known to seek freedom from fear through nationalism, terrorism, revolution, religious fundamentalism, racism, and even authoritarianism. Most of those Germans who voted for Hitler in 1932–1933 probably thought they were voting for freedom, as they understood it; some Russians today, as they contemplate the complications of life under *perestroika*, would just as soon have Stalin back. People fear different things for different reasons at different times; despite what we like to think, freedom from fear is not always a transferable or a fungible commodity.

The search for freedom from fear, then, tends to work against those processes of integration that are required to achieve freedom from want: the very idea of self-determination—which Americans originated, after all, also in 1776—involves breaking up large, potentially oppressive political structures and bringing government closer to the people, even if it makes no economic sense to do so. There is, therefore, a fundamental tension between the integration that is required for the satisfaction of material wants, and the particularization—or fragmentation—that is necessary to satisfy intangible (which is to say, intellectual, ideological, religious, or psychological) needs.

The industrial revolution of the late eighteenth and early nine-teenth centuries could only have taken place as a result of integra-tive processes that transcended national boundaries; but that same period also saw the rise of modern nationalism—the idea that dis-tinctive cultures should have their own state—which eventually undermined old integrative structures like the Austro-Hungarian, Russian, and Ottoman empires, and ruined the common markets that existed within them.

Late-nineteenth-century imperialism reflected the effects of a new and easily fungible technology that allowed Europeans to project power into parts of the world hitherto beyond their reach; but in doing so it set off national liberation movements that would, in time, overthrow the European colonial empires and create most of the some 170 separate sovereign states that now make up the United Nations.

World War I grew out of the combination of particularist or nationalist rivalries with a widely disseminated technology of modern warfare. Battleships, machine guns, and tanks worked in much the same way on both sides, but that fungibility failed to keep those nations who produced those weapons from using them against each other for four bloody and devastating years.

When Woodrow Wilson sought to redesign the international or-der after World War I, he took into account this tension between integrative and disintegrative forces: the Fourteen Points speech called, on the one hand, for economic interdependence, by which Wilson meant a world open to unrestricted flows of trade and in-vestment, and, on the other hand, for political independence, by which he meant self-determination for those peoples that had hith-erto been denied it.[15] Wilson thereby achieved, not peace, but a contradiction that has affected the conduct of United States for-eign policy ever since.

The great authoritarian ideologies of the twentieth century, fas-cism and communism, grew out of a search for intangible satisfac-tion that the integrated international economic order of the late nineteenth century had been unable to provide; unfortunately these ideologies wound up producing not only the greatest denials of

15 The Fourteen Points speech is in R. S. Baker and W. E. Dodds, eds., *The Public Papers of Woodrow Wilson: War and Peace*, 2 vols. (New York, 1927), 1:157–60.

freedom in modern history, but another world war and a Cold War following that.

We would be foolish to expect, therefore, that just because the Cold War has ended, the old historical fault line between integrative and disintegrative forces has disappeared. Indeed, it may well be that the Cold War temporarily stabilized that fault line, and that with the end of the Cold War, we can expect more frequent upheavals along it.

Historians are going to argue, I think, that the Cold War tilted the balance toward integrative processes in world politics and temporarily submerged—or absorbed, or coopted—their disintegrationist counterparts. In Western Europe, the Marshall Plan and NATO ended the old rivalry between France and Germany, paving the way for the eventual development of that most striking of integrationist institutions, the European Community. In Eastern Europe and the Balkans, the Warsaw Pact imposed a much harsher form of order on a part of the world where the fragmenting forces of nationalism, religion, language, and ethnicity had been extremely powerful. In much of the rest of the world, the coincidence of Soviet-American rivalry with decolonization forced new political entities to live within old colonial boundaries, because under the conditions of Cold War attempts to revise them seemed too risky. Meanwhile, the international economic institutions created in the wake of World War II—the International Monetary Fund, the World Bank, the General Agreement on Tariffs and Trade were producing a system that is as close as we have ever come to a truly global market.

But how much of this integration grew out of the peculiar conditions of the Cold War, and how much of it would have happened even if that struggle had never occurred? The question is a very important one now, for institutions and practices rooted only in the Cold War are likely to find the post-Cold War environment inhospitable. Already challenges to integration—which is to say, instances of fragmentation—are beginning to arise:

German reunification, together with Soviet withdrawal from Central and Eastern Europe, has created a volatile situation in which old nationalist and ethnic rivalries are reappearing—most noticeably in Yugoslavia but by no means exclusively there—with quite unpredictable results. The European Community, so far, has shown little effectiveness in handling them.

The Soviet Union itself has disappeared before our eyes as the central government's control has weakened and as the individual republics have taken more and more authority into their own hands. The process has been, so far, remarkably peaceful; but historical experience provides little basis for confidence that it will indefinitely remain so.

Now that Soviet boundaries have been revised, it is not at all clear why Middle East and African boundaries—most of them relics of empires long since dead—should not be also. Already in India, a sudden upsurge in separatist sentiment has raised questions about the survival of that enormous multinational state. And the forces of fragmentation have even arisen in so peaceful and stable a country as Canada, whose future as a confederation is now very much in doubt.

Meanwhile, other kinds of tension between integrative and disintegrative phenomena could cause new kinds of security problems:

The extension of the industrial revolution into many parts of the Third World—an integrative phenomenon—is causing disintegrative consequences in terms of pollution, rapidly expanding birth rates, mass movements of people from the countryside into cities not equipped to handle them, social tensions that arise from exposure to the lifestyle and culture of the industrialized "first" world, and frustrations that build when people feel they are losing control of their own destinies to international economic forces they do not understand. These trends would appear to call into question the theoretical proposition that everybody benefits from the maximum possible diffusion of market economies throughout the world.

The international market in energy and arms—both of them reflections of how market systems are supposed to work in theory—combined in practice to produce war in the Persian Gulf early in 1991. Saddam Hussein would hardly have invaded Kuwait had it not been for the arms he bought and the profits he thought he could make by seizing that country's oil fields. This unexpected intersection of Western energy dependency with Western eagerness to export arms could produce similar results in the future, thus calling into question the theoretical proposition that the maximum possible flow of commodities across international boundaries best guarantees peace.

Victories for self-determination in Eastern Europe and the Soviet Union—a fragmentationist phenomenon, but one most of us wholeheartedly applaud—could very well undermine integrationist institutions in Western Europe. What will happen to the European Community's plan for a wholly integrated market after 1992 if massive refugee flows begin to develop, either because minorities have been forced to flee as Yugoslavia and the USSR break up, or because of a general economic collapse in that part of the world resulting from exposure to market forces? These prospects could very well call into question the theoretical proposition that political freedom will lead to economic prosperity wherever it exists.

It is even possible to see tensions between integrative and fragmentationist forces developing inside the United States. Will the American people continue to support their long-time role as world policeman if there is no clear external threat and if their allies continue to resist playing that role themselves? How long will Americans continue to tolerate their economy's involvement in the global market if the only benefits they see are the export of jobs beyond borders, together with increasing foreign control over whatever economic activity remains? The very success of the United States in achieving its Cold War objectives could push it back toward a kind of pre-Cold War isolationism, thus confirming the counter-theoretical proposition that Great Powers do, at times, give power up.

One has to wonder, therefore, whether a dialectical relationship does not exist between integrative and disintegrative forces in world affairs. The things that work to integrate the life of one country, or one group of individuals, can have disintegrative consequences for others; actions that might appear disintegrative in certain situations can be profoundly integrative in others. Movement too far toward freedom from want can produce fear; movement too far toward freedom from fear can produce want. All of which suggests that we might best deal with the new world that confronts us by returning to the old practice of balancing power: the task this time, though, would be not to balance the forces of democracy against those of authoritarianism, as it was during the Cold War, but rather to balance the forces of integration and fragmentation against each other.

Statesmen often claim to seek "stability" in world politics, but they rarely explain what they mean by that term. Perhaps they themselves do not know: it is all too easy to regard stability as an end in itself, rather than as the means to larger ends it always is. For in statecraft as in evolution, the surest way of ensuring the survival of species—political or biological—is to perpetuate existing environments: stability tends to do that. But as the concept of evolution itself implies—and certainly that of "punctuated equilibrium"—the only thing certain about stability is that it will not remain stable. Environments do sooner or later shift, sometimes abruptly; at such times, definitions of "stability" must shift accordingly.

"Stability," for Western statesmen during the Cold War, meant containment: balancing democratic against authoritarian forces throughout the world. But the West's success in that task has created a new environment in which old definitions of "stability" no longer apply; familiar habits of thought and action no longer serve our interests. We can orient ourselves in this unfamiliar environment by simply trying to guess what lies ahead. Or we can take a long view of history—one that extends back through several "punctuations"—to look for fault lines that extend across time and space, and that therefore seem unlikely to disappear, however dramatically the environment has changed.

The tension between integrative and disintegrative processes, I think, is such a fault line: finding a balance between them would, I believe, most closely approximate, in the post-Cold War era, the stability that came to characterize the Cold War itself. No one can guarantee that the Long Peace will survive the end of the Cold War: earthquake prediction is an inexact science, and history is indeed an imperfect teacher. But one has to start somewhere.

4

Quiet Cataclysm:
Some Afterthoughts on
World War III

JOHN MUELLER

In the last few years we seem to have experienced something like the functional equivalent of World War III. The recent pleasantness (as Winston Churchill might have called it) was preceded, like its unpleasant and far noisier predecessors of 1914 and 1939, by a lengthy process in which rival countries jockeyed for position as they proclaimed competitive visions of the way the world ought to be ordered, armed themselves to the earlobes, made threatening noises, and confronted each other in traumatic crises. Like World Wars I and II, a consequence of the event was that a major empire was dismembered, important political boundaries in Europe were reorganized, and several nations were politically transformed. And, just as the ancient institution of monarchy met its effective demise in Europe in World War I and as the newer, but dangerous and seemingly virile ideologies of nazism and fascism were destroyed by World War II, so a major political philosophy, communism, over which a great deal of ink and blood had been spilled, was discredited and apparently expunged in World War III.

Following World War I and II it took a few years for the basic political order to be settled, after which it remained substantially stable until revised by the next war (or war-equivalent). A similar process of shaking-out seems to be going on now in Eastern Europe and in the former Soviet Union—and perhaps also in China, where aged leaders are trying to counter an apparently inevitable historic process. In addition, the victors of World War III, like their predecessors in 1918 and 1945 (and, for that matter, 1815),

I would like to thank Stanley Engerman, Carl Honig, and Karl Mueller for their comments.

have been given to proclaiming a new world order in which former enemies can expect to collaborate in international police work. After World Wars I and II, such hopes were rather short lived. We will have to see if history repeats itself in this respect.

Although there may be some merit in considering the experience of the last few years to have been the functional equivalent of a world war, there are at least two extremely important respects in which the conceit fails miserably. First, of course, the recent cataclysm, unlike its bloody predecessors, was astoundingly quiet: It took place almost completely without violence—and, to a very remarkable extent, without much in the way of recriminations, at least so far. Second, although World War III may have caused great changes in international politics, it did not, unlike World Wars I and II, notably change the world's military balance. Indeed, about the only thing that has *not* changed quickly in the last few years is the balance of weaponry, particularly the supposedly crucial nuclear weaponry, arrayed on both sides.

This last observation strongly suggests, I think, that, at base, the Cold War had much more to do with ideology than with armaments. Although it is frequently argued that it was the bomb that dominated and principally shaped the contest, it seems rather that the Cold War essentially sprang from the oft-proclaimed expansionary goals of communism: when these changed, everything changed, even though the bombs remained very much in place.

When it was formed in 1917 the Soviet Union took on as one of its essential beliefs the notion that international capitalism, or imperialism, was a profoundly evil system that must be eradicated from the face of the globe, and by violence if necessary. Any country designated "imperialist" by the Soviets would naturally tend to find such pronouncements threatening, particularly after they had been hurled thousands—perhaps millions—of times.[1] Of course,

---

1 As John Lewis Gaddis has observed, "Moscow's commitment to the overthrow of capitalism throughout the world had been the chief unsettling element in its relations with the West since the Russian revolution." See Gaddis, "Was the Truman Doctrine a Real Turning Point?" *Foreign Affairs* 52 (January 1974): 388. See also his *The Long Peace: Inquiries into the History of the Cold War* (New York, 1987), chap. 2. Hugh Thomas puts it this way: "The prime cause of the conflict opening up between the Russians and the Americans (and their allies) was the ideology of the Soviet leaders, and their conse-

the Soviet ideological challenge was particularly unsettling to the West after World War II because it was backed by an exceptional military capacity. If this capacity helped to concentrate the imperialist mind, however, it did not determine the essential shape of the contest. A Soviet Union that was militarily less capable might have been less worrisome, but, like Khomeini's Iran in the 1980s (or, for that matter, like the Soviet Union in the 1930s), it would still have been seen as a dangerous opponent.

Militarily—particularly in the area of nuclear weaponry—the United States and the Soviet Union remained at least as threatening to each other as ever in the late 1980s: At any time either country could have inflicted tens of millions of deaths on the other. Nevertheless, everything changed because the Soviet Union abandoned its threateningly expansionary ideology. As Francis Fukuyama has observed, "the role of ideology in defining Soviet foreign policy objectives and in providing political instruments for expansion has been steadily declining in the postwar period," and Mikhail Gorbachev "further accelerated that decline."[2] By December 1988, Gorbachev specifically called for "de-ideologizing relations among states"[3] and, more importantly, acted as if he believed it. With this change in ideology—which took place *before* the disintegration of the Soviet empire in Eastern Europe and well before the breakup of the Soviet Union—the Cold War evaporated, even though the nuclear arsenals remained. The *New York Times* proclaimed on 2 April 1989 that the Cold War was over, and George

quent incapacity, rather than their reluctance, to make permanent arrangements with the leaders of capitalist states. This was stated by Maxim Litvinov in June 1946, in one of those strange, candid remarks of his: the 'root cause' of the trouble was 'the ideological conception prevailing here that conflict between communist and capitalist worlds is inevitable'. When asked what would happen if the West were to concede to Russia all her aims in foreign policy, Litvinov replied: 'It would lead to the West being faced, in a more or less short time, with the next series of demands'." See Thomas, *Armed Truce: The Beginnings of the Cold War, 1945–46* (New York, 1987), 548. Analysts of the Cold War revisionist school would argue that, while there was some reason for people in the West to conclude that the Soviets were hostile, politicians and business leaders in the West vastly exaggerated the extent of the threat, particularly in its military aspects. See Thomas G. Paterson, *Meeting the Communist Threat: Truman to Reagan* (New York, 1988).

2 Francis Fukuyama, "Patterns of Soviet Third World Policy," *Problems of Communism* (September–October 1987): 12.

3 *New York Times*, 8 December 1988.

Bush was soon urging that Western policy should move "beyond containment" and should seek to "integrate the Soviet Union into the community of nations."

Thus the demise of the Cold War came about when ideas changed. Material factors have certainly helped to bring these changes about: Clearly the failure of the Soviet economic and administrative system helped to impel Gorbachev and others to reexamine their basic ideology. But it was the change in ideology that was crucial. A simple thought experiment may make this clear. Suppose that persistent material failure had caused the Soviet Union to lapse into steady Ottoman-like decline but that its ideological quest to overthrow international capitalism had continued unabated. Suppose, in other words, that it took on the characteristics of China in the 1950s or 1960s or of the Soviet Union in the 1920s or 1930s. The West might have become somewhat less concerned that a major war would develop from the contest, but its hostility would have continued and the Cold War would have prospered. On the other hand, suppose that the Soviet Union had *not* fragmented or lapsed into material stagnation or decline, but that its leaders had undergone an ideological conversion to democratic liberalism or for that matter to Burma-style isolation and xenophobia. In that case the Cold War would have abated.

Further suggesting the dependence of arms on politics (rather than the reverse), the ending of the Cold War has brought about what might be called a negative arms race. Hans J. Morgenthau once proclaimed that "men do not fight because they have arms." On the contrary, "they have arms because they deem it necessary to fight." If that is so, it follows that when countries no longer deem it necessary to fight they will get rid of their arms. This is what has been happening.[4] Indeed, as we venture through the aftermath of what I have characterized as World War III, it may

---

4 Hans J. Morgenthau, *Politics among Nations: The Struggle for Peace and Power* (New York, 1948), 327. As Winston Churchill put it on 13 July 1934 in a House of Commons speech, "It is the greatest possible mistake to mix up disarmament with peace. When you have peace, you will have disarmament." For a discussion see John Mueller, "Arms Reduction: Don't Talk, Just Do It," *Wall Street Journal,* 1 June 1988; idem, "A New Concert of Europe," *Foreign Policy* 77 (Winter 1989–90): 3–16; and idem, "Taking Peace Seriously: Two Proposals," in *Soviet-American Relations after the Cold War,* ed. Robert Jervis and Seweryn Bialer (Durham, NC, 1991), 262–75.

be useful to speculate on the prospects that substantial violence can be contained or avoided in the current version of the new world order.

The Prospects for World War IV. It may not be completely irrelevant to point out that in distant memory there was a time—a few years ago—when very many people were consumed by the concern that a major war might break out among developed nations. Remember the sword of Damocles? Remember the two scorpions in a bottle? Remember the ticking doomsday clock on the cover of the *Bulletin of Atomic Scientists?* "Nuclear war," observed Bruce Russett in 1983, "is the central terror of our time."[5]

As the doomsday clock kept suggesting, moreover, many thought calamity was imminent and/or nearly certain. In 1945, H. G. Wells declared that "the end of everything we call life is close at hand and cannot be evaded," and the usually prescient Joseph Grew concluded, "a future war with the Soviet Union is as certain as anything in this world." In 1950, Arnold J. Toynbee wrote, "in our recent Western history war has been following war in an ascending order of intensity; and today it is already apparent that the War of 1939–45 was not the climax of this crescendo movement," and Albert Einstein was certain that "unless we are able, in the near future, to abolish the mutual fear of military aggression, we are doomed." In 1960, strategist and futurist Herman Kahn wrote, "I have a firm belief that unless we have more serious and sober thought on various aspects of the strategic problem . . . we are not going to reach the year 2000—and maybe not even the year 1965—without a cataclysm," and C. P. Snow assured his listeners that unless nuclear weapons were restricted, it was a "certainty" that within "at the most, six years, China and several other states [will] have a stock of nuclear bombs" and that within "at the most, ten years, some of those bombs are going off." In 1979, Morgenthau concluded that "the world is moving ineluctably towards a third world war—a strategic nuclear war. I do not believe that anything can be done to prevent it. The international system is simply too unstable to survive for long." Three years

5 Bruce Russett, *The Prisoners of Insecurity* (San Francisco, 1983), 1.

later, William McNeill advocated that a "global sovereign power willing and able to enforce a monopoly of atomic weaponry" be fabricated because the "alternative appears to be sudden and total annihilation of the human species," and Jonathan Schell proclaimed, "One day—and it is hard to believe that it will not be soon—we will make our choice. Either we will sink into the final coma and end it all or, as I trust and believe, we will awaken to the truth of our peril . . . and rise up to cleanse the earth of nuclear weapons."[6]

These concerns may have been overdone,[7] but it is surely clear that the prospects of a global war are far lower today, whatever the likelihood may have been in the past. The most likely way such a war could have come about was out of the deep rivalries and disagreements between the well-armed Cold War contestants. With the evaporation of that contest, the prospects for major war have substantially diminished, even though the earth has hardly been cleansed either of trouble or of nuclear weapons.

The Frequency of Local Wars. As recent experience reminds us, local wars are still entirely possible, and there have been a lot of them since 1945—though the vast majority of these have been civil wars. In the wake of World War III, there are three factors that may work to reduce the incidence of local wars and perhaps to resolve ones that are ongoing.

First, as communism died, so did many romantic myths about revolution. For decades, communism had preached that successful revolutions and wars of liberation in the Third World would be followed by social, political, and economic bliss. Through the 1970s at least, quite a few people—not only Communists—were still

6 H. G. Wells, *The Last Books of H. G. Wells* (London, 1968), 67; Grew, quoted in Gaddis, *The Long Peace*, 218n; Arnold J. Toynbee, *War and Civilization* (New York, 1950), 4; Albert Einstein, *Einstein on Peace* (New York, 1960), 533; Herman Kahn, *On Thermonuclear War* (Princeton, 1961), x; C. P. Snow, "The Moral Un-Neutrality of Science," *Science*, 27 January 1961, 259; Morgenthau, quoted in Francis Anthony Boyle, *World Politics and International Law* (Durham, NC, 1985), 73; William H. McNeill, *The Pursuit of Power: Technology, Armed Force, and Society since A.D. 1000* (Chicago, 1982), 383–84; Jonathan Schell, *The Fate of the Earth* (New York, 1982), 231.
7 For an argument along those lines see my *Retreat from Doomsday: The Obsolescence of Major War* (New York, 1989), chaps. 4–10.

working up enthusiasm for violent, undemocratic revolution. In her multiple-award winning book about Vietnam, American journalist Frances Fitzgerald, in consonance with many people around the globe, fairly glowed with anticipation at what successful revolutionaries could bring to Southeast Asia. "When 'individualism' and its attendant corruption gives way to the revolutionary community," she breathlessly anticipated, "the narrow flame of revolution" will "cleanse the lake of Vietnamese society from the corruption and disorder of the American war."[8] But in each of the ten countries that edged or toppled into the Communist camp between 1975 and 1979, successful revolutionaries variously led their societies into civil war, economic collapse, and conditions of severe social injustice. Neither corruption nor disorder was eradicated when revolution's narrow flame sliced through Vietnam, and notable evils were perpetrated. The disasters that followed the successful revolutions in Vietnam and elsewhere principally cleansed the world of the notion that revolution can be cleansing. Increasingly, violent revolutionary movements in places like Peru, El Salvador, and the Philippines have come to seem anachronistic.

Second, although I am not terribly hopeful about this, there may be something of an exhaustion with war in much of what used to be known as the Third World (which is where virtually all warfare has taken place since 1945). At the time of writing there are no international wars going on anywhere in the world, and several civil wars have ended in the last couple of years, and many of the others may be in the process of winding down.[9] On the other hand, of course, the decline may very well prove to be a mere hiatus between periods of warfare.

Third, as violent revolution has become discredited, peaceful

8 Frances Fitzgerald, *Fire in the Lake: The Vietnamese and the Americans in Vietnam* (New York, 1972), 589–90.
9 It is interesting in this regard that many people found Saddam Hussein's invasion of Kuwait in August 1990 to be remarkably odd. Although the Iraqis had been building up troops on the border, the director of the U.S. Defense Intelligence Agency "just did not find it conceivable that Saddam would do something so anachronistic as an old-fashioned land grab. Countries didn't go around doing things like that anymore." See Bob Woodward, *The Commanders* (New York, 1991), 217. That perspective may be premature, because there have been a number of out-of-the-blue land grab efforts in recent memory—by such countries as India (1961), China (1962), and perhaps Iraq (1980)—but the general notion that that sort of behavior is going out of style may prove to have substance.

democratic reform has begun to look pretty good by comparison. As a result, the democratic idea has flared up—not unlike, perhaps, a narrow flame—throughout the world. Democracy is an imperfect, but often effective, method for resolving local conflicts peacefully.

Opposed to these three factors, however, are the escalating troubles in other areas, particularly in the former Soviet Union and Yugoslavia, where turmoil is clearly evident. I also suspect that the other shoe has yet to drop in China. In addition, there is another possible new source of war. If it becomes fashionable to use force to impose democracy (as in Grenada and Panama), one might expect to see a series of short, assertive wars in the Third World committed by the United States and its Western allies. Cuba might become a future arena. The Gulf war, however, seems to be leaving an unpleasant aftertaste, and the experience may not inspire great calls for repetition unless there are severe provocations.

The Extensiveness of Local Wars. Few wars since 1945 have been started by the major belligerents in the Cold War, but quite a few local wars have been exacerbated by interfering Cold War contestants. The central point of Communist ideology was that violent conflict was pretty much inevitable, and that the Communist states were duty-bound to help out.[10] And the Western policy of containment often suggested that force would have to be used to oppose this thrust. In addition to Korea, Vietnam, the Dominican Republic, Lebanon (1958), Afghanistan, and Grenada where troops from the United States, the Soviet Union, and/or China became directly involved, the Cold War could be said to have exacerbated violent conflict in Thailand, Burma, Guatemala, Nicaragua, El Salvador, Venezuela, Cuba, Greece, Peru, Uruguay, Argentina, Bolivia, Cambodia, Laos, Angola, India, Mozambique, Chile, the Congo, Brazil, Ethiopia, Algeria, Iraq, various Yemens, Hungary, Zanzibar, South Africa, Guyana, French Indochina, Malaya, Iran, Indonesia, and the Philippines.

10   In his memoirs, Nikita Khrushchev puts it this way: "Both history and the future are on the side of the proletariat's ultimate victory. . . . We Communists must hasten this process. . . . There's a battle going on in the world to decide who will prevail over whom." See *Khrushchev Remembers: The Last Testament* (Boston, 1974), 530–31.

With the demise of the Cold War, it is to be expected that such exacerbation will not take place. To the extent that this means that fewer foreign arms and less aid will now be infiltrated to the local contenders, violence will be lower. Unfortunately, experience suggests that encouragement and sophisticated arms are not required for local warriors to prosper and to commit mayhem.

The New World Order as a Policing Mechanism. In the wake of World War III, two contradictory, even paradoxical, lessons about the future of Great Power cooperation can be drawn. On the one hand, as the Gulf crisis demonstrated, cooperation between East and West has become far easier to arrange than before. On the other, the parties are likely to find few trouble spots worthy of their cooperative efforts.

During the Cold War, East-West cooperation was extremely difficult to bring about because the two sides were locked in an intensely competitive struggle. Now, however, they seem to agree that their interests are best served by "a reliable peace" and by "a quiet, normal international situation," as Mikhail Gorbachev once put it.[11] Thus, there is now a strong incentive to cooperate to generate peace and stability.

At the same time, the dynamic of the Cold War contest caused the two sides to believe that their interests were importantly engaged almost everywhere. The Western policy of containment was based on the notion that any gain for communism would lead to further Western losses elsewhere, while the Soviets held that they should aid anti-Western forces throughout the globe.

As this elemental contest has evaporated, most areas of the world have become substantially less important to the two sides. In the 1960s, a civil war in the Congo inspired dedicated meddling by both sides; no one wanted to become involved very much in the civil war in Liberia—still less in such intractable conflicts as those in Lebanon or Sri Lanka. Even costly conflicts in such once-important Cold War arenas as Ethiopia and Cambodia mainly elicit hand wringing from the former contestants—certainly neither has offered to send troops to pacify and police the situation.

11 Timothy J. Colton, *The Dilemma of Reform in the Soviet Union* (New York, 1986), 191.

Thus, although both sides have an interest in peace and stability, they probably will be stirred to significant cooperative action only in those few remaining areas, like the Persian Gulf, where they feel their interests to be importantly engaged. In this respect, the Gulf experience bodes rather well for at least two potential trouble areas: Eastern Europe and Korea. Should resurgent nationalism in the one case or persistent division in the other lead to international conflict or to substantial international crisis, it seems likely that the major countries will be launched into cooperative action, possibly even into military action, to contain damage and to rectify problems in these important areas. Although economic sanctions were never allowed to play themselves out in the Persian Gulf, they are relatively cheap to inflict on small-time aggressors and may play a productive role in some lesser areas as well.

Great Power cooperation will certainly be an improvement over the hazardous competition of the Cold War. But euphoria about the imminent emergence of a peaceful new world order or of global collective security is hardly justified. Moreover, with respect to the most likely form of violent conflict—civil wars—the big countries may not be able to stir themselves into anything like action.

The Persistence of Nationalism. Many people are concerned about what seems to be a resurgence of nationalism in Eastern Europe and the former Soviet Union.[12] Because nationalism, or hypernationalism, was a cause of World Wars I and II, this concern is certainly reasonable.

It is not clear, however, that nationalism has grown any less strong in peaceful Western Europe. It is certainly true that few national differences there are being expressed in violence, in threats of violence, or in once-fashionable messianic visions about changing the world to reflect the national perspective.[13] But that does not necessarily mean that Western Europeans are less nationalistic than they were in the 1920s or the 1890s. Do the British (many of them distinctly unamused by the prospects of the new Channel tunnel) love the French any more or less than in days of yore? Do

12   See, for example, John J. Mearsheimer, "Back to the Future: Instability in Europe after the Cold War," *International Security* 15 (Summer 1990): 5–56.
13   See Michael Howard, *The Lessons of History* (New Haven, 1991), chaps. 2, 4.

Italians think of themselves less as Italians? Closer economic relations in Europe may only suggest that it has finally dawned on those countries that there is benefit in economic cooperation, not that Europeans love each other any more or that they identify themselves more now as Europeans. (The United States is looking toward a free trade zone with Mexico, but that stems from economic expedience, not from dampened Mexican or American nationalism. And the same could perhaps be said about the U.S.-Canada agreement.) German unification was a spectacular (and peaceful) triumph of national desire: If German nationalism had been truly dampened, one might have expected two Germanys to have emerged when the Soviets left, but instead the general conclusion was that an independent East Germany made no sense, and the Germans rushed into each other's arms.

Nationalism can lead to war, of course, but as the experience in Western Europe suggests, it does not have to be eradicated for peace to prevail. France and Germany today do not by any means agree about everything but, shattering the pattern of the century previous to 1945, they no longer even conceive of using war or the threat of war to resolve their disagreements. As F. H. Hinsley has put it, in Europe and North America, once "the cockpit for the world's great wars," states "are coming to terms with the fact that war has ceased to be one of their options" at least in their dealings with one another.[14]

A hundred years ago, as Michael Howard has observed, "war was almost universally considered an acceptable, perhaps an inevitable and for many people a desirable way of settling international differences." Oliver Wendell Holmes told the Harvard graduating class in 1895 that war's message was "divine." John Ruskin found war to be the "foundation of all the higher virtues and faculties of men." Alexis de Tocqueville concluded that "war almost always enlarges the mind of a people and raises their character." Émile Zola considered war to be "life itself." Igor Stravinsky believed that war was "necessary for human progress."[15] Those views, so common then, are remarkably rare today in the developed world.

---

14   F. H. Hinsley, "Peace and War in Modern Times," in *The Quest for Peace,* ed. Raimo Väyrynen (Beverly Hills, 1987), 78–79.
15   Mueller, *Retreat from Doomsday,* 38–40, 45.

This may not quite be the "systematic evidence demonstrating that Europeans believe war is obsolete" that John Mearsheimer has called for.[16] But it does suggest that the appeal of war has diminished markedly, that war is going out of style on a continent that for centuries was the most warlike in the world.

It will be of great interest to see if that attitude has infected Eastern Europe as the countries there chart their destinies after the quiet cataclysm we have just experienced. As noted, they have done remarkably well at avoiding violence during their liberation from Soviet rule, and that may lead one to hope that, despite national surges and despite the Yugoslavia case, international war, at least, can be avoided in the area. Indeed, nationalism could well be a constructive force: If Poland survives its current test of trauma and turmoil, Polish nationalism will probably have been an important strength.

The Catastrophe Quota. This survey has been reasonably optimistic about most issues of war and peace in the post-World War III era. As the discussion of nationalism suggests, however, it should not be concluded that conflict itself will somehow go away. Conflict is inevitable, because it is impossible for everyone to have exactly the same interests. The issue is not whether conflict will persist, but whether countries will use war to settle these conflicts.

It seems safe to conclude, however, that for many observers, the catastrophe quota will always remain comfortably full. In his review of a new book by Michael Howard, for example, Herbert Mitgang managed to remain gloomy even when Howard concluded that it is "quite possible that war in the sense of major, organised armed conflict between highly developed societies may not recur, and that a stable framework for international order will become firmly established."[17] Given a half-century of terror and trauma about thermonuclear catastrophe, one might have thought Howard was bringing good, even giddily optimistic, news. Instead, Mitgang became preoccupied by Howard's prediction that local armed conflict will continue.

What seems to happen is that when big evils vanish, lesser ones

16 Mearsheimer, "Back to the Future," 41.   17 Howard, *Lessons of History,* 176.

are quickly promoted to take their place. At one point Mitgang argues that the following observation of Howard's is "prescient": "The one place in the world today where a global conflict might still conceivably originate is the Persian Gulf."[18] The only way that statement could be considered prescient would be if one elevated the recent conflict in the Middle East to the status of "global conflict." And Mitgang adds that "after two World Wars, it's hard to distinguish local wars from large-scale wars."[19] One would have thought it would continue to be easy to discriminate.

Even though the chances of thermonuclear catastrophe have diminished to the point where remarkably few even worry about it any more, some have espied a new enemy: Japan. Those of the FLASH! JAPAN BUYS PEARL HARBOR! school argue that we must now fear not "missile vulnerability" but "semiconductor vulnerability." And "economics," they apparently seriously warn us, "is the continuation of war by other means."[20] Others have sighted a more vaporous enemy—chaos, uncertainty, unpredictability—and some even have been given to yearning for the old Cold War days when we, like Damocles or like those scorpions in that legendary bottle, were comfortable in our certainty about what the danger was.

It can be a fundamental and analytically mischievous error to confuse peace with tranquility, certainty, or predictability. Peace is quite compatible with trouble, conflict, contentiousness, hostility, racism, inequality, hatred, avarice, calumny, injustice, petulance, greed, vice, slander, squalor, lechery, xenophobia, malice, and oppression—*and* with chaos, uncertainty, and unpredictability. It is also entirely compatible, as it happens, with economics.

To achieve peace, people do not necessarily have to become admirable or gentle. Neither do they need to stifle all their unpleasant instincts and proclivities and disagreements, nor to abandon eco-

18 Howard, *Lessons of History*, 169.
19 Herbert Mitgang, "Looking at History with a Military Slant," *New York Times*, 3 April 1991.
20 Samuel P. Huntington, "America's Changing Strategic Interests," *Survival* 33 (January/February 1991): 8, 10. The concept of economic war comes close to being oxymoronic. There are times when it may make some sense (as when the world ganged up in 1990 against Iraq), but while war is substantially zero sum, economic exchange, while not always fully fair or equal, is generally positive sum.

nomics (which, it seems, will always be with us). They merely need to abandon the rather absurd institution of war as a method for dealing with one another. The abolition of slavery may have made the world better, but it certainly did not make it perfect. Similarly, peace is not a utopian condition; it is merely better than the alternative. Thus, misanthropes can take unaccustomed cheer: Even in a state of considerable peace there will still be plenty to complain and worry about.

5

Some Lessons from the Cold War

ARTHUR SCHLESINGER, JR.

In those faraway days when the Cold War was young, the English historian Sir Herbert Butterfield lectured at Notre Dame on "The Tragic Element in Modern International Conflict." Historians writing about modern wars, Butterfield said, characteristically start off with a "heroic" vision of things. They portray good men struggling against bad, virtue resisting evil. In this embattled mood, they see only the sins of the enemy and ignore the underlying structural dilemmas that so often provoke international clashes.

As time passes and emotions subside, history enters the "academic" phase. Now historians see "a terrible human predicament" at the heart of the story, "a certain situation that contains the element of conflict irrespective of any special wickedness in any of the parties concerned." Wickedness may deepen the predicament, but conflict would be there anyway. Perspective, Butterfield proposed, teaches us "to be a little more sorry for both parties than they knew how to be for one another." History moves on from melodrama to tragedy.[1]

Butterfield made a pretty good forecast of the way Cold War historiography has evolved in the more than forty years since he spoke. In the United States the "heroic" phase took two forms: the orthodox in the 1940s and 1950s, with the Russians cast as the villains, and the revisionist in the 1960s, with the Americans as the villains. By the 1980s, American Cold War historians discerned what one of the best of them, John Lewis Gaddis, called an

---

1 Herbert Butterfield, "The Tragic Element in Modern International Conflict," was published in *Review of Politics*, April 1950, and reprinted in Butterfield, *History and Human Relations* (London, 1951), 9–36.

"emerging post-revisionist synthesis."[2] History began to pass from a weapon in the battle into a more analytical effort to define structural dilemmas and to understand adversary concerns. *Glasnost* permitted comparable historiographical evolution in the former Soviet Union.

Quite right: The more one contemplates the Cold War, the more irrelevant the allocation of blame seems. The Second World War left the international order in acute derangement. With the Axis states vanquished, the Western European allies spent, the colonial empires in tumult and dissolution, great gaping holes appeared in the structure of world power. Only two nations—the United States and the Soviet Union—had the military strength, the ideological conviction, and the political will to fill these vacuums.

But why did this old-fashioned geopolitical rivalry billow up into a holy war so intense and obsessive as to threaten the very existence of human life on the planet? The two nations were constructed on opposite and profoundly antagonistic principles. They were divided by the most significant and fundamental disagreements over human rights, individual liberties, cultural freedom, the role of civil society, the direction of history, and the destiny of man. Each state saw the other as irrevocably hostile to its own essence. Given the ideological conflict on top of the geopolitical confrontation, no one should be surprised at what ensued. Conspiratorial explanations are hardly required. The real surprise would have been if there had been no Cold War.

And why has humanity survived the Cold War? The reason that the Cold War never exploded into hot war was surely (and by providential irony) the invention of nuclear weapons. One is inclined to support the suggestion (Elspeth Rostow's, I think) that the Nobel Peace Prize should have gone to the atomic bomb.

At last this curious episode in modern history is over, and we must ask what lessons we may hope to learn from a long, costly, dark, dreary, and dangerous affair; what precautions humanity should take to prevent comparable episodes in the future. I would suggest half a dozen fallacies that the world might well forego in years to come.

2   John Lewis Gaddis, "The Emerging Post-Revisionist Synthesis on the Origins of the Cold War," *Diplomatic History* 7 (Summer 1983): 171–90.

The first might be called the fallacy of overinterpreting the enemy. In the glory days of the Cold War, each side attributed to the other a master plan for world domination joined with diabolical efficiency in executing the plan. Such melodramatic imagining of brilliant and demonic enemies was truer to, say, Sax Rohmer, the creator of Dr. Fu Manchu, than to shuffling historical reality.

No doubt Soviet leaders believed that the dialectic of history would one day bring about the victory of communism. No doubt Western leaders believed that the nature of man and markets would one day bring about the victory of free society. But such generalized hopes were far removed from operational master plans.

"The superpowers," as Henry Kissinger well put it,

> often behave like two heavily armed blind men feeling their way around a room, each believing himself in mortal peril from the other whom he assumes to have perfect vision. Each side should know that frequently uncertainty, compromise, and incoherence are the essence of policymaking. Yet each tends to ascribe to the other a consistency, foresight, and coherence that its own experience belies. Of course, over time, even two blind men can do enormous damage to each other, not to speak of the room.[3]

The room has happily survived. But the blind men meanwhile escalated the geopolitical/ideological confrontation into a compulsively interlocked heightening of tension, spurred on by authentic differences in principle, by real and supposed clashes of interest, and by a wide range of misperception, misunderstanding, and demagoguery. Each superpower undertook for what it honestly saw as defensive reasons actions that the other honesty saw as unacceptably threatening and requiring stern countermeasures. Each persevered in corroborating the fears of the other. Each succumbed to the propensity to perceive local conflicts in global terms, political conflicts in moral terms, and relative differences in absolute terms. Together, in lockstep, they expanded the Cold War.

In overinterpreting the motives and actions of the other, each side forgot Emerson's invaluable precept: "In analysing history, do not be too profound, for often the causes are quite simple."[4]

3 Henry Kissinger, *White House Years* (Boston, 1979), 522.
4 Ralph Waldo Emerson, *Journals*, ed. E. W. Emerson and W. E. Forbes (Boston, 1908–1914), 4:160.

Both superpowers should have known from their own experience that governments mostly live from day to day responding to events as they come, that decisions are more often the result of improvisation, ignorance, accident, fatigue, chance, blunder, and sometimes plain stupidity than of orchestrated master plans. One lesson to be drawn from the Cold War is that more things in life are to be explained by cock-up, to use the British term, than by conspiracy.

An accompanying phenomenon, at first a consequence and later a reinforcing cause of overinterpretation, was the embodiment of the Cold War in government institutions. Thus our second fallacy: The fallacy of overinstitutionalizing the policy. The Soviet Union, a police state committed to dogmas of class war and capitalist conspiracy and denied countervailing checks of free speech and press, had institutionalized the Cold War from the day Lenin arrived at the Finland Station. In later years the Cold War became for Stalin a convenient means of justifying his own arbitrary power and the awful sacrifices he demanded from the Soviet peoples. "Stalin needed the Cold War," observed Earl Browder, whom Stalin purged as chief of the American Communist party, "to keep up the sharp international tensions by which he alone could maintain such a regime in Russia."[5]

In Washington by the 1950s the State Department, the Defense Department, the Central Intelligence Agency, the Federal Bureau of Investigation, and the National Security Council developed vested bureaucratic interests in the theory of a militarily expansionist Soviet Union. The Cold War conferred power, money, prestige, and public influence on these agencies and on the people who ran them. By the natural law of bureaucracies, their stake in the conflict steadily grew. Outside of government, arms manufacturers, politicians, professors, publicists, pontificators, and demagogues invested careers and fortunes in the Cold War.

In time, the adversary Cold War agencies evolved a sort of tacit collusion across the Iron Curtain. Probably the greatest racket in the Cold War was the charade periodically enacted by generals and admirals announcing the superiority of the other side in order

5   Steven G. Neal, "A Comrade's Last Harrumph," *Philadelphia Inquirer*, 5 August 1973.

to get bigger budgets for themselves. As President John F. Kennedy remarked to Norman Cousins, the editor of the *Saturday Review*, in the spring of 1963, "The hard-liners in the Soviet Union and the United States feed on one another."[6]

Institutions, alas, do not fold their tents and silently steal away. Ideas crystallized in bureaucracies resist change. With the Cold War at last at an end, each side faces the problem of deconstructing entrenched Cold War agencies spawned and fortified by nearly half a century of mutually profitable competition. One has only to reflect on the forces behind the anti-Gorbachev conspiracy of August 1991.

A third fallacy may be called the fallacy of arrogant prediction. As a devotee of a cyclical approach to American political history, I would not wish to deny that history exhibits uniformities and recurrences. But it is essential to distinguish between those phenomena that are predictable and those that are not. Useful historical generalizations are mostly statements about broad, deep-running, long-term changes: the life-cycle of revolutions, for example, or the impact of industrialization and urbanization, or the influence of climate or sea power or the frontier. The short term, however, contains too many variables, depends too much on accident and fortuity and personality, to permit exact and specific forecasts.

We have been living through extraordinary changes in the former Soviet Union and in Eastern Europe, in South Africa and in the Middle East. What is equally extraordinary is that *no one foresaw these changes*. All the statesmen, all the sages, all the savants, all the professors, all the prophets, all those bearded chaps on "Nightline"—all were caught unaware and taken by surprise; all were befuddled and impotent before the perpetual astonishments of the future. History has an abiding capacity to outwit our certitudes.

Just a few years back some among us were so absolutely sure of the consequences if we did not smash the Reds at once that they called for preventive nuclear war. Had they been able to persuade the U.S. government to drop the bomb on the Soviet Union in the

6   Norman Cousins, *The Improbable Triumvirate* (New York, 1972), 114.

1950s or on China in the 1960s . . . but, thank heaven, they never did; and no one today, including those quondam preventive warriors themselves, regrets the American failure to do so.

The Almighty no doubt does know the future. But He has declined to confide such foresight to frail and erring mortals. In the early years of the Cold War, Reinhold Niebuhr warned of "the depth of evil to which individuals and communities may sink . . . when they try to play the role of God to history."[7] Let us not fall for people who tell us that we must take drastic action today because of their conjectures as to what some other fellow or nation may do five or ten or twenty years from now.

Playing God to history is the dangerous consequence of our fourth fallacy—the fallacy of national self-righteousness. "No government or social system is so evil," President Kennedy said in his American University speech in 1963, "that its people must be condemned as lacking in virtue," and he called on Americans as well as Russians to reexamine attitudes toward the Cold War, "for our attitude is as essential as theirs."[8] This thought came as rather a shock to those who assumed that the American side was so manifestly right that self-examination was unnecessary.

Kennedy liked to quote a maxim from the British military pundit Liddell Hart: "Never corner an opponent, and always assist him to save his face. Put yourself in his shoes—so as to see things through his eyes. Avoid self-righteousness like the devil—nothing is so self-blinding."[9] Perhaps Kennedy did not always live up to those standards himself, but he did on great occasions, like the Cuban missile crisis, and he retained a capacity for ironical objectivity that is rare among political leaders.

Objectivity—seeing ourselves as others see us—is a valuable adjunct to statesmanship. Can we be so sure that our emotional judgments of the moment represent the last word and the final truth? The angry ideological conflicts that so recently obsessed us may not greatly interest our posterity. Our great-grandchildren may well wonder what in heaven's name those disagreements could have

7 Reinhold Niebuhr, *The Irony of American History* (New York, 1952), 173.
8 John F. Kennedy, *Public Papers, 1963* (Washington, 1964), 460–61.
9 Arthur M. Schlesinger, Jr., *A Thousand Days: John F. Kennedy in the White House* (Boston, 1965), 110.

been that drove the Soviet Union and the United States to the brink of blowing up the planet.

Men and women a century from now will very likely find the Cold War as obscure and incomprehensible as we today find the Thirty Years War—the terrible conflict that devastated much of Europe not too long ago. Looking back at the twentieth century, our descendants will very likely be astonished at the disproportion between the causes of the Cold War, which may well seem trivial, and the consequences, which could have meant the veritable end of history.

Russians and Americans alike came to see the Cold War as a duel between two superpowers, a Soviet-American duopoly. But the reduction of the Cold War to a bilateral game played by the Soviet Union and the United States is a fifth fallacy. The nations of Europe were not spectators at someone else's match. They were players too.

Revisionist historians, determined to blame the Cold War on an American drive for world economic hegemony, have studiously ignored the role of Europe. Washington, they contend, was compelled to demand an "open door" for American trade and investment everywhere on the planet because American capitalism had to expand in order to survive. The Soviet Union was the main obstacle to a world market controlled by the United States. So, by revisionist dogma, American leaders whipped up an unnecessary Cold War in order to save the capitalist system.

No matter that some fervent open door advocates, like Henry A. Wallace, were also fervent opponents of the Cold War. No matter that the republics of the former Soviet Union now want nothing more than American trade and investment and full integration into the world market. And no matter that most Western European nations in the 1940s had Socialist governments and that the democratic socialist leaders—Clement Attlee and Ernest Bevin in Britain, Leon Blum and Paul Ramadier in France, Paul-Henri Spaak in Belgium, Kurt Schumacher, Ernst Reuter, and Willy Brandt in West Germany—had powerful reasons of their own to fear the spread of Stalinist influence and Soviet power.

Such men could not have cared less about an open door for American capitalism. They cared deeply, however, about the future of democratic socialism. When I used to see Aneurin Bevan, the leader of the left wing of the British Labour party, in London in 1944, he doubted that the wartime alliance would last and saw the struggle for postwar Europe as between the democratic socialists and the Communists. "The Communist party," Bevan wrote in 1951, "is the sworn and inveterate enemy of the Socialist and Democratic parties. When it associates with them it does so as a preliminary to destroying them."[10] Many in the Truman administration in the 1940s espoused this view and, dubbing themselves (in private) NCL, favored American support for the non-Communist Left.

The democratic socialists, moreover, were in advance of official Washington in organizing against the Stalinist threat. Despite his above-the-battle stance at Notre Dame, Herbert Butterfield himself wrote in 1969, "A new generation often does not know (and does not credit the fact when informed) that Western Europe once wondered whether the United States could ever be awakened to the danger from Russia."[11] The subsequent opening of British Foreign Office papers voluminously documents Sir Herbert's point.

Far from seeing President Truman in the revisionist mode as an anti-Soviet zealot hustling a reluctant Europe into a gratuitous Cold War, the Foreign Office saw him for a considerable period as an irresolute waffler distracted by the delusion that the United States could play mediator between Britain and the Soviet Union. Ernest Bevin, Britain's Socialist foreign secretary, thought Truman's policy was "to withdraw from Europe and in effect leave the British to get on with the Russians as best they could."[12] A true history of the Cold War must add European actors to the cast and broaden both research nets and analytical perspectives.

The theory of the Cold War as a Soviet-American duopoly is sometimes defended on the ground that, after all, the United States and the Soviet Union were in full command of their respective alliances. But nationalism, the most potent political emotion of the age, challenged the reign of the superpowers almost from the start:

10 Aneurin Bevan, foreword, *The Curtain Falls*, ed. Denis Healey (London, 1951).
11 Herbert Butterfield, "Morality and an International Order," in *The Aberystwith Papers: International Politics, 1919–1969*, ed. Brian Porter (Oxford, 1972), 353–54.
12 Alan Bullock, *Ernest Bevin: Foreign Secretary, 1945–1951* (London, 1983), 216.

Tito, Mao, and others vs. Moscow; De Gaulle, Eden and others
vs. Washington. Experience has adequately demonstrated how
limited superpowers are in their ability to order their allies around
and even to control client governments wholly dependent on them
for economic and military support. Far from clients being the prisoners of the superpower, superpowers often end as prisoners of
their clients.

These are lessons Washington has painfully learned (or at least
was painfully taught; has the government finally learned them?) in
Vietnam, El Salvador, Israel, Saudi Arabia, Kuwait. As for the Soviet Union, its brutal interventions and wretched Quislings in Eastern Europe only produced bitterness and hatred. The impact of
clients on principals is another part of the unwritten history of the
Cold War. The Cold War was *not* a bilateral game.

Nor was it—our sixth and final fallacy—a zero-sum game. For
many years, Cold War theology decreed that a gain for one side
was by definition a defeat for the other. This notion led logically
not to an interest in negotiation but to a demand for capitulation.
In retrospect the Cold War, humanity's most intimate brush with
collective suicide, can only remind us of the ultimate interdependence of nations and of peoples.

After President Kennedy and Premier Khrushchev stared down
the nuclear abyss together in October 1962, they came away determined to move as fast as they could toward détente. Had Kennedy lived, Khrushchev might have held on to power a little longer,
and together they would have further subdued the excesses of the
Cold War. They rejected the zero-sum approach and understood
that intelligent negotiation brings mutual benefit. I am not an unlimited admirer of Ronald Reagan, but he deserves his share of
credit for taking Mikhail Gorbachev seriously, abandoning the zero-
sum fallacy he had embraced for so long, and moving the Cold
War toward its end.

And why indeed has it ended? If the ideological confrontation
gave the geopolitical rivalry its religious intensity, so the collapse
of the ideological debate took any apocalyptic point out of the
Cold War. The proponents of liberal society were proven right.
After seventy years of trial, communism turned out—by the
confession of its own leaders—to be an economic, political, and

moral disaster. Democracy won the political argument between East and West. The market won the economic argument. Difficulties lie ahead, but the fundamental debate that created the Cold War is finished.

6

Nuclear Weapons and European Security during the Cold War

SAMUEL F. WELLS, JR.

The surprise that all students of the Cold War felt when the Berlin Wall was breached on 9 November 1989 remains a vivid memory. Other surprises followed as we came to know more about the societies that had existed behind the Iron Curtain. A surprise that has been widely commented upon was the hollow quality of the Communist regimes, such as those in the German Democratic Republic (GDR) and in Czechoslovakia, that had appeared from the Western perspective to be so solid. Not only did these regimes collapse quickly but it also became apparent, and was in itself surprising, that their economies had been highly dysfunctional. Some officials within the Communist states realized the seriousness of their economic problems. But in the absence of market prices and interaction with market economies to test how these systems really functioned, outside analysts consistently overestimated the productivity of all of the member states of the Council for Mutual Economic Assistance (COMECON). More surprising was the fact that the Soviet military and the leadership of the Soviet Communist party allowed the governments of Eastern Europe to be overthrown when it could be clearly forecast that one result would be the forced withdrawal of Soviet troops from the former satellites. It is now reasonably clear that as the revolutions of 1989 gained momentum, Mikhail Gorbachev and some of his close advisers came to accept this result, just as it is equally clear that the vast majority of the Soviet military, the leadership of the Communist party, and the KGB (Committee of State Security) did not want to relinquish control of Eastern Europe. It remains unclear, however, why these conservatives did nothing to prevent such an undesirable outcome.

The realization that the Communist bloc was composed of hollow regimes with weak economies has encouraged historians to take a new look at whether or not the Cold War was justified and whether it might have been pursued with too much vigor and military force by the West. Some of the recent academic analysis asserts that U.S. officials greatly exaggerated the Soviet threat and responded with aggressive military policies that produced a more dangerous confrontation than would have otherwise developed. Unfortunately, neither this interpretation nor the more traditional arguments are based on Soviet archival materials. Some evidence from the Communist governments of Eastern Europe and from the People's Republic of China is becoming available, however, and serious efforts are under way to explore these sources so that we can write about the Cold War from both sides.

In reassessing the origins and dynamics of the Cold War from the admittedly one-sided evidence that is currently available, several fundamental conclusions emerge. American officials on occasion did exaggerate the magnitude of the Soviet threat and the malignant intent of Soviet leaders, but in acknowledging these exaggerations it is incorrect to contend that there was no serious Soviet threat. A Soviet challenge to a stable world and to U.S. interests in democratic political systems and open economies clearly existed. A forthcoming book by David Holloway of Stanford University on Stalin's nuclear policy demonstrates that at a time immediately after World War II, when the Soviet Union was in need of top scientific and technical personnel as well as material resources to rebuild the country, immense human and physical resources were devoted to the construction of a nuclear weapons program. By early 1947 the Soviet military had developed a plan for a strategic counteroffensive using nuclear weapons and long-range bombers, and by 1950 Stalin was pressing his aircraft design teams to develop an intercontinental bomber.[1]

The fact that these plans continued has become obvious with the end of the Cold War. Documents from the GDR, seized by

1   David Holloway, *Stalin and the Bomb* (Yale University Press, forthcoming).

West German forces only hours after formal unification on 3 October 1990, show that the Warsaw Pact had developed war plans for an invasion of Western Europe. These war plans, as described by a reporter for the *Wall Street Journal,* indicate that the objective was not simply to defend Warsaw Pact members. Under the guise of countering an offensive by the North Atlantic Treaty Organization (NATO), the pact members planned to move through all of Western Europe with the goal of seizing and holding territory. Their plan included detailed arrangements for operating transportation systems in West European countries and for providing occupation money in a transition period to Warsaw Pact rule. These plans also indicate a clear intent to use chemical, biological, and tactical nuclear weapons in an attack that was premised on advancing through Western Europe at the rate of thirty miles per day.[2] Other disclosures in the eastern part of Germany show that a massive Soviet presence formed what one reporter has called a "Soviet state that operated within" the GDR. Senior officials in NATO have disclosed that a twenty-two-thousand-mile Soviet-controlled road network linked Soviet bases throughout East Germany, a network whose existence was unknown to the East German military as well as to Western intelligence. The total territory reserved for Soviet military use and denied to East German military officials totaled more than 2 percent of the former GDR. East Germany held the largest proportion of Soviet offensive forces, including roughly one thousand separate installations, among which were at least twenty air bases. One training area near Potsdam was as large as 290 square miles.[3] In the months ahead, a wealth of additional evidence about the offensive military preparations of the Soviet Union and its allies will become available.

Although the United States may at times have used military power excessively or wrongly, U.S. military strength was a fundamental element in containing Soviet expansionism and in forcing the Warsaw Pact to disintegrate and the Soviets to acknowledge the need

2 Timothy Aeppel, "East German Papers Yield War Scenario: Plan Included Nuclear Attack on Western Europe," *Wall Street Journal,* 13 June 1991. For greater detail on Warsaw Pact war plans and training exercises see Lothar Rühl, "Offensive Defence in the Warsaw Pact," *Survival* 33 (September–October 1991): 442–50.
3 Joseph Fitchett, "The Iron Curtain Hid Soviet Military Ministates," *International Herald Tribune,* 29–30 June 1991.

for fundamental reform. The West, and the United States in particular, did rely too heavily on military power in its contest with the Soviet Union. In instances such as the attempt to destabilize the Castro regime in Cuba, military power was used excessively. It was used wrongly in the Korean War, when UN forces crossed the 38th parallel in an attempt to unify Korea by force, and throughout the Vietnam War as well. Yet, the testimony of numerous civilian and military officials from the Soviet Union and Eastern Europe indicates that U.S. military strength, especially the significant buildup beginning in the late Carter administration and extending through both Reagan terms, did prove to be a significant factor in forcing the Eastern European regimes and the Soviet Union to change.

Evidence from recent months now makes it clear that U.S. support for democratic institutions and human rights through even the darkest days of the Cold War had a much greater effect inside Eastern Europe and the Soviet Union than most American foreign policy specialists believed at the time. We have graphic testimony by members of underground organizations and opposition groups, such as the Solidarity movement in Poland, that American support for human rights and democratic institutions, broadcasts of the Voice of America and Radio Free Europe, and activities of Americans at review conferences by the Conference on Security and Cooperation in Europe (CSCE) were fundamental in maintaining their hope and in giving them mechanisms through which they could resist repression in their own countries.[4] Ernst Kux, a distinguished commentator on Communist affairs, even argues that the Helsinki process, as the meetings and procedures of the CSCE are commonly called, "had a greater influence on developments in Europe than Gorbachev's *perestroyka.*"[5]

Although democracy was always part of the superpower competition and human rights became an important element in the Western agenda after the early 1970s, the Soviet-American rivalry

---

4 For details on the human rights campaign see Max M. Kampelman, *Entering New Worlds: The Memoirs of a Private Man in Public Life* (New York, 1991), chaps. 13–18 passim.

5 Ernst Kux, "Revolution in Eastern Europe—Revolution in the West?" *Problems of Communism* 40 (May–June 1991): 6.

basically focused on the nuclear arms race. This was in large part due to the tremendous destructive power of nuclear weapons and to the dramatic way in which the atomic bombs dropped on Hiroshima and Nagasaki brought World War II to a swift and successful conclusion. But it was also in some measure due to the drama of the weapons competition in which the United States held a monopoly on nuclear weapons for some years only to be shocked when the technologically inferior Soviets detonated their first atomic device in 1949. Even though U.S. officials gave no serious consideration to using nuclear weapons in the Korean War, each military service wanted a nuclear mission and built part of its force structure around nuclear weapons. For the American public, the nuclear menace quickly became part of every citizen's consciousness through the films of Hollywood and the civil defense drills that were held in every community beginning in the 1950s.

Nuclear technology allowed the United States to dominate NATO in a way that would have been impossible under a nonnuclear regime. The United States always had superior technology, especially in the nuclear area, and it invested huge resources in laboratories and delivery mechanisms to maintain that advantage. This technological lead, especially in nuclear weapons, allowed the United States to avoid heavy expenditures on conventional forces after the Korean War and was the basis for the lower cost New Look strategy of the Eisenhower administration. In addition, the heavy symbolism of the nuclear era, conveyed in such images as Strategic Air Command (SAC) alerts and the "football" containing the codes for the release of nuclear weapons that accompanies the president of the United States in his every movement, enhanced the power of the president and his staff, especially the national security adviser. The prestige and symbolism of nuclear weapons was further reinforced by the elaborate theology surrounding nuclear doctrine, a theology that was almost purposefully designed to be impenetrable for laymen. Leadership in nuclear affairs almost automatically gave the United States the priority position in shaping NATO decisions and studies through the power of the U.S.-uniformed Supreme Allied Commander in Europe (SACEUR) and through the ability to chair all of the key groups and committees within the alliance.

Nuclear weapons also had a significant influence on U.S. relations with its allies. Nuclear cooperation, along with intelligence sharing, was a key element of the special relationship with Great Britain. It gave the British the prestige of being the second member of the nuclear club at minimum cost. But it left Britain hostage to U.S. weapons decisions such as the cancellation of the Skybolt missile that nearly toppled the Macmillan government. The special relationship also posed problems for British ties to Europe. It gave Charles de Gaulle the basis for twice vetoing British membership in the European Economic Community and diluted the British commitment to an integrated Europe when membership later became possible.

For France, the development of an independent nuclear weapons program became the most critical reason for withdrawing from NATO's integrated military command. The French nuclear program did not begin with this objective, because the basic development of a nuclear weapons program occurred under the Fourth Republic, when France assumed that it would remain part of the military arm of the alliance. But the rearmament of Germany, Britain's favored nuclear relationship with the United States, and the American assertion of dominance in military affairs within the alliance persuaded General de Gaulle to pursue an independent course in nuclear affairs when he returned to power in 1958. The general demanded a role equal to Britain's in directing the alliance and requested U.S. assistance in nuclear development. When both requests were rejected, and when the United States provided support for the Algerian rebels against France, de Gaulle decided to withdraw France from the integrated command.

Gaining access to nuclear weapons and being included in the nuclear planning process became the principal goals of the West German government after the Korean War. Konrad Adenauer was quick to realize that having a seat at the table when nuclear decisions were made was the only way for Germany to influence its own future. Given Soviet conventional superiority and the U.S. adoption of its New Look strategy in 1954, Germany had to argue for forward defense and an early use of nuclear weapons in order to minimize damage to German territory in any war. As Soviet nuclear capability increased after Sputnik, and with Soviet nuclear and political blackmail in the Berlin crises after 1958, the United States led the process of giving Germany access to nuclear decision making. The Bundeswehr had possession of tactical nuclear weapons by 1960, although the United States and Great Britain still retained control over their use, and German representatives were included on nuclear and Berlin contingency planning in 1961. This new political participation gave the Federal Republic a role in nuclear targeting, participation in changes of strategy, and access to all command channels. Taken together, these new roles were a major step toward including Germany as an equal partner in the Atlantic alliance.

Germany has always shown a profound ambivalence about this partnership. Even as he was negotiating to gain a seat at the nuclear table of the alliance, Adenauer had deep reservations about allied plans to use nuclear weapons to defend Berlin and worked resolutely to head off situations that might require such use. When in 1961 *Der Spiegel* published the results of a NATO staff exercise showing the effect of a number of nuclear explosions over the Federal Republic, the German public began to press for a new strategy, and this became a critical element in developing flexible response, with its forward defense doctrine. Although forward defense was not militarily sound at a time when the West was conventionally inferior to the Warsaw Pact, it was a politically necessary doctrine for a German public increasingly anxious about the effects of war. By the mid 1960s, German popular antipathy toward nuclear warfare had so solidified that the Federal Republic gradually turned against the early use of nuclear weapons.

In the course of the Cold War, Germany replaced Great Britain as the principal ally of the United States. While U.S. relations with Great Britain retained special qualities, by the early 1960s, Germany had become more important to Washington in a variety of ways. One can almost date the change from the summer of 1961, when Germany was included for the first time in formal Berlin crisis contingency planning. Chancellor Adenauer had always tried to promote close ties to Washington, but just as he achieved this goal, the McNamara regime in the Defense Department began to develop policies that called for the use of tactical nuclear weapons in Europe and a reduction in conventional forces. In the winter of

1961–62, Adenauer turned against the United States and moved closer to France and General de Gaulle. By the time of his death, Adenauer was thoroughly anti-American. Thereafter, Germany would remain the principal alliance partner for the United States. But whenever new deployments of nuclear weapons were proposed, strong political opposition would develop in Germany—opposition that ended the political careers of leaders such as Helmut Schmidt and forced his Social Democratic party to reorient its policies.

French withdrawal from the integrated military command significantly affected alliance dynamics. Because both Britain and Germany were in different ways dependent on the United States, agreement was easier among these three on key military questions, such as the new strategy of flexible response. Brigadier Kenneth Hunt, a central participant in the negotiations within the Defense Planning Committee of NATO in 1966 and 1967, declared recently that "after months of inconclusive debate, a consensus began to develop around the American position only to have France totally obstruct negotiations for over three months. But when the French withdrew from the committee, agreement on Flexible Response came fairly quickly."[6] From the mid-1960s through the mid-1980s, NATO decisions tended to be driven by the prospect of new technologies that generated proposals from Washington every few months. Representatives from London and Bonn would race to Washington to try to influence these proposals before they were formally submitted, and many useful channels of communication and influence developed within this process, channels in which the French played no role as a result of their decision to withdraw from the integrated command. Still, some means of coordination with the French were created. The principal device was using the agreements on the joint occupation of Berlin to include the French in all aspects of contingency planning for Berlin, including possible use of nuclear weapons. Many specialists, including some French analysts, would agree that the French withdrawal from the integrated command allowed the development of a strong

6   Brigadier Kenneth Hunt, statement at a conference of the Nuclear History Program, Ebenhausen, Germany, 29 June 1991.

internal consensus in support of an independent French defense program built around a national nuclear force, but that this domestic consensus came at a high cost in influence within the alliance and in East-West relations more broadly.

Beyond alliance relationships, nuclear weapons had a number of important effects during the Cold War. Nuclear threats were made in a number of superpower crises, ranging from Korea and Berlin to the Taiwan Straits and Cuba. American leaders resorted to nuclear coercion more frequently than Soviet officials, and most of these threats came in the first two decades after 1945. Threats were most often issued when domestic political credibility was under challenge, or when allies were in danger and needed a reinforced guarantee of protection. Strategic analysts have often claimed that the development of powerful nuclear arsenals and the occasional threats to use them constrained military adventurism and prevented general war in Europe for over forty-five years. This argument has some plausibility, but its force is diminished by confused and contradictory official thinking about whether nuclear weapons could ever be used, under what circumstances, and with what results.

Whether or not nuclear weapons contributed to stability in the Cold War, the nature of nuclear competition changed after 1965. The Cuban missile crisis had a generally sobering effect on both sides. The Soviet Union invested heavily in a drive to achieve nuclear parity, a goal that it had achieved by 1970. The United States, increasingly committed to an expanding war in Southeast Asia, wanted to avoid clashes with Moscow. Early in the 1970s, two other developments altered the Soviet-American rivalry. The superpowers reached a general political accommodation in Europe through agreements on the status of Berlin and the Helsinki accords, and the United States reduced the chances of conflict with China by initiating détente with Beijing. Concurrently with these developments, and perhaps as a result of them, the incidence of nuclear threats declined and their locus shifted away from such high-value points as Berlin and Cuba to less vital areas in the Third World. Nuclear issues in Europe continued to receive attention as the debate on the deployment of new theater weapons raged through the 1980s, but this was essentially a political competition that no official believed would lead to a threat of nuclear war.[7]

Nuclear weapons, one can argue, had the further effect of lengthening the Cold War by making it less expensive. After 1948, military and political officials consistently viewed a robust and modernized nuclear force as a way to keep the number of troops under arms to a minimum. When the Korean War forced a large expansion of the armed forces, planners in the Truman administration prepared for a sharp reduction of manpower after the war on the basis of an expanded reliance on nuclear weapons. When he became president, Dwight D. Eisenhower endorsed and expanded these plans in implementing the New Look strategy and the nuclear doctrine of massive retaliation.[8] The Vietnam War posed a more complicated problem, because of the intense domestic opposition to the war, much of which focused on the draft. The Nixon administration met this issue and the need to reduce military expenditures by instituting an all-volunteer military force and reducing active duty personnel by almost 1.5 million, while dramatically increasing nuclear power through the decision to deploy MIRVed (Multiple Independently-targeted Re-entry Vehicle) missiles, each with between three and fourteen separately targetable warheads.

Further complicating any effort to wind down the Cold War was the difficulty of making compromises on nuclear arms levels when an opponent held your population hostage to near-instant destruction. For the United States, there clearly were periods during the last forty-five years when political preferences and economic stringency would have combined to create a less active foreign policy and a sustained era of détente with the Soviet Union. But the existence of a large Soviet nuclear arsenal targeted on American cities and military installations and a form of domestic politics that made it perilous to appear conciliatory toward the Communists joined to make serious arms reduction difficult.

Acknowledging the obstacles on both sides to any concessions in nuclear arms negotiations only increases the importance of an-

7 For a full and discriminating analysis of nuclear threats see Richard K. Betts, *Nuclear Blackmail and Nuclear Balance* (Washington, 1987).
8 Samuel F. Wells, Jr., "The Origins of Massive Retaliation," *Political Science Quarterly* 96 (Spring 1981): 31–52.

swering the question of why the Soviet leadership chose the path of internal reform and external conciliation. The short answer to this large and complex question is that George F. Kennan was correct in his "X" article prediction that a policy of steady and coordinated containment would lead the Soviet Union to make internal changes. The political, economic, and technological pressure exerted by the West increasingly put the Soviet Union at a disadvantage. When the Reagan administration introduced massive defense programs involving the challenge of new technology, such as that projected for the Strategic Defense Initiative (SDI), Soviet leaders began a reassessment of their system. This evaluation started in 1983 shortly after the announcement of SDI by President Reagan. The initial stages of the Soviet process of reform, under discussion before Gorbachev came to power and instituted in his early months in office, were designed to improve the Soviet system and could easily have led to new levels of rivalry with the West. But the pace of political reform could not be controlled, and the Communist system came apart before serious economic reform had really begun. Domestic weaknesses were the fundamental cause of the collapse of the Soviet system, but competition with the West was an important contributing factor.[9]

The reform process could not be held back in Eastern Europe either. The revolutions of 1989 ended the threat to Western Europe from the Warsaw Pact. The new governments in Eastern Europe demanded the withdrawal of Soviet troops, and these have begun. All organized Soviet military units of the former Soviet Union have left Hungary and Czechoslovakia, and the last are due to leave Poland by the end of 1992 and Germany by 1995. Changes in force levels began quickly to reflect these events. The United States announced plans to reduce its armed forces by 25 percent on 1 August 1990. A treaty further reducing conventional forces in Europe was signed in Paris on 19 November 1990, and the START I Treaty was signed on 31 July 1991.[10]

The unsuccessful coup in Moscow of 19–22 August 1991 began

9 Georges Soutou, "New Europe and the International Historian," *Cambridge Review of International Affairs* 5 (Spring–Summer 1991): 2–3.
10 R. Jeffrey Smith, "The Soviet Summit: Treaty Looks Back, Forward," *The Washington Post*, 1 August 1991.

what might be called the Second Russian Revolution. The refusal by important segments of the Soviet public to accept a Communist party-led reversal of the democratic reforms and the refusal of vital military and KGB units to support the conservative seizure of power doomed the efforts of those George Bush referred to as "the coup people." Mikhail Gorbachev was returned to his office as president, but his power and that of the whole central government was greatly reduced. The breakup of the Soviet Union was under way and would be completed with dramatic speed by the end of 1991. The situation today remains in a high state of confusion; it is not at all clear that the future will witness a gradual evolution of democratic politics in most of the republics or even a weakened commonwealth held loosely together by economic, political, and security mechanisms similar to those envisioned for the European Community after 1992.

The end of the Cold War has changed many of the national and institutional perspectives and strategies of the last four decades. Issues of military security will be less important. NATO must reorient itself to a very different security environment in which general war in Europe is highly unlikely, and the most probable threats in Europe will be ethnic conflict and social and political unrest resulting from economic need. The relationship between the United States and Europe will be quite different as military issues decline in salience and economic questions take center stage. The chances of major nuclear war are greatly reduced, and the most significant issues will be unauthorized seizure and use of nuclear weapons or their proliferation among smaller states, such as Iraq. President Bush's proposal on 27 September 1991 for unilateral nuclear cuts and Gorbachev's response in kind on 5 October 1991 reflect these primary concerns. The role of international organizations such as the United Nations and the Conference on Security and Cooperation in Europe will be increased, and new approaches must be created to deal with conflicts that occur within a state. Any new world order worth its name should include mechanisms to protect the rights of individuals, as well as ethnic and religious groups, from persecution by majorities or governments within their states.

The Cold War leaves more open questions than it does clear

lessons. For example, two scholars have recently analyzed some new archival materials in Prague and question whether firmer Czech resistance, along with greater Western support for the Dubček government, could not have prevented the Soviet invasion of Czechoslovakia in 1968 and thereby hastened the process of liberating Eastern Europe by twenty years.[11] Their basic question and subsequent analysis are indeed provocative, but we cannot begin to shape a full answer until the records in Moscow, Washington, and other capitals are open for research. Many scholars of recent history are eager to provide answers to these important questions when the records become fully available.

11 Jiří Valenta and Jan Moravec, "Could the Prague Spring Have Been Saved?" *Orbis* 35 (Fall 1991): 581–601.

7

Victory in the Postwar Era: Despite the Cold War or Because of It?

ALEXEI FILITOV

It is natural to analyze war in terms of victory and defeat, and so it is almost inevitable that the end of the Cold War will be analyzed in these terms. But is the concept of victory and defeat an appropriate analytical framework for understanding the outcome of the Cold War? What state can possibly claim victory in the Cold War—certainly not the former Soviet Union? But can the United States be considered the victor either?

It seems unlikely that either superpower "won" the Cold War when one compares their relative positions in the world prior to the Cold War with their positions afterward. In 1945 the United States had a monopoly on atomic weapons and was virtually invulnerable to attack. By the end of the Cold War both superpowers had massive atomic arsenals and shared equal insecurity under the regime of Mutual Assured Destruction, a situation that left the Soviet Union no better off than before and that clearly marked a decline in American power.

That the Cold War resulted in the relative decline of both superpowers is also clearly discernible when one examines their economic situations. The military competition of the Cold War left the Soviet Union as economically devastated as it was after World War II. The United States came through the Cold War with its economy much more intact, just as was the case after 1945. But unlike forty-five years ago, its economy is only better off in comparison with its former adversary. It has suffered real economic decline when compared with its allies, a far more important fact for international relations in the post-Cold War era than the fact that the former Soviet Union is in even worse condition.

Given the decline of both superpowers, perhaps Germany and
Japan are more properly regarded as the true winners of the Cold
War. The history of the Federal Republic of Germany makes a
most convincing case for this argument. The Federal Republic can
boast not only of extraordinary economic growth but also of a
political achievement of the first magnitude—reunification. It is
important to note, however, that West Germany did not succeed
by adopting the assumptions of the Cold War. The ideology of the
Cold War emphasized an arms race, confrontation, and an insistence that the eastern frontier of Germany (and NATO's frontline)
be moved well beyond the Oder-Neisse line. West Germany not
only rejected these assumptions but took nearly the opposite course.
It avoided pressure and confrontation; it did not engage in a massive arms buildup; and it accepted the Oder-Neisse line. NATO
did not become an instrument for German revanchism. Germany's
victory was not a victory as defined by the terms of the Cold War.
Rather, the German spirit triumphed over the mentality of the Cold
War and achieved victory in spite of, not because of, the superpower confrontation.

This perspective on Germany's success may perhaps be taken
with a grain of salt. Historians of the "missed opportunities" school
(to which I admittedly belong) will argue that there existed the
possibility that the Cold War could have been aborted and that
Soviet-American cooperation on the German problem could have
begun on several occasions during the last forty-five years, notably
in 1947 and 1948, or from 1953 to 1955, or even, as one historian
has argued, from 1955 to 1958.[1] Such cooperation would have
produced a settlement of the German problem similar to the one
that was achieved in 1990, with much less waste of human and
material resources. Perhaps the only real winner of the Cold War
is a state like Finland—simply because it managed to abstain from
the competition.[2]

Many writers have suggested that a better way to examine the
issue of winners and losers in the Cold War is to shift the question

1 W. Loth, "Die Deutschen und die deutsche Frage von 1949 bis 1969: eine Bilanz,"
   Bundesrepublik Deutschland: Geschichte. Bewusstsein (Bonn, 1989), 45.
2 See R. M. Berry, *American Foreign Policy and the Finnish Exception: Ideological Preferences and Wartime Realities* (Helsinki, 1987).

from which state to which ideology won. Arthur Schlesinger, Jr., provides an illuminating example of this perspective:

The collapse of the ideological debate obviously concluded the Cold War. Communism in the form practiced in the Soviet Union and imposed on Eastern Europe—an absolutist polity based on the dictatorship of an infallible creed, an infallible party, and an infallible leader—is simply and palpably an economic, political, and moral disaster. Democracy has won the political argument between the East and the West. The market has won the economic argument.[3]

Schlesinger's verdict, although basically fair, is not really balanced. While communism in the former Soviet Union and in Eastern Europe has been judged a failure, in other parts of the world the ideological debate is far from over. Still, putting aside semantic debates and fruitless speculation as to the future prospects of ideologies, I strongly disagree with the tendency of Schlesinger and others to equate the Cold War with the ideological debate between East and West. Victory or defeat in the East-West debate over socioeconomic systems and ideologies must not be confused with victory or defeat in the Cold War. This confusion is probably due to the fact that no commonly accepted definition as to what constituted the Cold War exists. In my opinion, the Cold War was simply the unrestricted arms race between the superpowers and the state of hostility between them that continually threatened to erupt into a worldwide holocaust.

Given this definition of the Cold War, it is clear that it did not begin until 1948. Only then did military spending, the American atomic stockpile, and the numbers of men under arms in both camps begin to rise suddenly. Churchill's "Iron Curtain" speech at Fulton, the Truman Doctrine, and the Soviet rejection of the Marshall Plan were all largely irrelevant to the outbreak of the Cold War. The Cold War as a concept and set of assumptions is much narrower in scope than is the East-West ideological conflict. It is, in fact, essentially unrelated to the ideological debate. Far from being merely one aspect of the East-West clash, the Cold War actually

3 Arthur Schlesinger, Jr., "Some Lessons from the Cold War" (Paper presented at Soviet-American Seminar on the Origins of the Cold War, Meshcherino, USSR, 27 June 1990), 12.

obscured, distorted, and retarded the historical debate between these opposing socioeconomic systems in much the same way that the Dynastic Wars of the sixteenth and seventeenth centuries retarded and distorted the emergence of modern capitalism from the feudal system of the Middle Ages.

This analogy is far from perfect. There were real winners and losers in past wars, while the Cold War was an unwinnable contest. There could be no victory within the Cold War, for its premises did not admit victory. What could be defined as victory in an arms race—the outbreak of real war? This is obviously nonsense. If victory did exist, it was victory over the Cold War; it was the defeat of its premises and a concomitant reduction of tensions and demilitarization. In that case the true victor was Mikhail Gorbachev, together, indeed, with Ronald Reagan.

Still, the analogy seems relevant. Regardless of who won the War of Spanish Succession and regardless of whether it even took place, it did not reverse or halt the world trend toward capitalism—although it certainly could be argued that the militaristic society created by that era's "cult of war" did tend to aggravate the birth pangs of the emerging bourgeois social order. Much the same thing can be said about the interaction between the Cold War and the emerging world civilization of our times, which I shall simply term "market and democracy." Although "market and democracy" is too short and inadequate a definition of the emerging world order, because both existed even in ancient Athens, I will stick to it as a shorthand description. Had the Cold War not militarized the historical dialectical argument between East and West, the triumph of "market and democracy" would have come much sooner and would have cost much less. The case of Germany that I cited earlier is but one example of how this might have occurred.[4]

Examined in this context, it is neither surprising nor paradoxical that the Cold War culture perfectly suited those who opposed the emergence of "market and democracy." More surprising and ironic was the fact that the assumptions of the Cold War were willingly accepted and perpetuated by those who supported the "market and democracy" paradigm, despite the fact that the Cold

4 Terms like "militarization of the Cold War" seem to me analogous to phrases like "oily oil" or "wet water."

War only served to strengthen Stalinist structures in the Soviet camp and also, in the long run, began to undermine the "market and democracy" foundations of American society. McCarthyism was just an early harbinger of the steady erosion of American society that was to be brought about by the Cold War.

Some Western scholars have simply blamed the Cold War on misperceptions. This approach is quite in vogue among Russian scholars too, but I do not believe that it is very useful.[5] Misperceptions certainly occurred on both sides, but it was hardly inconceivable that Joseph Stalin, Nikita Khrushchev, or Leonid Brezhnev would have outwitted their Western counterparts in assessing the usefulness for either side of continuing confrontation. Totalitarian societies are more prone to misjudge the world situation than are democratic ones. For the West the problem is different, as Ronald Pruessen pointed out in his study of John Foster Dulles. Dulles's "intellectual grasp," "sophisticated perceptions," and "shrewd analysis" simply did not express themselves in the actual decisions he made.[6] One can argue that Western Cold Warriors were not so much concerned with victory or even superiority as they were with maintaining a continuing enemy that served their own particular goals. Thus, misperceptions were not especially important. The maintenance of their own particular perceptions was what counted. The Cold War cannot be viewed as a war against Stalinism—despite the fact that this is what some Soviet scholars concluded.[7]

Because the Cold War tended for both sides to undermine democracy as well as common sense and rationality in politics generally, it is pertinent to ask why there emerged in the Western world many useful innovations in ways to approach both internal and external social organization so that the "market and democracy" paradigm was able to triumph so rapidly following the end of the Cold War. There were at least two factors that accounted for the success of "market and democracy," despite the retarding

5 See, for instance, the article by E. Yegorova and K. Pleshakov in *International Affairs* (Moscow) 8 (1988): 87–95.

6 Ronald W. Pruessen, "John Foster Dulles and the Predicament of Power," in *John Foster Dulles and the Diplomacy of the Cold War,* ed. Richard H. Immerman (Princeton, 1990), 43.

7 N. Popov, "Vse my v odnoi lodke" [All of us in a single boat], *Literaturnaya gazeta* [Literary newspaper], 3 March 1989.

effect of the Cold War. First, some of the social structures and ideology of the new order already existed, or had at least been proposed, prior to the Cold War. These included aspects of the New Deal in the United States, the *Soziale Markwirtschaft* in Germany, and the concept of supranationality (internationalism). Second, the Cold War was not a constant reality that abruptly ended in one day. The process of dismantling the Cold War did not begin in 1989 or even in 1985, with all due respect to Gorbachev's achievements. Nor can the 1972 détente agreements, or the 1963 Test Ban Treaty, or even the death of Stalin and the Korean armistice in 1953 serve to mark the beginning of the "end" of the Cold War.[8] Rather, starting with American cuts in military spending in 1951, a series of turning points occurred that slowly dismantled the Cold War.[9] Thus, "market and democracy" did not emerge all at once following an abrupt end to the Cold War, but instead developed during the various recesses, lulls, or loops in the Cold War that appeared on and off at various times during the last forty-five years.

Unfortunately, while the West was able to exploit these periodic lulls, the East was unable to make any progress. A telling example of Western success and Eastern failure is the history of European integration. Initially, both East and West put the cart before the horse and tried in vain to organize and impose political and military integration from above without a solid economic foundation. This action was natural in the heat of confrontation generated by the Cold War. But with the achievement of the first prolonged détente after Stalin's death, and following the French Parliament's defeat in 1953 of the EDC, Western Europe switched to what ironically could be called a genuine Marxist approach. Integration now focused on economics first, to be followed later by the creation of a political superstructure. Again ironically, the professed Marxists of the Eastern camp persisted in focusing on military and political integration and, emulating NATO, created the Warsaw Treaty

8 See Robert Tucker, *Evolving Patterns in U.S.-Soviet Relations, 1933–1986* (Washington, 1987), 25, which asserts that "on March 5, 1953, at approximately 9:30 in the morning, the Cold War ended when Josef Stalin breathed his last."

9 This subject was dealt with perceptively by Ernest R. May at a seminar of Soviet and American historians on Soviet-American relations from 1950 to 1955 that was held at Ohio University in Athens, Ohio, in October 1988.

Organization (WTO) and blocked the long-overdue depoliticization of Comecon. The new results are visible today: The European Community has good prospects of evolving into a political and economic body of great vitality, while the WTO and Comecon have collapsed, leaving a potentially dangerous power vacuum in the East.

Some of my colleagues would urge me at this point to take it easy and would argue that concepts such as "power vacuum" or "balance of power" are obsolete relics and should be tossed into the dustbin of history. They stress that a "balance of interests" is what counts in the modern world. If a recent working session of Soviet historians is any indication of the general mood, however, this new approach will not generate much enthusiasm. The session's discussions, which were held in March 1991 and were, I admit, under the influence of the Gulf crisis, essentially concluded that the "balance of interests" approach would not supersede the "balance of power" approach to world affairs and that both would somehow continue to coexist. The vagueness of, and the inability to quantify, the "balance of interests" was duly noted; as Mme Volokhova observed, "it is not a useful input for a computer."

Did the session's conclusions represent a retreat from "new thinking" and suggest a renewed conservative and militaristic approach to the study of world events? I do not think so. Hardly anyone less deserves the title of "conservative" or "militarist" or to be portrayed as an advocate of force than British liberal Socialist and pacifist H. N. Brailsford, whose World War II pamphlet discussing what form the postwar settlement should take attracted my attention as I researched the subject.[10] Brailsford, a supposedly naïve "softy" of the type most disliked by Stalin, was harshly attacked by the wartime Soviet press and was even called pro-Nazi by Ilya Ehrenburg, despite his essentially neutral attitude toward the Soviet Union.[11] The key point, however, is that despite his Socialist and pacifist ideology, Brailsford discussed not only moral "re-education" but also the "problems of power." He discussed at some length the intricacies of "maintaining the stable balance of

10 H. N. Brailsford, *Our Settlement with Germany* (New York, 1944).
11 I. Ehrenburg, "Advocat dyavola" [Devil's advocate], *Voina i rabochiy klass* [War and working class] (1944): 15, 25–27.

power in Europe" and also advocated the creation of an international "World Guard."[12] Thus, in itself, a focus on the problems of power, force, and security need not represent a militaristic mentality—unless one accepts Ehrenburg's and Stalin's logic. It would be an error to see a renewed focus on the "balance of power" as an indication of a conspiracy led by conservative "hawks."

I do not propose to join the debate on the political merits of specific plans or proposals concerning what form the new world balance of power should take. But I do not think it would be misplaced to address a word of caution as a historian to political analysts who are wrestling with these issues. I would summarize my concerns in three "don'ts," although I sincerely disclaim any intention of posing as a mentor by offering this advice.

First, do not discard everything simply because it is associated with the Cold War era. For example, every deed or word that helped to encourage nuclear nonproliferation must not be discarded or abandoned. Despite Richard Ullman's ideas, Germany must be discouraged from becoming a nuclear power. Ullman's idea of a European Security Organization is sound, and I agree with most of it, except for his suggestion that Germany join the nuclear club.[13] In addition, despite my own critical view of NATO, its experience in solving the problems posed by the coexistence of an integrated supranational force alongside national armies must not be neglected. The problem of the coexistence of supranational and national forces created a headache for Brailsford, and is a problem that may face the republics of the former Soviet Union. NATO's success shows that history may sometimes teach optimism toward the resolution of contentious issues.

Second, do not repeat the mistakes of the Cold War. There are some serious problems with the idea of using the EDC concept as a model for a future all-European security structure, despite the fact that some aspects of the idea, as set out recently by James G.

---

12 Brailsford, *Our Settlement*, 105, 121–25. Although Brailsford's book contains many errors of judgment, it also contains several sober, if somewhat somber, predictions that accurately anticipated later developments in the Cold War, along with several shrewd but unheeded recommendations for avoiding that conflict.

13 See R. Ullman, "Enlarging the Zone of Peace," *Foreign Policy* (Fall 1990).

Hershberg, may initially seem quite attractive.[14] Historically, the EDC was a failure, even as an idea, and recent attempts by certain leftist writers to depict its predecessor—the Pleven Plan—as a genuine European response and alternative to U.S. hegemony and militarism are not very convincing.[15]

Third, do not ignore the projects that the Cold War abandoned. The idea of a multinational nuclear force that was suggested some time ago by a group of the most progressive elements of the old Soviet military is an interesting development in this respect. It reminds me of an idea from the past that deserves to become a reality in the future. That idea is not the MLF project of the 1960s, or the "World Guard" idea of Brailsford, but rather the grand design of Roosevelt, his "World Policemen" scheme and its concomitant plan to deploy an Anglo-American-Soviet "air corps" to patrol the world. Today of course, China and France might also be included. The fear of adopting such an approach needs to be overcome.

For the average Russian, foreign military bases abroad are the main symbol of imperialism and represent an acute threat. For many Westerners, any kind of combination among the Great Powers smacks of imperialism and hegemonic domination. Historians must play a role in overcoming these attitudes. John Lewis Gaddis has done much to dispel the myth that American efforts to establish bases overseas were part of a sinister anti-Soviet plot that aimed right from the very beginning at the encirclement of the Soviet Union.[16] The Cold War was not begun by Roosevelt; the foundations were not laid by his administration, for he would not have tolerated it. Soviet scholars and American "revisionist" writers were wrong when they referred to "growing expansionist ambitions" among the "ruling circles" of the United States as World War II

14 James G. Hershberg, "Pan-European Military? Combining Blocs Could Answer Everyone's Security Needs," *Washington Post,* 17 June 1990.
15 H. W. Kahn, *Der Kalte Krieg. Bd. 1. Spaltung und Wahn der Starke, 1945–1955* (Köln, 1986), 228.
16 John Lewis Gaddis, *The Long Peace: Inquiries into the History of the Cold War* (New York, 1987), 27–28. The degree of oversimplification of the complex origins of the Cold War is illustrated by the assertion, in a serious Soviet monograph, that America had "196 atomic bombs" in its possession in late 1945. See A. Gromyko and V. Lomeiko, *Novoye mishleniye v vadernyi vek* [New thinking in the nuclear age] (Moscow, 1984), 53.

entered its final phase. Such ambitions existed, but they were contained by a sense of realism about world conditions.

Gaddis was wrong in describing the "World Policemen" concept as a scheme for dividing the world into spheres.[17] By doing so he misrepresented the nature of the anti-Hitler coalition and the intention implicit in the Yalta and Potsdam accords. Criticism of Yalta and Potsdam has subsided in the West, increased in the East. But despite the many drawbacks of the accords, it would be unwise to throw the baby out with the bath water. The accords reflected the responsibility of the Great Powers for maintaining the world order, a responsibility that found its best expression in the Charter of the United Nations. It is neither politically nor historically wise to deny that the Great Powers were and still are responsible for keeping the world at peace. The end of the Cold War must not be used as a pretext for them to abandon this role.

17 Gaddis, *Long Peace*, 50

8

The Wicked Witch of the West is Dead. Long Live the Wicked Witch of the East

BRUCE CUMINGS

What was the Cold War? Ostensibly it was a global struggle between communism and democracy, with frightening military formations arrayed along the central front in Europe. Three "Berlins" seemed to typify the conflict and to place the appropriate emphasis on Europe: the airlift in 1948 at the Cold War's reported beginning, the crisis in 1961 that summed up its bipolar and intractable nature, and the dismantling of the wall in 1989 that presumably ended it. Hardly any lives were lost along the central axis of division in Europe, which encourages historians like John Lewis Gaddis to speak of a "long peace" in our time.[1] Gaddis argues for the success of George Kennan's containment doctrine, conceived as a long twilight struggle to hold the existing lines of the postwar settlement, until the Soviet Union saw the error of its ways and reformed itself. When Gorbachev proceeded to dismantle the Soviet empire, Kennan's wisdom seemed triumphant. Only a myopic Eurocentrism could yield such conclusions.

In fact, Europe fought a "shadow conflict," obscuring the real history of the past four decades.[2] Kennan's strategy had a curiosity in an unspoken premise: The doctrine was meant both to contain the enemy, the Soviet Union, *and* the allies—mainly West Germany and Japan. Kennan was one of the architects of a strategy in which West Germany and Japan were shorn of their previous military and political clout during the period of American occupation,

---

1 John Lewis Gaddis, *The Long Peace: Inquiries into the History of the Cold War* (New York, 1987).
2 Mary Kaldor calls it an "imaginary war." See Mary Kaldor, *The Imaginary War: Understanding the East-West Conflict* (London, 1990).

but their industrial economies were encouraged to revive, and they were posted as engines of growth in the world economy. Meanwhile, the United States kept both countries on defense dependencies and shaped the flow of essential resources to each, thus to accumulate a diffuse leverage over all of their policies and to retain an outer limit veto on their global orientation.

The major wars of the "long peace" were part of this American hegemonic project, which was articulated and developed coterminous with the Truman Doctrine to bolster regional positions of strength. In Korea, the United States picked up the glove of the Japanese empire and sought to keep South Korea and Taiwan within Japan's historic economic area, thus to aid its reviving industry. In Vietnam, we picked up the French glove, but again for reasons connected to the needs of the French and Japanese economies. Lesser interventions, like those in Greece in 1947 and Iran in 1953, were similarly connected to the revival of the industrial economies and the American desire to police the lines of resource flow to the industrial states.

The real reason for the long European peace between the superpowers was that the Soviet Union shared the American perspective to a much greater degree than is generally recognized. Stalin's doctrine, which became the life-long doctrine of Foreign Minister Andrei Gromyko, was to contain not just the United States but also any hint of *revanche* in Germany and Japan; to contain an Eastern Europe that had been fertile ground for conflict before both world wars (Soviet domination froze the "Balkan problem" that wells up before our eyes today) and also a restive Third World with clients who might draw Soviet might and prestige into unwanted peripheral clashes with the United States. When push came to shove the Soviet Union pulled its forces out of northern Iran in 1946, cut off the Greek guerrillas, distanced itself from direct involvement in the wars in Korea and Vietnam, and withdrew from the brink over Cuba in 1962. Meanwhile it laid siege against West Germany and Japan.

Thus, when the United States found itself in the best of all possible worlds in 1990, having won the Cold War but still retaining immense leverage over Germany and Japan, it was not by accident, because the Cold War consisted of two systems: the containment project, providing security against both the enemy and the ally; and the hegemonic project, providing for American leverage over the necessary resources of our industrial rivals. Both the hegemonic project and the allied-containment system survive today.

The shadow conflict of the Cold War period shaded our vision, obscuring the hegemonic project and highlighting threats that could never stand the glare of realpolitik analysis: above all the obsession with China beginning in 1949, which for a generation made the People's Republic seem far more important than it really was, both to the Nixons who clamored about its expansionism in the 1950s and to the Nixons who inflated it into a strategic ally in the 1970s. Notice how China has faded from view as a strategic asset, coterminous with the end of the Cold War. More importantly, Russia is now seen for what many "revisionists" always argued it to be, a regional power of the second rank (except in regard to inherently unusable nuclear weapons), inflated out of all proportion by the hot air of Cold War ideology. Finally, the United States can now be seen to be what it always has been since the 1940s— the only hegemon, the Great Britain of our time.

That the Cold War ended essentially through the unilateral acts of the Soviet Union also helps to explain why the American projects of global hegemony and allied containment continue: Nothing really changed in American policy.[3] It was as if two horses were racing around a track, one broke its leg, and the other kept on running anyway. But our treatment of U.S. global policy is not sufficient to explain why Reagan and Bush kept on racing. The rise of the Cold War system had a domestic corollary as well in the emergence of mechanisms that served the twin projects of containment and hegemony: a military-industrial complex and a national security state. Although the twin projects were conceived in 1947, the system necessary to service them took several years to develop.

A diverse American coalition of left and right, located in small business, labor, and farming constituencies and known colloquially as "isolationists," resisted the Roosevelt-Truman march toward world power, and up until 1950 had been unwilling to counte-

3   This point is made strongly by Hans Magnus Enzensberger, "New Europe," *Granta* 30 (Winter 1990): 140–42.

nance the major defense expenditures deemed necessary to service
the new global commitments. It was the Korean War that "came
along and saved us," as Secretary of State Dean Acheson later remarked, a necessary crisis that galvanized Congress and the public.[4] Only with the Korean War did the mechanisms and bureaucracies of hegemonic maintenance proliferate in the federal
government and the defense industries (the CIA, for example, was
still little more than a rump operation in early 1950).

This domestic system, like the hegemonic project, showed little
effect from the much-vaunted "end of the Cold War." Although
the first months of 1990 were filled with optimism about a big
"peace dividend" just around the corner, Iraq's invasion of Kuwait had an evil genius: Just in time, it snatched defense contracts
and military production lines from the jaws of oblivion. The
American response to this invasion also bore close comparison with
Korea in 1950: After years of warning about threats to Third World
resources, contingency plans for intervening in the Middle East,
the elaboration of rapid deployment forces and the like, Saddam
Hussein's invasion touched off an astonishingly rapid intervention, as if the forces had been pre-placed at the ready. But there is
nothing surprising in this, either: The end of the shadow conflict
with the Soviet Union has merely revealed what the Cold War was
really about for Americans—interventions in the Third World, from
Korea through Iran, Guatemala and Cuba, to the debacle in Vietnam.

The only thing about the Gulf crisis that really bespoke the end
of the Cold War is this: Iraq felt free to invade Kuwait not because
the United States was likely to respond in some way, but because
the Soviet Union was *not*. At any previous time, Iraq's invasion
would have invoked Soviet credibility and a distinct threat of superpower conflict. And so Saddam knew that the Soviets or the
Americans or both would have stepped in to block him.

Otherwise, this crisis partook of the untouched elements of the

---

4   In a seminar held at Princeton University on 9 July 1953 an unidentified person says,
    "we were having a hell of a time figuring out how we were going to get the NSC 68
    program," whereupon another person says, "Korea came along and saved us—do the
    job for us." Acheson then replied, "I think you can say that." (Harry S. Truman Li-
    brary, Princeton seminars transcript, box 82.)

Cold War system. First, it was part of the long-standing hegemonic project to shape the flow of resources to Japan and Western Europe, and thereby to retain leverage on America's economically worrisome allies. Second, it was part and parcel of the real conflict we have fought for the past four decades, that between the United States and the Third World. Third and most important, if Korea was the alpha of the military-industrial complex, Iraq was the omega. The end of the Cold War had done little or nothing by 1992 to dismantle the enormous machine set in motion in the 1950s, a perpetual-motion machine that was built for war and that advances its interests in making war. Joseph Schumpeter's interpretation of imperialism as an atavism is precisely relevant here: Institutions built for service to empire continue onward with a clanking automaticity, in spite of dramatic changes in the world or strong constituencies calling for an end to empire. Made to fight old wars, the systems call forth new ones.

The Schumpeterian perspective makes understandable the atavism of American behavior amid the welter of transformations in Europe. It tells us why the Bush horse keeps running. At the precise moment when Gorbachev was dismantling his empire and calling for a new world order, and when the last of the Eastern European Stalinist systems was crumbling, George Bush decided to invade Panama. For the umpteenth time in this century, American forces intervened in Central America, as if nothing whatever had changed.

The Soviet Union withdraws its troops and closes bases in Eastern Europe, the United States keeps its troops and bases in Western Europe. The Soviet Union dismantles the Warsaw Pact, and the United States places a unified Germany in NATO. The Soviets disabuse themselves of a client state in Iraq, whereupon it is immediately embroiled in war with the United States. The Soviet Union moves a major logjam in another grave trouble spot by opening diplomatic relations with South Korea (in September 1990), and the United States continues to lay siege against North Korea, hoping it will collapse on the Romanian model.

President Bush dramatically pulled back American tactical nuclear weapons from around the world in 1991, but hardly anyone in the press pointed out the background to this move: The American military has wanted out of tactical nuclear warfare for some time, believing that high-yield conventional explosives in precision-guided carriers do what the nukes can do, without the attendant "fallout." (The Gulf war was an important demonstration of this fact.) Other changes are mostly incremental, like the overweeningly modest reduction of the defense budget to $293 billion for fiscal 1992.

The ultimate atavism of the Bush administration's policy and the real meaning of its "New World Order," however, rest in its remarkable desire to have its cake and eat it too, that is, to continue in place the domestic and global structures of the Cold War, while moving toward trilateral accommodation with a newly emerging Europe and Japan—thus to deal with the really critical problem facing the United States: relative hegemonic decline.

From the onset of the Cold War into the mid-1960s, American industrial and military dominance was so complete and American allies so relatively weak that an expensive unilateral role was the only one available to American policy, creating an era of indulgence in which the United States transferred enormous resources of capital, aid, and technology to the industrial allies. But that was an anomalous period, sure to end when the other industrial allies revived from the war and sure to spawn a move toward multilateralism when they did.

The intractibility, stupidity, and gross expense of the Vietnam War hastened this process, and hastened a modest American retreat from empire—known as the Nixon Doctrine for a while, and articulated by trilateralists in the Carter administration as a move from being the world's policeman to the world's "night watchman." The more important watchwords of the 1970s, however, were "free trade" and "interdependence," both of which were responses to Nixon's brief flirtation with neo-mercantilism in his "New Economic Policy."

If Republicans experimented with détente in the early 1970s and then declared it a non-word in the Ford administration, Carter revived the policy during the first years of his presidency. Trilateralists correctly gauged the Communist weakness to be primarily economic and technological and understood that nearly everywhere in the Communist sphere revolutionary socialism had given way to bureaucratic conservatism; they thought that through loans, aid, and open markets the Communist nations could be tamed and brought into the world system. There was, in fact, supreme confidence that these nations would sooner or later join the world economy, largely on American terms. Although trilateral strategy had failed with the Soviet Union by 1979, it succeeded in enveloping China in a broad-ranging economic relationship (with the key Chinese internal reforms coming at the end of 1978), and in making unprecedented inroads into the Soviet sphere in Eastern Europe (especially through big loans to Poland, Hungary, Romania, and other countries).

From this brief sketch we can predict a continuing policy of multilateralism in the First World, accommodation of the (formerly Socialist) Second World, market-*perestroika* and arms control for Russia and Eastern Europe, and Indian Summer for the American military-industrial complex. In other words, the new trilateralism would mean cooperation among the advanced capitalist states and accommodation and envelopment of the formerly Socialist regions.

What about the Third World? It will likely continue to get what it got throughout the Cold War period: American unilateralism and confrontation against local upstarts, combined with heightened domination and exploitation of the Third World in everyone's interest (except that of Third World peoples themselves).

The rosy-fingered dawn occasioned by the end of U.S.-Soviet rivalry ignores a Third World that remains dominated by the advanced countries and that has fewer alternative paths and models than at any point since 1945. Furthermore, with a few notable exceptions it is largely left out of the prosperity of recent years, and thus is the prime source of war, instability, and class conflict.

Our sketch thus far suggests that Stalinism and Cold War bipolarity seem to be the only certain casualties of the 1980s. There is still the possibility of global depression as a result of the frantic deregulation of Reaganism and Thatcherism in the 1980s, not to mention intercapitalist conflict: Germany and Japan resurgent, America in decline. Or perhaps, global depression and then withdrawal into three regional economic blocs, followed by intercapitalist conflict on the 1930s pattern.

Yet, the 1990s hold much promise for First World cooperation, not crisis and closure but prosperity and opening: a genuine common market and the restriction of many national barriers in Europe, the demise of closed economies throughout Eastern Europe and the Soviet Union, the open possibilities of people throughout Europe who have regained or newly exercised their democratic rights in recent years. We can also see a "peace interest" today like that of the nineteenth century.

It is not simply that the "anti-system" now wants to join up, although the re-connecting of the old Soviet Union and Eastern Europe will mean large new markets for the West (just as China's opening in the 1970s did the same in the East) and will distinctly reduce the chances for global war. More importantly, like the "long peace" of the nineteenth century (again, only for Europe) we also find several great powers of roughly equivalent weight that are more interested in creating wealth than in accumulating power. The new technologies of the information age, which have increased labor productivity and expanded the service industries so dramatically, combined with the existence of six reasonably dynamic, advanced capitalist economies, should keep the world from plunging into a new depression, assuming the creation of new markets in Central Europe and East Asia.

If the above analysis is correct, the tendency in the First World ought now to be toward multilateral great power cooperation, rather than unilateralism or the formation of regional blocs. If, as I think, the United States is in the middle age rather than the alpenglow of hegemony, it ought to do what the British did in the face of incipient but relative decline roughly a century ago: ally with the rising capitalist powers. In that time this meant British cooperation with the United States and alliance with Japan (from 1902 to 1922)—although the British sought outright alliance with the United States as well. (At that time, of course, it also meant hostility to the other rising capitalist power, Germany.) Today the logic would suggest a multilateral arrangement focusing on New York, Berlin, and Tokyo, with Washington still hegemonic.

In East Asia (except for Korea) the Cold War ended in the mid-1970s with the opening to China and the end of the Vietnam War. Nonetheless, structures elaborated in the wake of World War II still govern: In spite of its world-beating industrial prowess, Japan is still firmly within the constraints of the postwar system. This was obvious in the delicate *kabuki* dance carried on by Japan's leadership in regard to the Gulf crisis. Japan gets about 65 percent of its oil from that region, yet even in timidly venturing to send a handful of "non-combatant" forces to the Middle East, the leadership was quickly forced to backtrack. Then it pledged an additional $9 billion (bringing the total to $13 billion) to the effort in January 1991, a substantial sum, only to run into a firestorm of domestic criticism before pushing the measure through the Diet. But one grasps Japan's situation more clearly by imagining this headline: "Tokyo Dispatches Large Naval Task Force to the Persian Gulf." It is still an impossible headline, and if it appeared, it would touch off a spate of American comment about Japanese militarism and a frenzy of outrage in Japan's near reaches.

It is perhaps a paradox that whereas Nazi Germany was more aggressive, violent, and virulent than militarist Japan, its near neighbors are less worried about its new unity than are Japan's about any hint of Tokyo again taking up a military role—except for Poland, that is, which unlike the United States or Great Britain was occupied by Nazi Germany, and unlike occupied Vichy France was nearly destroyed by the ordeal. Korea and China look upon Japan the way the Poles look upon Germany, because both were occupied and brutally subjugated. The Communist movements that still govern China and North Korea were outgrowths of an anti-Japanese struggle and are still governed by Chinese octogenarians and Korean septuagenarians who fought the Japanese. Moreover, the general Japanese population has yet to shake off the long-standing (and very welcome) pacificism that was an important residue of military defeat—and that national security pundits have long derided as Japan's "nuclear allergy." In this sense the World War II settlement has not ended in East Asia—we are still not in a "post-postwar" era.

Japan is a rising power and it may one day be the hegemonic power of the Pacific region or even the world, but it is today about where the United States was in regard to Great Britain in the first decades of this century: happy to play second fiddle, content to let the hegemon police the world and rule the waves. Nor is this any-

thing new for Japan: as the dean of diplomatic historians of East
Asia, Akira Iriye, has shown in several books, through this entire
century save for one (disastrous) decade Japan has assiduously
sought cooperation with the dominant powers in East Asia—first
Great Britain and then the United States.

For much of the postwar period the United States has given every
support to Japan and the other East Asian capitalist economies. If
in the 1940s the United States structured a situation where Japanese industry could revive, in the 1960s the Kennedy administration placed strong pressures on Japan and its near neighbors (especially South Korea) to restore Japan's economic influence in the
region. This resulted in the normalization of relations between Korea and Japan in 1965 and in a bundle of Japanese grants and
loans that helped the ROK's economy to take off. It was also in
the Kennedy period, however, that for the first time American leaders
began criticizing Japan for its "free ride" in security affairs. It is
daunting to realize that this rhetoric now is entering its third decade, with Japan still recalcitrantly limiting defense spending to
about 1 percent of its GNP and with American politicians still
carping about it. But what is the alternative—a Japanese fleet in
the Persian Gulf?

Elsewhere in East Asia we also see continuity rather than change.
Even the Communists have failed again, this time to understand
that, according to the Americans, their system has failed or to learn
that bureaucratic planning equals nightmarish inefficiency and that
only the market can save us (Japan, South Korea, and China all
have rapidly growing economies and strong central bureaucracies). The East is still Red, with Communist leaderships that emerged
in the 1930s and that pursued revolutionary-nationalist strategies
still holding power in China, North Korea, and Vietnam. But perhaps because of the nationalist credentials of these leaders, most
of them have found it easier to open themselves to capitalist interests (especially Japanese) than have their counterparts in the former Soviet Union or the more hard-line Eastern European states,
at least before the changes of the late 1980s.

Japan seems to be hedging against its possible exclusion from
the European community after 1992 by building its position in
East and Southeast Asia. Its direct investment in the region has

grown six-fold since 1985, its trade with Taiwan tripled in the same period, and its manufactured imports from the Asian region as a whole more than doubled from 1985 to 1988 (contrary to pundits who argue that its economy is basically closed). Japanese investors have been especially active in Thailand: On the average, one new Japanese factory opened every working day in 1989.

According to current projections, the Pacific region inclusive of Northeast Asia, the ASEAN countries, and Australia will have a GNP of $7.2 trillion by the year 2000, which will be bigger than that of the EC; as stated earlier, the number of effective consumers in the region will be at least as large as in Europe. Japan has also been assiduous in breaking barriers to trade with the Asian Communist countries: it is North Korea's biggest capitalist trading partner and may normalize relations with P'yongyang soon; it went back into China much more quickly than other investors in the wake of the Tiananmen bloodletting in June 1989.

All of this regional investment is grist for the mill of those who find a developing tendency toward regional economic blocs. But as argued earlier, this is unlikely short of a major world depression; a trilateral regime of cooperation and free trade linking Europe with the Far East and the Americas is much more likely, with the three great markets of each region underpinning and stabilizing intercapitalist rivalry in the world system and encouraging interdependence rather than go-it-alone strategies that would be deleterious to all.

If "partnership" and "cooperation" are the trilateral watchwords, however, why is Germany still a member of NATO, in spite of the collapse of the Warsaw Pact? Why do American military bases still dot the Japanese archipelago, even though North Korea is about the only remaining "threat" in the East? In thinking through the problems of Japan and Germany today, we can grasp that a kind of "trilateral cooperation" has been the name of the game since the late 1940s. Furthermore, if the Cold War ended by 1990, the project of American hegemony did not, and that project was always trilateral.

Perhaps nothing would have surprised George Frost Kennan more in 1947 than if someone had told him that the major wars that the United States would fight in pursuit of "containment" would be in

Korea and Vietnam, two countries that never held more than his momentary attention, and then only as he figured out how they might make themselves useful to someone else (usually Japan). Nor could Kennan have imagined that when the Cold War finally ended and the Soviet Union returned to its Russian roots, the Cold War would persist intractably in Korea. Yet distant, remote Korea provides an optic that highlights almost all of the important history of the Cold War.

Korea was there before the beginning of the Cold War and it is still there after the end. The full panoply of conflict that we associate with the Cold War appeared in Korea in the last months of 1945. In 1992, Korea is a museum of that awful conflict, the only place in the world where Cold War confrontation remains predominant. What does this have to teach us about the Cold War?

It teaches us that the Cold War was only indirectly about U.S.-Soviet strategic conflict. No realpolitik worthy of the name, no military doctrine before, during, or after the Korean War could sustain the argument that possession of Korea (or half of it) made a significant difference militarily or strategically in the balance of power. That Soviet power occupied northern Korea in 1945 simply intensified a different conflict, that between Japanese and American power and indigenous popular forces seeking to orient Korea's future independently. This struggle began in the waning period of Soviet-American cooperation in 1945 and would have happened had Korea been on the other side of the globe: let's say, in Central America.

In other words, the Cold War was also about confrontation between the First and Third worlds, and this is where its major violence came: four million deaths in Korea, nearly an equal number in Vietnam. It was a conflict between core and periphery, especially in that contingent, intermediate zone that Immanuel Wallerstein terms the semi-periphery. And here we find the logic of American policy in Korea; all sorts of historical conundrums can be unpacked when we understand that Korea's primary significance for the United States was not its proximity to the Soviet Union, but its proximity to Japan.

When traditional American noninvolvement in Korea was reversed during World War II, it was Japanophiles in the State Department who did the about face, linking postwar Korean security to that of Japan and the Pacific. When Secretary of State George Marshall, at the onset of "the fifteen weeks" in 1947, gave post facto blessing to the American Occupation's eighteen-month-old effort to contain revolution and establish a separate southern government, he did so to "connect [Korea] up" with Japan. When his successor Dean Acheson spoke publicly in 1950 about a "defense perimeter" in Asia, he was thinking privately about a "great crescent" delineating a 1940s "Pacific Rim" political economy, linking Tokyo with the East Asian rim and ultimately with the oil of the Middle East. Acheson's decision six months later to take American forces into the Korean War had to do internationally with holding the lines of this developing political economy and domestically with finding a crisis that would win congressional approval of NSC 68 and thus commit the American people to maintaining an enormous, far-flung, and historically unprecedented hegemony.

What Acheson and Truman found in Korea was quite different from their expectation. The Koreans fought tenaciously and ultimately pulled a rabbit called China out of their hat. By December 1950, U.S. policy was in ruins, and a crisis beyond imagination was at hand that destabilized and ultimately destroyed the Truman administration (according to Acheson). Paradoxically, this dark moment stabilized the Cold War system financially and strategically. By December 1950, authorized defense spending had nearly quadrupled from its $13 billion level in June 1950. More generally, Korea was a crisis enabling the second major wave of statebuilding in this American century: The New Deal was the first, and the national security state was the second, with security bureaucracies growing exponentially from the early 1950s onward.

Furthermore, an unstable compromise on containment from 1947 to 1950, lacking bipartisanship on Asia and on how to respond to the dynamism of communism, was brought together into a temporary consensus via the march to the Yalu; when this exploded in everyone's face, centrists like Acheson and Dulles retreated to de facto containment thereafter, even though Dulles continued to give voice to rollback rhetoric in the 1950s. In this sense, the Chinese limited the war for an America that could not. China understood that the wars in Korea and Vietnam were proxy wars for the United

States, that the Chinese revolution was the real issue. Therefore, China established definitive limits on American expansionism in these two former tributary states, and in so doing taught a lesson that lasted down to the worldwide end of the Cold War: Communist territory was off limits, except to covert forays.

Fear of China then decisively affected the course of the Vietnam War by deterring an American invasion of North Vietnam and causing successive administrations to define "success" as a permanently divided Vietnam. Within the American state and polity, the failed rollback attempt in Korea and the crisis it caused also explain the stalemate between conservatives and liberals over the Bay of Pigs in 1961 and over Nicaragua throughout the 1980s. From this standpoint the Korean War was far more important to the construction of postwar American foreign policy than the Vietnam War. Only the latter, however, stuck itself irrevocably in the American heart.[5]

The enemy in Korea did not seek or want any of this. The North Koreans and the Chinese sought to drive a stake into the heart of Acheson's "great crescent" political economy, to declare their territories off limits to American hegemony and Japanese economic influence. Today it appears that they merely succeeded in delaying for two decades the dynamism of the regional Northeast Asian economy, which had its origin in colonial development in the 1930s. Neither North Korea nor China could contain the automaticity of a dynamic regional capitalist economy once it got going again in the mid-1960s. In the 1990s, capitalism laps at their doors, and increasingly integrates the most advanced parts of the Chinese economy.

North Korea, however, remains outside this realm, and dangerously so. The only question Americans have ever wanted to ask about the Korean War was "who started it?"—a snapshot in time that buries the war's origins and embodies its own ideological answer. So also Americans today view Korea through one "snapshot" that seeks to silence and bury the history that explains why the Cold War lives on in Korea: satellite photos showing some sort of nuclear facility at Yongbyôn. American policy points at that

5 See my *Origins of the Korean War, II* (Princeton, 1990), for elaboration and evidence on the points in this text.

issue and at North Korea as another "renegade state" like Iraq; the media uncritically repeats the line, or goes beyond it (*Chicago Tribune* editors have twice called for a military attack on Yongbyôn); hardly anyone points out that we are still technically at war with North Korea, that the real reason that the Bush administration points the finger at P'yôngyang's unusable (and as yet nonexistent) nuclear weapon is to keep Japan from going nuclear, to keep American troops in Korea and Japan to retain leverage on both, and to continue the postwar settlement regardless of the ostensible end of the Cold War.

The wicked witch of the West is dead. Long live the wicked witch of the East. (And welcome to Oz.)

9

The End and the Beginning

RONALD STEEL

During the darkest periods of the Cold War, parallels were sometimes drawn to World War I. Armed conflict, it was said, could
break out, as it had in 1914, through miscalculation, rhetorical
posturing, and the technological imperatives of the new weaponry.
What was not imagined, however, was that the Cold War might
suddenly come to an end in a way strikingly similar to that in
which the war had ended on the eastern front in 1918: through
the internal collapse and unconditional withdrawal of one of the
belligerents. That one of the two superpowers might simply retire
from the contest, that it would lose its empire and its internal
cohesion, seemed no less improbable seventy-five years ago than,
in a different context, does the demise of its successor today.

The collapse of the Russian state, which allowed the Bolsheviks
to seize power, and the withdrawal of Russia from the war after
the surrender at Brest-Litovsk, resulted from the rigidities of autocratic rule, the costs of fighting an interminable war, and the loss
of faith by the nation's elite in the system itself. After the event,
what had hitherto seemed unthinkable became strikingly obvious:
Of course the Russian state, so outwardly formidable and unyield-
ing, was merely a shell. Beneath the façade of invincibility, however, it was ripe for disintegration. It was almost inevitable, considering the toll of war, that the Romanov dynasty would fall. Was
this not evident?

Yet, of course, it was not evident at the time because virtually
no one in a position of power wanted to believe it. The Allies
sought Russian help in the war with Germany, and thus it fit their
purposes to assume that its government was strong and its people

103

united in a common purpose. Because the Allies needed a partner equal to the fervor of their endeavor, they suffered from a self-willed political blindness.

Now this all seems abundantly clear. But are there not clear parallels between the years 1917 and 1918 and the period 1989–1991? In both cases political leaders were stunned by a course of events in Russia for which their analyses and assumptions had not prepared them. They had viewed Russia through the lenses of their own preoccupations. As in World War I, Western policy in the Cold War was based on assumptions repudiated by events. Soviet Russia was clearly not the adversary that American policymakers thought it was: not in internal cohesion, not in military strength, and probably not even in geopolitical ambitions. To an important degree the United States was involved in a deadly struggle with a phantom Russia, just as Russian leaders—themselves bedeviled by suspicion, fear, and ideology—were with a phantom America.

The Cold War was not supposed to have ended as it did, with the demise of the Soviet empire in Europe, the dissolution of the Soviet state, and the repudiation of communism itself by those thought to be its most ardent adherents. Such a situation normally results from a catastrophic defeat in war. According to the Cold War scenario, over a period of several more decades the conflict would gradually be reduced as the two superpowers worked out mutually beneficial arms control arrangements to lessen the cost of maintaining their respective spheres of influence. In effect, the Cold War was not supposed to end at all. The advantages it offered to both major contestants were so manifest, and its cost seemingly so manageable, that there seemed little incentive on either side to end it. Indeed, a political negotiation to end the Cold War in Europe, its focal point, had from the beginning been firmly rejected by American policymakers.

For these reasons, the way that the Cold War ended requires us to make a fundamental reassessment of the assumptions on which American actions were based. Unquestionably, the Soviet Union was far weaker ideologically, politically, structurally, and, of course, economically, than was generally assumed. Some of these assumptions were based on fear and exaggeration, others seemed spun out of thin air to serve political purposes. Among the most fatuous of these was the theory advanced by one of Ronald Reagan's academic advisers, that totalitarianism by its very nature was irreversible. The purpose of this theory was to justify American support of rightist authoritarian regimes; its rationale was that these regimes, unlike Communist ones, might one day evolve into democratic ones. Adherence to such exaggerated, self-serving, and even delusional assumptions about what was generically labeled the "Communist threat" clouded our understanding of what was happening in the Soviet Union, impeded the course of orderly change, and inflicted terrible misery on the Cold War arenas of the Third World, where the contest between "good" and "bad" forms of authoritarianism was taking place.

The problem has not been one merely of a self-blinding dogma. The enormous apparatus of government intelligence and spy operations, of generously endowed think tanks and research institutes, and of the entire discipline of "strategic studies" failed to anticipate or even intellectually to prepare the ground for an understanding of what is arguably the most momentous political event of this century. In understanding the collapse of communism and the Soviet state, the strategists in government, at universities, and in the well-financed limbo in between have been virtually irrelevant.

In part, this is a failure of American social science, with its blind faith in quantification, its indifference to history and political culture, and its aggressive ethnocentrism. In a larger sense, it is also a failure of political intelligence, a failure to penetrate into the realities of an adversarial society. Americans saw the Soviet Union that they wanted to see: a society of automatons mesmerized by a messianic ideology and intent on applying all of its energies to gaining Soviet domination over the entire world.

This was the Soviet Union of George Kennan's "Long Telegram," which, lacking the nuances of his later writings, combined concerns over both totalitarianism and communism to portray a state that was relentlessly expansionist and implacably hostile to the West. This is the state found, in exaggerated form, in NSC-68 of 1950, which, in calling for a vast expansion of U.S. military power, declared that "the Soviet Union, unlike previous aspirants to hegemony, is animated by a new fanatic faith, antithetical to our own, and seeks to impose its absolute authority over the rest of the world."[1]

Revisionism in its early and later forms undercut the self-justification of such analyses. Yet, as late as 1967, when the Vietnam War had brought the argument over revisionism to a fever pitch, one of the most eminent of American liberal historians wrote of the early Cold War period that "Leninism and totalitarianism created a structure of thought and behavior which made postwar collaboration between Russia and America—in any normal sense of civilized intercourse between national states, inherently impossible."[2] To this Walter Lippmann, America's most influential political columnist, replied in a private letter that such an explanation failed to take into account the "political and strategic vacuum" in Europe after the war that at once "provoked and lured Moscow and Washington to fill it." Furthermore, Lippmann warned against exaggerating Soviet motives and paying no attention to opportunity, and of failing to take notice of "how often the search for security and the assembling of an empire are two sides of the same coin."[3] Later, as postrevisionism sought to embrace both the revisionists and their critics, a leading scholar of that school admitted that early scholarship on the Cold War self-servingly "absolved the United States of responsibility for the breakdown of wartime cooperation; it made any future relaxation of tensions dependent upon changes of heart in Moscow, not Washington."[4]

One does not have to be a revisionist to recognize that Washington's interpretation of a global military and ideological struggle for dominance corresponded more to postwar America's ambitions and capacities than to the ability of the Soviet Union to control politically significant areas outside of Eastern Europe. Even without Soviet activism the United States would have dominated the post-World War II world—but not to the degree that it did.

1   "NSC-68: United States Objectives and Programs for National Security," 14 April 1950, U.S. Department of State, *Foreign Relations of the United States, 1950,* 1: 237–92.
2   Arthur Schlesinger, Jr., "Origins of the Cold War," *Foreign Affairs* 46 (October 1967).
3   Walter Lippmann to Arthur Schlesinger, Jr., 25 September 1967, Walter Lippmann Collection, Sterling Memorial Library, Yale University, New Haven, Connecticut, quoted in Ronald Steel, *Walter Lippmann and the American Century* (Boston, 1980), 580.
4   John Lewis Gaddis, *The Long Peace: Inquiries into the History of the Cold War* (New York, 1987), 40.

The Soviets, with their brutal methods and hostile behavior, provided the challenge that permitted American policymakers to block a retreat to prewar passivity and to engage the nation's formidable energies in a global vocation. Soviet power and ruthlessness in Eastern Europe were real enough, and required an American response in the West. But Soviet brutality was also fortuitous, for it permitted an engagement, and a global extension, of American power that otherwise could not have been justified domestically. The Cold War served a useful political function for both Soviet and American policymakers. If it provided the United States with a global vocation, it also elevated to theoretically equal world status an economically backward and politically primitive Soviet state.

We now know more about the Soviet Union than we did before: its inner weakness, both material and psychological, its vulnerability, and the structure of lies, intimidation, and apathy on which rule by the Communist party bureaucracy rested. This was not a state inspired by a proselytizing ideology, as so many of our political leaders and ostensible experts told us, but rather one sustained by habit, a custom of deference to authority, the lack of a democratic tradition, and the absence of a realistic alternative. The Soviet people did not embrace communism, or outside the Russian core even the union itself; they merely acquiesced in it.

American diplomacy during the Cold War would have been more successful, and its instruments less politically costly, had it confined itself to its supposed goal, the containment of Soviet military power. The forcible imposition of Soviet control on the peoples of Eastern Europe, Moscow's potential threat to the great industrial centers of Western Europe and Japan, the arsenal of nuclear weapons that could be used to intimidate the United States and its European allies—these needed to be checked by the only military power capable of doing so. Even though the Russians, as Kennan, Lippmann, and others had long insisted, showed no intention of using military force against Western Europe, it was prudent to deny them opportunities for exerting political pressure. The scale of the military effort on both sides was, however, grossly disproportionate to the political situation, which was, in fact, quite stable. Neither side had the least interest in disturbing the political equilibrium by force. Europe, for all of the excessive arms that the two sides ranged against one another, was the quietest frontier of the Cold War.

The reason that the Cold War produced such violence, entailed such cost, and periodically threatened to go out of control was not because of containment in Europe, but because of the links made between communism and radical social upheavals in the Third World. It was the attempt to control such social change, particularly in the former colonial areas, that transformed the Cold War from a dispute over the political orientation of Eastern Europe into a global conflict. The stated justification for U.S. intervention in the Third World was that the Soviet Union was the chief inspiration for such change and would be its primary beneficiary. This was the formula used to justify the interventions, either covert or overt, within the self-declared spheres of influence, notably Cuba, the Dominican Republic, Panama, Guatemala, El Salvador, Brazil and Chile—and also in Africa and Asia, notably Angola, the former Congo, Indonesia, Korea, and Vietnam.

That the expansion of the European quarrel to a global level would also enable the United States greatly to expand its military and political reach enhanced its appeal to American foreign policy elites eager to embrace the nation's new opportunities. The collapse of the former centers of global power—Britain and France no less than Germany and Japan—made this expansion not only easier but also seemingly necessary and inevitable. Thus, the Cold War was not simply a response to Soviet expansion, the containment of its geopolitical ambitions in Europe, but the framework by which American policymakers were able to extend globally the reach of American power and influence.

Without the Soviet factor such a policy would never have been able to achieve the widescale public support it required. The smothering of domestic dissent, as evidenced in the loyalty programs of the late 1940s and the 1950s, and a climate of fear intensified by the Korean War, made possible the vast expansion of the American security state. Thus, an understanding of the Cold War must be found not only in the ambitions, real or hypothetical, of the Soviet Union but also in the anxieties and ambitions of American policymakers suddenly confronted with a world, so different from that of a decade earlier, when opportunities seemed unlimited. That expansionism was simply the other side of the coin of containment was one of the ironies of the Cold War.

The two strands of Soviet containment and global expansion were there almost from the beginning and were linked in the Truman Doctrine of 1947. At the time a number of centrists objected to this linkage, including Lippmann, who, even while approving an aid program to Greece and Turkey, warned against the globalist implications of an avowedly counterrevolutionary policy. But the exigencies of the Cold War, particularly over the political and economic control of Germany, and its spread to Asia with the triumph of the Communists in China and the expansion of the civil war in Korea, effectively transformed the containment of Soviet military power in Europe into a global struggle against what was glibly, but for policymakers usefully, termed the "international Communist conspiracy."

Although the Cold War was waged on many fronts and took a terrible toll in resources and human lives, it was, with one major exception, kept within bounds that the United States and the Soviet Union considered tolerable. That exception was, of course, the Cuban missile crisis of 1962: a near-catastrophic confrontation resulting from miscalculation, bravado, expediency, and duplicity on a scale that frightened both sides. After that crisis, the two antagonists made sure that their competition for advantage and influence was waged through either proxy or semicolonial wars. The American war in Vietnam and the Soviet war in Afghanistan were aspects of the Cold War: Each superpower justified its intervention as directed toward the containment (not only military, but also psychological[5]) of the other; both sought to preserve spheres of influence. But these two conflicts also bore strong resemblance to the colonial wars that the French had fought in Indochina and North Africa and that Russian tsars had waged in central Asia.

What one must ask about the Cold War is not why it ended so soon but why it lasted so long. There were a number of reasons

---

5 In this regard the response by Robert F. Kennedy to an interviewer in 1964 is particularly interesting. When asked why President Kennedy felt it necessary "to keep and hold on to" Vietnam, he replied: "He reached the conclusion that probably it was worthwhile for psychological, political reasons more than anything else." See *Robert Kennedy: In His Own Words*, ed. Edwin O. Guthman and Jeffrey Shulman (New York, 1988), 288.

for its longevity: the preference of the Europeans and the Japanese to grow rich rather than to resume the game of power politics; the eagerness of both the United States and the Soviet Union to inherit those roles; the transformation of the Soviet-American geopolitical quarrel into an ideological one that respected no frontiers; and the utility of the conflict in establishing Soviet or American hegemony within their respective areas. Without the Cold War, U.S. and Russian positions, especially within Europe, would have been significantly weaker.

Most important, in the European context, the Cold War offered a solution of sorts to the perennial German problem. Partition had at last made it possible for the Europeans to live without serious anxiety about German power and to build in the West a European construction that Germany would neither threaten nor dominate. So long as the Soviets stood in the way of unification, there was no longer a German problem in the old sense. Even the Germans did not seem to be particularly troubled by their partition. They had found a new place of honor and respectability in the West with which they were quite satisfied. And during the long course of the Cold War they had at last achieved a democratic transformation of their society. Further, within the Soviet empire the Cold War was keeping deadly East European tribal hatreds in check. By the mid-1960s, with Western Europe moving gradually toward integration under the comforting and inexpensive umbrella of American protection, the Cold War had become quite institutionalized.

The Cold War had, in fact, developed into an eminently workable international system. It was predictable, economically manageable, politically useful, and militarily unthreatening. This was so because the Soviets, too, had developed a vested interest in its preservation. The Americans kept the Germans in check, and the Europeans kept the Americans in check. The Cold War allowed the Japanese to gain extraordinary economic power as America expended its resources on potlach objectives, and it gave the Soviets, despite their primitive economy and retrograde social structure, the attributes of a Great Power. For all practical purposes it permitted the Americans to control the foreign policies of their major allies (and potential challengers): the Europeans and the Japanese. And it gave the Chinese a privileged position as the "good"

Communists who would antagonize the Russians on their Asian flanks. Despite its considerable costs, the Cold War thus provided something desirable for all of the major participants. No nation had a compelling interest in ending it. From an American perspective it had a particular appeal. The Soviets were unquestionably the weaker power and posed no serious threat to American interests. As one astute critic has written: "The purpose of the Cold War was not victory but the maintenance of a controlled contest."[6]

The demise of the Cold War system inevitably means a sharp reduction of the influence of the two major adversaries. While this is obvious in the case of the former Soviet Union, it is no less true of the United States. To a far greater degree than has generally been realized, American political influence has rested significantly on the Cold War. It was concern over the reality of Soviet power and the uncertainty of Soviet ambitions that induced the Europeans and the Japanese to put their security in American hands to play a historically passive role in world affairs. So long as fear of Soviet power was real, the most prudent, as well as the most economic, course for these countries was to rely on American leadership. For this they paid a certain price, both economic and political, of deference to the United States, whether in the form of trade concessions, financing of the U.S. treasury's deficits, purchases of U.S.-made military equipment, or allowing Washington alone to negotiate with Moscow.

So long as such deference seemed necessary, it was largely unchallenged by the allies, with the exception, of course, of Gaullist France in the 1960s. But the retreat of the Soviet Union from the contest, indeed the disappearance of that state itself, has dramatically altered the balance within the former Cold War coalition led by the United States. Today, the United States—in part because of exaggerated Cold War preoccupations, in part because of irresponsible fiscal and economic policies of its own making—has lost both its economic and its political freedom of action. Washington cannot finance its unquenchable deficits without the willingness of the Europeans and the Japanese to buy treasury bonds; it cannot

6 Michael Cox, "From the Truman Doctrine to the Second Superpower Détente: The Rise and Fall of the Cold War," *Journal of Peace Research* 27:1 (1990): 25–41.

undertake large-scale military interventions without their financial contributions, as the Gulf war of early 1991 demonstrated. The United States fought the Cold War, but today it is the Western Europeans who are financing, organizing, and influencing the political future of what was once the Soviet Cold War empire.

Unavoidably, the end of the Cold War means a dramatic decline in the ability of the United States to determine the course of events. This has not yet become fully apparent to foreign policy elites. Some, in the wake of the U.S.-initiated and mostly U.S.-fought Gulf war, and of the collapse of the Soviet Union, refer to the United States as the only superpower. To be a "superpower" in a world where the instruments of power are either restricted by economic dependency or directed against a foe that has largely ceased to exist, however, is to render the term meaningless. It took two to fight the Cold War, two to ensure abdication by the lesser players, two to give American leaders a sense of mission and freedom of action, two to justify the suppression of American domestic social and economic needs to the exigencies of a Great Power struggle.

Two have been reduced to one, and the contest has shifted to other arenas. It is no longer between the United States and the Soviet Union, no longer over the pretensions of ideology, no longer waged by military interventions or by the accumulation of nuclear weaponry. With the end of the Cold War, the United States will be forced to adjust to a competition where its familiar instruments are inapplicable and where its allies and dependencies are increasingly rivals. It is not merely the end of the Cold War, but a dramatic reshifting of the world power balance. For the American economy, distorted by a half-century of reliance on military spending, for American political elites, who had come to believe that they were "born to lead," and for an American public, deprived of an enemy to justify its sacrifices, the experience will be a wrenching and possibly threatening one.

10

A Balance Sheet: Lippmann, Kennan, and the Cold War

RICHARD J. BARNET

Such reputations as present day pundits enjoy owe much to the fact that the newspaper columns they wrote forty-three days ago have already become recycled paper. Re-reading Walter Lippmann's columns on George Kennan's "X" article forty-three years after they were first published—in my case on the very day that the World War II conquerors relinquished their powers over Germany—is an unsettling experience. What are we to make of these twelve columns that Lippmann published a few months later as *The Cold War?*[1] The clarity, the intellectual power, and the breadth of the analysis cannot fail to impress the reader, whatever one thinks of Lippmann's argument. As the United States stands on the threshold of another series of fateful choices, the contemporary relevance of the Lippmann-Kennan debate is striking.

The Cold War lays out a surprisingly coherent view of politics and diplomacy. It is a traditionalist, realist argument for a path not taken. Embedded in these columns and in Kennan's "Sources of Soviet Conduct" are many of the concerns that are likely to engage future historians of the Cold War.[2] What was the Cold War? Was it inevitable? Could it have ended sooner? Is it reasonable to think that it could have ended differently under happier circumstances? (It is easy to imagine it ending under far worse.) What were the costs? Were any of them avoidable?

It is most unlikely that these questions will ever be put to rest. Probably the best we can hope for from historians are intimations

---

1 Walter Lippmann, *The Cold War: A Study in U.S. Foreign Policy* (New York, 1947).
2 X [George Kennan], "The Sources of Soviet Conduct," *Foreign Affairs* 25 (July 1947): 566–82.

of truth, not answers. Why, then, are the questions even interesting? Just as Lippmann and Kennan viewed the conflict with the Soviet Union and its Communist ideology through the prism of the struggle against Hitler and fascism, so today political analysts and politicians view the emerging order of the 1990s through the prism of the Cold War. The understanding of what that struggle was about, what was gained and what was lost, will have a profound influence on the paths to national security that will be taken in the months ahead.

Both Kennan and Lippmann cast themselves in the twin roles of prognosticator and counsellor. As prognosticator about the trajectory of the Soviet Union, Kennan had the better of the argument. Lippmann took aim at Kennan's prediction that "Soviet power . . . bears within itself the seeds of its own decay, and that the sprouting of these seeds is well advanced."[3] All of this seemed to fly in the face of Stalin's vaunted monolithic power, his huge standing armies, and the fanatical devotion demonstrated by the Russian masses to the Great Genius, impassive in his marshal's uniform atop Lenin's mausoleum. According to Lippmann, Kennan's prescription of "containment" ended up in political eschatology—the faith that when the Kremlin was forced to "face frustration indefinitely" the result would be "either the breakup or the gradual mellowing of the Soviet power."[4] Kennan suggested, however, that it would take ten or fifteen years for Stalin's empire to mellow, not forty-three.

Lippmann ridiculed Kennan's optimism since the policy prescriptions he wished to discredit depended on it. According to the columnist, Kennan's position of "holding the line and hoping for the best" was utterly dependent on "an extra strong dose of wishful thinking about the United States."[5] By his own admission Kennan's policies would take many years to work, and the notorious impatience of the American people—a favorite Lippmann theme— would render the strategy unworkable. But in fact, the United States maintained the "containment" policy for forty-three years. The Soviet Union not only mellowed but no longer exists.

3 Lippmann, *The Cold War*, 11.   4 Ibid., 18.
5 Ibid., 12.

But how much did U.S. Cold War policy have to do with what has happened to the Soviet Union? The spin doctors are already at work on the history books. Ronald Reagan's defenders argue that the willingness of the United States to challenge the Soviet Union to a technological arms race and a spending race strained the Communist system to the breaking point. The president's insistence on spending almost $2 trillion over five years, on confronting the Soviet leadership with Hollywood fantasies of miracle weapons, and on mounting an ideological offensive against communism and all forms of statism caused Mikhail Gorbachev to throw in the towel. The eight-year Cold War II that began even before the Afghanistan invasion was more than the Soviet system could take. In short, the Cold War ended in a military victory for the United States, a historic triumph because, for all the threats and feints, a shooting war between the United States and the Soviet Union was avoided.

This judgment appears to contradict most of the evidence. The arms race actually increased both the risk and the perception of risk of a war between the superpowers. It did not deter a Soviet intention to challenge the United States to a test of arms because, as virtually all U.S. intelligence estimates concluded in the years 1945–1950, the Soviet Union had neither the intention nor the capability of resorting to war. The U.S. nuclear monopoly neither contained Soviet expansion outside of Europe—that is, the acquisition of clients, spies, and propaganda assets—nor prevented Stalin from consolidating his hold over Eastern Europe. From the first the United States took the lead in the arms race. The Soviets struggled to keep up and thereby created the only military threat to the United States taken seriously by U.S. planners—the threat that Stalin's successors would acquire enough intercontinental planes and missiles to deter the United States from the vigorous pursuit of containment in the political arena. The extreme case, as NSC-68 put it, contemplated the possibility that the Kremlin might in some future "year of maximum danger" achieve the capability of launching a surprise attack. Should that happen, given the fundamentally evil nature of the system, the Soviets would resort to nuclear blackmail or "pre-emptive" war. These ideas kept the nuclear arms race going, raised the risk of war by miscalculation, and contributed to the proliferation of nuclear and nonnuclear military technology throughout the world.

The Cold War ended because internal failures and disappointments forced fundamental changes in the Soviet system. The Communist party lost legitimacy because it felt compelled to confirm the realities of Stalinist terror, to admit the widespread corruption of its leadership, and to come to terms with the fact that the system was working badly. The disastrous war in Afghanistan and the dawning realization that the Soviet Union would never develop a strong economic base as an autarchic command economy and could never compete in the global economy as a nation of regimented, unmotivated, and terrorized workers pushed Gorbachev down the road to *perestroika* and *glasnost*.

The disintegration of the Soviet system came about exactly in the way that Kennan had predicted. The system contained the seeds of its own destruction. The expensive pursuit of military equivalence no doubt accelerated the process, and for this the United States can take some dubious credit for hooking the Soviets into a spending race that was more precipitously disastrous for the Soviet system than for American society and its economic base. But the Cold War also helped to strengthen the hard-line leadership. Indeed, some reformist historians in the former Soviet Union believe that an earlier readiness of the United States to negotiate with Stalin's successors, or even with Stalin, over the fate of Europe would have caused the winds of change to blow earlier, harder, and faster, and that some Soviet leader might well have taken the risks of *perestroika* in the 1950s or the 1960s. Who knows? But as Kennan noted, the myth of capitalist encirclement was an important Stalinist weapon of social control. Beginning in the late 1940s, the extravagant rhetoric of officials, generals, and politicians in the United States about the inevitability of war with the Soviet Union—and the need to get it over with before the year of maximum danger arrived—served to confirm Stalinist paranoia and to reinforce the climate of fear on which the dictator built his regime. The hostility of the West also served to explain to two Soviet generations why the workers' government could not deliver on its promises to the workers.

But George Kennan neither predicted nor advocated a military victory, not even one that rested on a spending race and the demonstration of superior technological prowess. He has spent the second half of his life explaining away his "X" article, apologizing for its excessively militaristic ring, and lamenting the uses to which it was put. Yet, it was Kennan's eloquent distillations of his complex, contradictory thought (backed by a reputation for expertise on the Soviet Union that few could match)—in such phrases as the "adroit and vigilant application of counter-force," or "the Russians look forward to a duel of infinite duration,"[6] or the emphasis on the Soviets' "neurotic view of world affairs," or the "instinctive Russian sense of insecurity"[7]—that took official Washington by storm in early 1946. The picture that emerged from Kennan's analysis was of an ambitious power in the grip of an irrational ideology and impervious to conventional diplomacy. His "Long Telegram" was leaked to *Time* a year before the "X" article appeared, and his message was amplified and distorted as a brief for policies that he never supported, and indeed would at a much later stage publicly oppose.

Because Secretary of the Navy James V. Forrestal and others emphasized the passages that seemed to support the big military buildup and the across-the-board get-tough policy with Stalin that they advocated, the most prescient passages in Kennan's piece were ignored. He pointed out that "we have in Russia today a population which is physically and spiritually tired. The mass of the people are disillusioned, skeptical and no longer as accessible as they once were to the magical attraction which Soviet power still radiates to its followers abroad."[8] Kennan talked about the inherent weakness of the Soviet system. Not only did he identify the weakening hold of Stalinist ideology on the Russian people, but he was sensitive to the fundamental vulnerabilities of the Stalinist economy.

Russian Communists who speak of the "uneven development of capitalism" should blush at the contemplation of their own national economy.

---

6   Kennan, "The Sources of Soviet Conduct," 576.
7   George Kennan, "The Long Telegram" in *The Forrestal Diaries*, ed. Walter Millis (New York, 1951), 136.
8   Ibid.

Here certain branches of economic life, such as the metallurgical and machine industries, have been pushed out of all proportion to other sectors of economy. Here is a nation striving to become in a short period one of the great industrial nations of the world while it still has no highway network worthy of the name and only a relatively primitive network of railways. . . . And in vast sectors of economic life it has not yet been possible to instill into labor anything like that general culture of production and technical self-respect which characterizes the skilled worker of the west.[9]

Today it is commonplace to read almost identically self-critical analyses in Russian publications.

Lippmann was unwilling to assume that the "neurotic world view" and the totalitarian organization of Stalinist society meant that the Soviet Union was so inexorably committed to an expansionist course as to be beyond the influence of adroit diplomacy. Given the obvious Soviet weakness that Kennan identified, why was it so clearly impossible for the most powerful nation on earth to press the heirs of the Russian empire to accept a settlement?

I am contending that the American diplomatic effort should be concentrated on the problem created by the armistice—which is on how the continent of Europe can be evacuated by the three non-European armies which are now inside Europe. This is the problem which will have to be solved if the independence of the European nations is to be restored. Without that there is no possibility of a tolerable peace. But if these armies withdraw, there will be a very different balance of power in the world than there is today, and one which cannot easily be upset. For the nations of Europe, separately and in groups, perhaps even in unity, will then, and then only, cease to be the stakes and the pawns of the Russian-American conflict.[10]

It is hard to read the "X" article and come to any conclusion about when negotiation with the Soviet Union would make sense, if ever. Read literally, the article seems to say that there could be no useful diplomacy until the mellowing process was well advanced. We know that Kennan had misgivings about the division of Germany, German rearmament, and the deployment of NATO armies beyond the temporary "modest shield" behind which

9   Kennan, "The Sources of Soviet Conduct," 578.   10 Ibid., 579.

Western Europe would recover its economic and political stability. He was appalled by the global pretensions of the Truman Doctrine. But no one could guess it from the cold print that was so effectively used to support all of these policies.

Lippmann attacked Kennan for not keeping his eye on "the material cause and reason of the conflict,"[11] which was the future of Germany and the military balance in Europe. The columnist appeared more pragmatic and hard-headed than the suddenly famous diplomat. If Kennan was right that communism was already a weakening ideology and that the economic foundations of Soviet power were shaky, then the only reason that this underdeveloped country should have been considered a serious political rival was the presence of the Red Army in the middle of Europe. Given the uniquely dominant role of the United States in the world economy and its unique strength as the only big power not crippled by the war, not to mention the attraction its democratic system held for the entire war-shattered world—even Ho Chi Minh was celebrating Washington and Jefferson in 1945—why did the Truman administration not set as its overriding policy objective the redeployment and demobilization of Stalin's land forces and the avoidance of a nuclear arms race? For it was only in the military sphere that the Soviet Union had the chance to be a serious rival to the United States, and as Lippmann pointed out, a deal with the Soviet Union to withdraw and demobilize its forces in Europe would be largely self-verifying. Such an agreement would provide little employment "for the dialecticians, the ideologists, the sophists, and the casuists" who were then building political careers on the murky text of the Yalta accords. Soviet disengagement "is not a matter which can be hidden behind an iron curtain. It is a matter of plain and quite obvious fact."[12]

Lippmann made a strong case. A German settlement and withdrawal of the armies would "divide the Red Army from the Red International."[13] It would avoid the "continual and complicated intervention" of the United States in the affairs of its allies and would spare the effort and expense of "recruiting, subsidizing, and supporting a heterogeneous array of satellites, clients, dependents,

11 Lippmann, *The Cold War*, 35.   12 Ibid.   13 Ibid., 40.

and puppets . . . around the perimeter of the Soviet Union."[14]
(Lippmann correctly saw these imperial roles as sources of weakness, not strength, and certainly not as the badge of preeminent or
long-lasting power.)

Why did the United States not put Lippmann's strategy to the
test? Why did the Truman administration launch its containment
strategy by concentrating on the fringes of Europe—Turkey and
Greece—rather than on its center? Why did it move so quickly to
conclude that military pressure rather than diplomacy was the key
to containing Russian power?

In 1947 the United States had a monopoly on nuclear weapons,
produced about half the world's goods on its soil, and had most
of the world's gold reserves in Fort Knox. The Soviet Union was
still in ruins, and Stalin had already begun to destroy the "magical
attraction" of communism for people around the world. All over
Western Europe, Communists were out of government, although
Stalinist parties were still very strong in France and Italy. Stalin
was actually taking a conservative approach to revolution, coun-
seling caution to the comrades in Greece, France, and China. In
retrospect, it seems inexplicable that the United States at the height
of its military and economic hegemony should wish to delay the
grand settlement that Lippmann proposed until, in Dean Acheson's words, it had built "situations of strength." Given the conviction that the Soviet Union would acquire nuclear weapons and
that, as later suggested in NSC-68, Stalin would use them against
the United States whenever he deemed it advantageous to do so,
why was nuclear disarmament not the centerpiece of U.S. policy?
Why would the United States have a greater edge over the Soviet
Union after ten or fifteen years of containment than it already enjoyed in 1947?

I would suggest as an explanation four powerful political ideas
that gripped the Truman administration; each reinforced the other,
causing the architects of U.S. Cold War policy to reject the course
that Lippmann proposed without even giving it serious consideration. The first was the notion that the atomic bomb was a "win-

14   Ibid., 21.

ning weapon" under the cover of which the United States could successfully challenge Soviet power at the periphery of the Eurasian land mass. The geopolitical faith that the balance of power would be decided by the control of raw materials, sea lanes, bases, and internal political developments outside of Europe caused the Truman administration to put greater emphasis on military pressure and less on diplomacy. Two years after Japan's surrender in the wake of the atomic attack, it seemed reasonable to expect a more favorable outcome in Europe once the world was organized against Stalin and once the United States had clearly demonstrated, contrary to Roosevelt's comments to Stalin during the war, that the newly proclaimed leader of the Free World was in no hurry to withdraw its forces from the Continent.

The second idea that guided American policymakers was that Stalin was a reincarnation of Hitler, a man of boundless appetite, a barbarian whose word was worthless, and an ideologue as removed from the world of conventional politics as *Der Führer*. You could not do business with Stalin, and even to make the attempt would weaken political support for containment, giving the Soviet dictator an opportunity to divide the coalition against him and to confuse the American people.

The third and perhaps most important strain in American official thinking that pushed Truman's advisers toward a military rather than a diplomatic strategy for dealing with the Soviet Union was concern about Germany. The fear that a Germany that was not locked in an American embrace might conclude a new Rapallo agreement with the Soviet Union and that together the two land powers would attract Japan to a revived totalitarian alliance to challenge American hegemony was the driving force for the policy of partition on which NATO was founded. Within the Truman administration the distrust of Germany two years after the war was too strong to permit a deal with the Soviets based on the "neutralization" of Germany. Worse than the Red Army on the Elbe was the prospect of a power vacuum in Germany. A long-term U.S. military presence on German soil would serve as the glue for the economic integration of an Atlantic community in which the leading role of the United States would be assured for years to come. The military alliance would exert a profound influence on the domestic politics of every Western European country, ensuring that their governments would remain pro-American and centrist.

The fourth and final strain was a deep concern about the volatility of U.S. public opinion. The American people were demanding demobilization and the armed forces were melting away. In 1946, one third of American exports were being financed through various programs of economic assistance. But conservatives, divining the public mood, were gearing up to block the "giveaway programs" on which the administration's economic and political strategies depended. Impassioned oratory about unpaid World War I war debts echoed through the chamber of the House of Representatives. According to a Gallup poll, a majority of Americans favored high tariffs. The Council of Economic Advisers worried that "a drastic reduction in public outlays plus the rapid demobilization of our armed forces, would lead to heavy unemployment and business dislocation for a substantial period of time."[15] Acheson and Secretary of Defense George C. Marshall had run into trouble with Congress when they tried to present a nuanced view of the situation in Europe, and a consensus swiftly developed in the administration that scaring the hell out of the American people, in Vandenberg's famous phrase, was essential for combatting the isolationist mood. The containment strategy required that Americans believe that Stalin represented a threat to their own security. To sell Marshall Plan aid the only way it could be sold, as an instrument of containment, it was important to close off avenues of hope that the problems of Europe could be settled through negotiation with Stalin. "I think it is a mistake," Dean Acheson told the Senate Foreign Relations Committee, "to believe that you can, at anytime, sit down with the Russians and solve questions."[16]

Lippmann showed no interest in challenging Kennan on his judgments about Russia's vulnerabilities, much less on the facts

15 Council of Economic Advisers, *Midyear Review,* July 1950, 27, quoted in Richard M. Freeland, *The Truman Doctrine and the Origins of McCarthyism: Foreign Policy, Domestic Politics, and Internal Security, 1946–1948* (New York, 1985), 49.

16 Acheson quoted in Walter Isaacson and Evan Thomas, *The Wise Men: Six Friends and the World They Made* (New York, 1986), 403.

the Soviet expert used as the basis for his judgments. His rejoinder rested rather on his assessment of American vulnerabilities that would be likely to develop in a long Cold War. Why, asked Lippmann, do we think that it is ordained that the Soviet Union must break its leg "while the United States grows a pair of wings to speed it on its way?"[17] In his own way Lippmann was as prescient about what would happen to the United States as Kennan was about the fate of the Soviet Union. He was wrong about American staying power through nine administrations, but forty-three years later his columns do serve as an unheeded reminder of the extraordinary costs of containment.

Lippmann sounded like the George Kennan of the 1970s when he zeroed in on the rhapsodical coda of the "X" article. Kennan professed "a certain gratitude to a Providence which, by providing the American people with this implacable challenge [Soviet power and Stalinist ideology], has made their entire security as a nation dependent on their pulling themselves together and accepting the responsibilities of moral and political leadership that history plainly intended them to bear."[18] Lippmann did not question the assertion that it was America's destiny to lead, but he did challenge both the definition of leadership and the strategy for exercising leadership. He was clearer about why he did not like the strategy. Would it not take "a blank check on the Treasury?" How could the American constitutional system be maintained if containment of communism became the national purpose? How would the president know when he was to intervene? Or was the idea to intervene everywhere? Either the president would be too little and too late with his application of "counterforce" or he would have to bypass the Constitution. "A policy of shifts and maneuvers may be suited to the Soviet system of government, which, as Mr X tells us, is animated by patient persistence. It is not suited to the American system of government."[19]

Lippmann argued that a "free and undirected economy like our own" cannot "be used by the diplomatic planners to wage a diplomatic war against a planned economy."[20] Forty-three years later it is tempting to say that Lippmann was wrong on this score. The

17 Lippmann, *The Cold War*, 13.   18 Kennan, "The Sources of Soviet Conduct," 582.
19 Lippmann, *The Cold War*, 15–16.   20 Ibid., 16.

"arsenal of democracy," with the world's largest GNP and the world's most formidable military force, has its problems after forty years of unrelenting military budgets, but no one at this point would exchange these difficulties for the problems in the former Soviet Union. Yet the challenge of containment caused profound changes in the American system that Lippmann feared, correctly, would be destructive. The pressures of the military competition, which was assumed in the highest reaches of the Truman administration to be the likely outcome of their policies, forced the "free and undirected economy" to develop its owned planned sector; the Pentagon and the huge network of weapons procurement and maintenance facilities it fed is a market system in name only. The impact of four decades of permanent mobilization on the U.S. economy is the subject of considerable contention, but it is obvious that this mobilization transformed the nature of American capitalism—and certainly not in a direction advocated by free-market ideologues. My own view is that despite the periodic stimulus provided by cycles of military spending, military Keynesianism has been a disaster, contributing to budget deficits, loss of competitive position, and the siphoning of investment funds from both public infrastructure—schools, bridges, and the like—as well as from needed industrial and technological development. The spending priorities adopted in the pursuit of containment have had a great deal to do with the decline in American economic power. Lippmann did not exactly predict this, but he raised the issue. Kennan did not.

Lippmann also foresaw some of the constitutional problems of permanent mobilization—he touched on the atrophy of Congress's war-making powers and hinted at the rise of the imperial presidency—but he could not predict the huge impact the Cold War has had on the two-party system, the electoral process, and the political culture of the United States. Lippmann and Kennan shared a common worldview. Both were conservatives who were uneasy about American democratic culture. Lippmann made his reputation in the early 1920s by puncturing the platitudes of the day about public opinion and offering in their stead an unapologetically elitist view of government. He called the public a "willful despot," and thought that at critical junctures public opinion was "destructively wrong."[21] He despaired of conducting a sensible foreign policy in a democratic culture because voters could not be "aroused to the exertions and sacrifices of struggle" unless they were "incited to passionate hatred" or "intoxicated with unlimited hope."[22] George Kennan, the midwesterner who always seemed to be something of a pilgrim and stranger in his own country, could barely conceal his impatience with the crowd-pleasing yahoos in Congress who wielded such power over the national destiny.

Both shared the view that the United States was the custodian and guardian of Western civilization in a world in which the highest achievements of that civilization had barely survived the savage assault of a virulent, deformed populism. Kennan's peroration about how containment of the "implacable challenge"[23] of Soviet Russia would force the American people to exercise leadership smacks of the then-popular Toynbee thesis, and in challenging it Lippmann did not develop the full implications of his argument. Despite his mention of the economic and constitutional problems of fighting the Cold War, Lippmann, like Kennan, largely ignored domestic policy. Both presented themselves as foreign policy experts, offering critiques of alternative options as if the domestic political and economic sources of American strength were largely unaffected. Ironically, Kennan's prescience about the fate of the Soviet Union rested on his understanding of its shaky legitimacy. The irrationality and unattractiveness of the Communist system would eventually erode the popular support that even a totalitarian system needs to survive. Lippmann, who for all his scorn for the role public opinion plays in American politics, also understood that legitimacy is the essential foundation for the exercise of stable power. In the age of democracy the legitimate exercise of power depended on the ability to project a vision of the good society and to move forward toward its realization.

After almost fifty years the Cold War struggle has destroyed the Soviet Union. In the hands of Russian, Belorussian, Ukrainian, and Kazakhstani leaders are thousands of nuclear warheads that can

21   Walter Lippmann, *Public Policy* (New York, 1955), 21.   22   Ibid., 24.
23   Kennan, "The Sources of Soviet Conduct," 582.

destroy this country, and who will gain control of them in the months ahead is by no means certain. The collapse of Soviet power and the failure of Socialist institutions open up long-term possibilities of democratic transformation. But the prospects for the immediate future may be more political upheavals and economic distress. All of this is adding to the world's immense capital needs at a moment when the United States, debt ridden and more dependent on foreign capital than at any time in this century, can do almost nothing to meet them. The costs of the prolonged political-military struggle that Lippmann called the Cold War can be counted not only in the neglect and deterioration of domestic institutions but also in the loss of American capacity to exercise constructive influence abroad. The world's only global military superpower lacks the material resources to maintain a competitive industrial base, the infrastructure on which a strong economy depends, or even the necessities, much less the amenities, of a good society.

How ironical it is that as Leningrad has been renamed St. Petersburg and as the seventy-five-year obsession with the Soviet Union comes to an end, the United States is now obsessed with talk of its own decline. In 1991, it once again reasserted its strength and staying power by fixing on another underdeveloped country against which it waged a crushing but indecisive war. The United States has paid dearly for its Cold War victory and for the satisfaction of creating the foundations of the Cold War order. But the consequence—as Lippmann rightly predicted and as the last forty-three years have shown—has been political and moral exhaustion.

11

Why Did the Cold War Arise, and Why Did It End?

RAYMOND L. GARTHOFF

The fundamental underlying cause of the Cold War was the reinforcing belief in both the Soviet Union and the United States that
confrontation was unavoidable, imposed by history. Soviet leaders
believed that communism would ultimately triumph in the world
and that the Soviet Union was the vanguard Socialist/Communist
state. They also believed that the Western "imperialist" powers
were historically bound to pursue a hostile course against them.
For their part, American and other Western leaders assumed that
the Soviet Union was determined to enhance its own power and to
pursue expansionist policies by all expedient means in order to
achieve a Soviet-led Communist world. Each side thought that it
was compelled by the very existence of the other side to engage in
a zero-sum competition, and each saw the unfolding history of the
Cold War as confirming its views.

The prevailing Western view was wrong in attributing a master
plan to the Kremlin, in believing that Communist ideology impelled Soviet leaders to advance, in exaggerating Communist abil-
ities to subvert the Free World, and in thinking that Soviet officials
viewed military power as an ultimate recourse. But the West was
not wrong in believing that Soviet leaders were committed to a
historically driven struggle between two worlds until, ultimately,
theirs would triumph. To be sure, other motivations, interests, and
objectives played a part, including national aims, institutional interests, and personal psychological considerations. But these influ-
ences tended to enhance the ideological framework rather than
weaken it. Moreover, the actions of each side were sufficiently

consistent with the ideological expectations of the other side to sustain their respective worldviews for many years.

Within the framework of ideological conflict, the Americans and the Soviets waged the Cold War as a geopolitical struggle, more in terms of traditional balance-of-power politics than in terms of class struggle or global containment/deterrence theory. If ideology was the only thing driving the superpowers in the Cold War, why do we see that conflict as arising from the ashes of World War II rather than as stemming from the October Revolution of 1917? The answer is clear. In 1917 and over the next twenty-five years the Soviet Union was relatively weak and only one of several Great Powers in a multipolar world. By the end of World War II, on the other hand, Germany and Japan had been crushed, Britain, France, and China were weakened, and the enlarged Soviet Union, even though much weaker than the United States, seemed to pose an unprecedented threat by virtue of its massive armies and their presence deep in Central Europe. Under these circumstances, Joseph Stalin's reassertion in 1946 and 1947 of the division of the world into two contending camps seemed truer and more threatening than ever before.

So the Cold War had both an ideological and a geopolitical dimension. A Manichean Communist worldview spawned a Manichean anti-Communist worldview. Each side imputed unlimited objectives, ultimately world domination, to the other. In addition, each side's operational code looked to the realization of its ambitions (or its historical destiny) over the long term and thus posited an indefinite period of conflict. But even though both sides envisioned a conflict of indefinite duration, and even though policy decisions were pragmatic and based on calculation of risk, cost, and gain, there was always the hazard of a miscalculation that could be especially dangerous, given the historical coincidence of the Cold War and the first half-century of the nuclear age. Nuclear weapons, by threatening the existence of world civilization, added significantly to the tension of the epoch; the stakes were utterly without precedent and beyond full comprehension.

This is not to deny that nuclear weapons also helped to keep the Cold War cold, to prevent a third world war in the twentieth century. Indeed, in the final analysis and notwithstanding their awesome power, nuclear weapons did not cause, prevent, or end the Cold War, which would have been waged even had such weapons never existed. But it is to argue that the arms race and other aspects of the superpower rivalry were driven in part by ideological assumptions. As a result, while the Cold War and the nuclear arms race could be attenuated when opportunities or constraints led both sides to favor a relaxation of tensions, they could not be ended until the ideological underpinnings had also been released. This occurred under Mikhail Gorbachev's leadership, which saw a fundamental reevaluation in Moscow of the processes at work in the real world, a basic reassessment of threats, and finally a deep revision of aims and political objectives.

The West did not, as is widely believed, win the Cold War through geopolitical containment and military deterrence. Nor was the Cold War won by the Reagan military buildup and the Reagan Doctrine, as some have suggested. Instead, "victory" for the West came when a new generation of Soviet leaders realized how badly their system at home and their policies abroad had failed. What containment did was to successfully stalemate Moscow's attempts to advance Soviet hegemony. Over four decades it performed the historic function of holding Soviet power in check until the internal seeds of destruction within the Soviet Union and its empire could mature. At that point, however, it was Gorbachev who brought the Cold War to an end.

Despite the important differences between them, all Soviet leaders from Lenin until Gorbachev had shared a belief in an ineluctable conflict between socialism and capitalism. Although Gorbachev remained a Socialist, and in his own terms perhaps even a Marxist-Leninist, he renounced the idea of inevitable world conflict. His avowed acceptance of the interdependence of the world, of the priority of all-human values over class values, and of the indivisibility of common security marked a revolutionary ideological change. That change, which Gorbachev publicly declared as early as 1986 (though insufficiently noted), manifested itself in many ways over the next five years, in deeds as well as in words, including policies reflecting a drastically reduced Soviet perception of the Western threat and actions to reduce the Western perception of the Soviet threat.

In 1986, for example, Gorbachev made clear his readiness to ban all nuclear weapons. In 1987 he signed the INF Treaty, eliminating not only the Soviet and American missiles deployed since the late 1970s but also the whole of the Soviet strategic theater missile forces that had faced Europe and Asia for three decades. What is more, the treaty instituted an intrusive and extensive system of verification. In 1988, Gorbachev proposed conventional arms reductions in Europe under a plan that would abandon the Soviet Union's numerical superiority, and also launched a substantial unilateral force reduction. In 1988 and 1989 he withdrew all Soviet forces from Afghanistan. At about the same time, he encouraged the ouster of the old Communist leadership in Eastern Europe and accepted the transition of the former Soviet-allied states into non-Communist neutral states. By 1990, Gorbachev had signed a CFE Treaty accepting Soviet conventional arms levels in Europe to the Urals that were considerably lower than the levels for NATO. By that time as well he had not only accepted Germany's reunification but also the membership of a unified Germany in NATO. A year later he had jettisoned the Warsaw Pact and the CMEA economic union and had agreed to verified deep cuts in strategic nuclear forces.

Although Gorbachev may not have expected the complete collapse of communism (and Soviet influence) in Eastern Europe that occurred in 1989 and 1990, he had made clear to the 27th Congress of the Soviet Communist Party as early as February 1986 that a new conception of security had to replace the previous one and that the confrontation of the Cold War had to end. No longer speaking in Leninist terms of contending Socialist and capitalist worlds, Gorbachev spoke instead of one world, an "interdependent and in many ways integral world." He denied that any country could find security in military power, either for defense or deterrence. Security, he said, could only be found through political means, and only on a mutual basis. The goal, he asserted, should be the "creation of a comprehensive system of international security" that embraced economic, ecological, and humanitarian, as well as political and military, elements. Hence, the Soviet decision to give new support to the United Nations, including collective peacekeeping, and to join the world economic system. Hence, the cooperative Soviet efforts to resolve regional conflicts in Central America, Southern Africa, the Horn of Africa, Cambodia, Afghanistan, and the Middle East, not to mention the Soviet Union's support for the UN's collective action against Iraq. And hence, Moscow's willingness to countenance the dissolution of the Eastern European alliance and Socialist commonwealth, which had been fashioned to meet security requirements and ideological imperatives that had now been abandoned. These moves were all prefigured in the new approach that Gorbachev laid down in early 1986.

In the final analysis, only a Soviet leader could have ended the Cold War, and Gorbachev set out deliberately to do so. Although earlier Soviet leaders had understood the impermissibility of war in the nuclear age, Gorbachev was the first to recognize that reciprocal political accommodation, rather than military power for deterrence or "counterdeterrence," was the defining core of the Soviet Union's relationship with the rest of the world. The conclusions that Gorbachev drew from this recognition, and the subsequent Soviet actions, finally permitted the Iron Curtain to be dismantled and ended the global confrontation of the Cold War.

Gorbachev, to be sure, seriously underestimated the task of changing the Soviet Union, and this led to policy errors that contributed to the failure of his program for the transformation of Soviet society and polity. His vision of a resurrected socialism built on the foundation of successful *perestroika* and *demokratizatsiya* was never a realistic possibility. A revitalized Soviet political union was beyond realization as well. Whether Gorbachev would have modified his goals or changed his means had he foreseen this disjunction is not clear, probably even to him. In the external political arena, however, Gorbachev both understood and successfully charted the course that led to the end of the Cold War, even though in this area, too, he almost certainly exaggerated the capacity for reform on the part of the Communist governments in Eastern Europe.

As the preceding discussion suggests, the Western and above all the American role in ending the Cold War was necessary but not primary. There are a number of reasons for this conclusion, but the basic one is that the American worldview was derivative of the Communist worldview. Containment was hollow without an expansionist power to contain. In this sense, it was the Soviet threat, real or imagined, that generated the American dedication to waging the Cold War, regardless of what revisionist historians have to say. These historians point to Washington's atomic diplomacy and to its various overt and covert political, economic, paramilitary, and military campaigns. Supposedly designed to counter a Soviet threat, they argue, these initiatives actually entailed an expansion of American influence and dominion.

The revisionist interpretation errs in attributing initiative and design to American diplomacy, but it is not entirely wrong. American policymakers were guilty of accepting far too much of the Communist worldview in constructing an anti-Communist antipode, and of being too ready to fight fire with fire. Indeed, once the Cold War became the dominant factor in global politics (and above all in American and Soviet perceptions), each side viewed every development around the world in terms of its relationship to that great struggle, and each was inclined to act according to a self-fulfilling prophecy. The Americans, for example, often viewed local and regional conflicts of indigenous origins as Cold War battles. Like the Soviets, they distrusted the neutral and nonaligned nations and were always more comfortable when countries around the world were either their allies or the satellites and surrogates of the other side. Thus, many traditional diplomatic relationships not essentially attendant on the superpower rivalry were swept into the vortex of the Cold War, at least in the eyes of the protagonists and partly by their actions.

It is true, of course, that the Cold War led in some instances to constructive American involvements. The Marshall Plan is a prime example, as Michael J. Hogan has shown,[1] not to mention American support for some democratic movements, for the Congress for Cultural Freedom, and for the liberal journal *Encounter*. But other overt and covert involvements were more frequently less constructive, and often subversive, of real liberalism and democracy. Apart from the loss of American lives and treasure in such misplaced ventures as the Vietnam War and in the massive over-investment in weaponry, one of the worst effects of forcing all

1 Michael J. Hogan, *The Marshall Plan: America, Britain, and the Reconstruction of Western Europe, 1947–1952* (New York, 1987).

world developments onto the procrustean bed of the Cold War was the distortion of our own understanding and values. By dividing the globe into a Communist Evil Empire controlled by Moscow and a Free World led by Washington, American policymakers promoted numerous antidemocratic regimes into rewarded members of the Free World so long as they were anti-Communist (or even rhetorically anti-Communist). Washington also used the exigencies of the Cold War to justify assassination plots, to negotiate deals with drug lords and terrorists, and to transform anti-Communist insurgents, however corrupt, into Freedom Fighters. Alliance ties, military basing rights, and support for insurgencies were routinely given priority over such other American objectives as the promotion of nuclear nonproliferation, economic development, human rights, and democracy.

Parallel Soviet sins were at least as great. While Soviet foreign assistance to Socialist and "progressive" countries was sometimes constructive (construction of the Aswan Dam, for example, or economic assistance to India), it was also skewed by both the ideological expectation of moving the world toward communism and by expectations of geopolitical advantage in the Cold War. Often dictatorial regimes, "Marxist" or "Socialist" only according to the cynical claims of their leaders, provided the basis for Soviet support, as with Siad Barre in Somalia, for example, or Mengistu in Ethiopia. In addition, the Soviet Union engaged in many covert political operations and lent support to national liberation movements (some authentic, others less so) that sometimes included elements engaged in terrorism. On both sides, then, ideological beliefs combined with geopolitical considerations to fuel a Cold War struggle that left many victims in its wake.

Although the decisive factor in the end of the Cold War was a change in these beliefs, it is worth repeating that the Soviets could discard a long-encrusted and familiar ideology only because of a powerful transformation in the way Gorbachev perceived reality and because he was ready to adapt domestic and foreign policies to the new perception. Over time the extent of these changes became evident and their validity compelling. I earlier noted some of the cumulative changes in Soviet foreign policy that brought the Cold War to an end. The critical culimating event was the Revolution of '89. The year between the destruction of the Berlin Wall in November 1989 and the European conference in Paris in November 1990 saw the removal of the most important concrete manifestation of the Cold War—the division of Germany and Europe. The division of Europe had symbolized the global battle between the two ideological and geopolitical camps in the years immediately after World War II. When that division came to a conclusion, the consequences for the international balance of power were so substantial that even the most hardened Cold Warriors in the West were forced to acknowledge that the Cold War had ended—even before the collapse of Communist rule in the Soviet Union or of the Soviet Union itself. Moreover, the Revolution of '89 in Eastern Europe was decisive not only in demonstrating that the ideological underpinnings of the Cold War had been removed but also in shifting the actual balance of power. The removal of Soviet military power from Eastern Europe dissolved the threat to Western Europe and also restored a reunified Europe to the center of the world political stage. Russia, and more gradually the United States, even though still closely linked to Europe, will now become less central.

History, including the history of international relations, inexorably moves forward. The Cold War was an important episode, but with roots in earlier history and with ramifications that continue to influence the post-Cold War world. Emerging features of the new world illuminate not only the new agenda of world politics but also the Cold War. We see a return to multipolarity in a system of great and lesser powers. Related to this development is a shift to wider security concerns and therefore a shift in the elements of world power. Military power is by no means without continuing and, in the most ominous sense, ultimate influence. But military force as a means of registering and influencing power has declined while other factors—above all, economic ones—have become more important. One consequence is an increase in the relative weight of Japan and the European Community (especially with a unified Germany) and a decrease in the relative weight of the United States and the former Soviet Union. There will also be a new pattern of relationships between these countries and the rest of the globe (formerly termed the "Third World," but regarded mainly as an arena for competition between the two worlds led by the superpowers). There are those who see, clearly with some foundation but hopefully in exaggeration, economic and sociopolitical North-South tension replacing the ideological and politico-military East-West confrontation of the Cold War.

Military power will be less salient in world politics, but will remain a factor and on occasion will be used. The Gulf war waged against Iraq in 1991 by a U.S.-led coalition and supported by the Soviet Union was the first significant example. Although probably atypical, that experience did illustrate the enormous change in relations between the former Soviet Union and the West. The possible proliferation of nuclear and other weapons of mass destruction, and the efforts to deal with that danger, will be important elements of the new political agenda—again, in contrast to the nuclear confrontation between East and West during the Cold War.

Above all, there will be a return to the more traditional pattern of shifting blends of cooperation and competition among all nations, including former Cold War allies as well as former adversaries. Countries will pursue their own perceived interests in a more open international context. They will engage not only in new forms of cooperation but also in shifting rivalries and conflicts similar to those that preceded the Cold War. In short, the world will resume a pattern of political relationships free of bipolar superpower and coalition rivalry. We can hope for a new world order, and strive to fashion one. But numerous local and regional conflicts that were largely subsumed into the global confrontation of the Cold War will now assume their own places in the world order—or disorder—and new ones will arise. The most striking new source of potential conflict lies in the former, now-fractured Soviet empire.

U.S.-Russian relations in the new era will remain mixed, although probably with more cooperation and certainly with less competition than U.S.-Soviet relations during the Cold War. There is a distinct possibility that relations, already advancing beyond détente, will move toward an entente, though that outcome would depend on a number of things that cannot yet be confidently predicted. In all, diplomatic history promises to become richer and more varied, though let us hope not *too* exciting.

It is not, however, my present purpose to look into the future, except to sketch how the emerging future differs from the receding Cold War. While attention will naturally and properly be directed forward, it remains useful also to take the opportunity to look to the past. Much has been written about the Cold War and its near half-century of confrontations and crises, and some of it is very good. We know a great deal. But there remains much to learn, both about specific episodes and various dimensions of the epoch and about its underlying causes and effects. With the benefit of new sources, and from a new vantage point, it will now be possible to expand our knowledge of history and understanding of international politics.

12

A View from Below

NOAM CHOMSKY

There have been important changes in the international order in the past several decades, but the continuities are no less significant, particularly with regard to North-South relations. Although U.S. policies toward the Third World were framed within a Cold War context, that was more a matter of doctrinal utility than of fact. The North-South conflicts, with their deep roots in the colonial era, are likely to continue as the policies of the United States and other advanced industrial powers are adapted to changing circumstances, of which the end of the Cold War is only one aspect.

By the 1970s, the United States had lost its post-World War II position of overwhelming dominance, and there was speculation about competing trading blocs (dollar, yen, European Currency Union). While it remains the leading economic power, the United States faces serious internal problems, exacerbated by policies of the past decade whose social and economic costs cannot be indefinitely deferred. At the same time, Soviet military expenditures were leveling off and internal problems were mounting, with economic stagnation and increasing pressures for an end to tyrannical rule. A few years later, the Soviet system had collapsed. The Cold War ended with the victory of what had always been the far richer and more powerful contestant. The Soviet collapse was part of a much more general economic catastrophe of the 1980s, more severe in the Third World domains of the West than in the Soviet empire.

As commonly observed, the global system has become economically tripolar but militarily unipolar. The Soviet empire is gone, and in much of the Third World economic decline and violence, often conducted or backed by the West, have left a grim and ominous legacy. These developments have elicited much triumphalism in the West, but Third World reactions have been different, not surprisingly.

In concluding its report *The Challenge to the South,* the non-governmental South Commission called for a "new world order" that would respond to "the South's plea for justice, equity, and democracy in the global society," though its analysis offers little basis for hope.[1] Some months later, George Bush appropriated the phrase "new world order" as part of the rhetorical background for his war in the gulf. The Third World did not join in the enthusiastic U.S. welcome for the vision proclaimed by the president. Most shared the interpretation of *Die Zeit* editor Theo Sommer, who saw "an unabashed exercise in national self-interest, only thinly veiled by invocations of principle."[2] In a typical Third World reaction, the Jesuit journal *Proceso* (El Salvador) warned of the "ominous halo of hypocrisy, the seed of new crises and resentments." "This hypocrisy," it continued, "is extreme in the case of the United States, the leader of the allied forces and the most warmongering of them all, whose recent history includes the invasion of Grenada and the military occupation of Panama."[3] Cardinal Paulo Evaristo Arns of Sao Paolo captured the general mood when he wrote that in the Arab countries "the rich sided with the U.S. government while the *millions* of poor condemned this military aggression." Throughout the Third World, he continued, "there is hatred and fear: When will they decide to invade us," and on what pretext?[4]

When the president declared that the United States "has a new credibility" and that dictators and tyrants everywhere know that "what we say goes," few voices in the South celebrated the dawn of "an era full of promise."[5] Bush's words were more likely to evoke memories of Palmerston declaring that the capture of an Afghan fort would "cow all Asia and make everything more easy

1 *The Challenge to the South,* Report of the South Commission, Julius K. Nyerere, Chairman (Oxford, 1990), 287.
2 *Guardian* (London), 13 April 1991.   3 Editorial, *Proceso,* 23 January 1991.
4 Foreword, Thomas Fox, *Iraq* (Kansas City, 1991), ix.
5 Bush, 1 February 1991, quoted in Robert Parry, "The Peace Feeler that Was," *Nation,* 15 April 1991. James Baker, "Why America is in the Gulf," address to the Los Angeles World Affairs Council, 29 October 1990.

for us."[6] "Credibility" and "prestige" have always been the watchwords of empire. It is hardly surprising that the *Times of India* would describe Bush's Gulf war as an effort to establish a "regional Yalta where the powerful nations agree among themselves to a share of Arab spoils," a war that "revealed the seamiest sides of Western civilisation: its unrestricted appetite for dominance, its morbid fascination for hi-tech military might, its insensitivity to 'alien' cultures, its appalling jingoism."[7] And Third World observers readily understood that Bush's words were not directed to dictators and tyrants, but to anyone who stepped out of line. The United States and its allies have been happy to support the most murderous brutes—Saddam Hussein is only the most recent example—and to destroy democratic forces, as calculations of self-interest dictate.

In the old world order, the South was assigned a service function: for example, to provide resources, cheap labor, markets, and opportunities for investment and for the export of pollution. The primary threat to U.S. interests has therefore always been "radical and nationalistic regimes" that are responsive to popular pressures for "immediate improvement in the low living standards of the masses" and for diversification of the economies, tendencies that conflict with the need to protect sources of raw materials and to encourage "a political and economic climate conducive to private investment" and to the repatriation of "a reasonable return" on foreign investment.[8] Applauding the overthrow of the parliamentary Mosaddeq regime, the *New York Times* editors warned that "underdeveloped countries with rich resources now have an object lesson in the heavy cost that must be paid by one of their number which goes berserk with fanatical nationalism."[9] The record is also replete with self-congratulatory flourishes. As in the case of any state, these should be evaluated in terms of the historical record, which conforms well to the harsher doctrines.

6 Quoted in V. G. Kiernan, *European Empires from Conquest to Collapse 1815–1960* (London, 1982), 158.
7 Quoted in William Dalrymple, "Crazy for Saddam," *Spectator* (London), 23 February 1991.
8 NSC 5432/1, 3 September 1954, U.S. Department of State, *Foreign Relations of the United States, 1952–1954* (Washington, 1984), 4: 81ff.
9 Editorial, *New York Times,* 6 August 1954.

The North-South conflict has taken new forms with changing circumstances, but the basic themes are resilient. After World War I, British imperial managers realized that it would be more efficient to rule the Middle East behind an "Arab Facade," with "absorption" of the colonies "veiled by constitutional fictions as a protectorate, a sphere of influence, a buffer State, and so on."[10] Today, there are gestures to formal democracy and diversity, but within strict limits. Summarizing policies conducted "with the best of intentions," Robert Pastor writes that "the United States did not want to control Nicaragua or the other nations in the region, but it also did not want to allow developments to get out of control. It wanted Nicaraguans to act independently, *except* when doing so would affect U.S. interests adversely."[11] One consequence of this interpretation of freedom of choice is the persistent U.S. opposition to democracy, unless the rule of reliable business and land-owning interests is assured. Another is the resort to coercive means: subversion, terror, aggression, economic warfare.

Fear of what is called "communism" was rooted in the same concerns. One important study identified the threat as the economic transformation of the Communist powers "in ways that reduce their willingness and ability to complement the industrial economies of the West."[12] Unlike us, the "Communists" could "appeal directly to the masses," Eisenhower complained.[13] The Dulles brothers, in private conversation, deplored the Communist "ability to get control of mass movements," "something we have no capacity to duplicate." "The poor people are the ones they appeal to and they have always wanted to plunder the rich." The same concerns extended to "the preferential option for the poor" of the Latin American bishops and other commitments to independent development or democracy in more than form, and also to

10 Lord Curzon (and Eastern Committee), 24 April 1918, and Curzon memorandum, 12 December 1917, cited by William Stivers, *Supremacy and Oil: Iraq, Turkey, and the Anglo-American World Order, 1918–1930* (Ithaca, 1982), 28, 34.
11 Pastor, *Condemned to Repetition* (Princeton, 1987), 32.
12 William Yandell Elliot, ed., *The Political Economy of American Foreign Policy* (New York, 1955), 42.
13 Eisenhower to Harriman, quoted in Richard H. Immerman, "Confessions of an Eisenhower Revisionist," *Diplomatic History* (Summer 1990).

such friends as Mussolini, Trujillo, Noriega, and Saddam Hussein when they "get out of control."[14]

From 1917 to the 1980s, the "Communist threat" provided the ideological framework for intervention, including intervention in Russia itself after the Bolshevik revolution. This was a defensive action, John Lewis Gaddis argues, "in response to a profound and potentially far-reaching intervention by the new Soviet government in the internal affairs, not just of the West, but of virtually every country in the world," namely, "the Revolution's challenge ... to the very survival of the capitalist order."[15] The reasoning applies to a huge country or a speck in the Caribbean: intervention is entirely warranted in defense against a change in the social order, a disruption of the service function, and a declaration of revolutionary intentions. The danger is magnified because "the rot may spread" and the "virus" may "infect" others, to borrow familiar terms. Although the Sandinista "revolution without borders" was a government-media fabrication, the propaganda images reflected an authentic and traditional concern: from the perspective of a hegemonic power, declaration of an intent to provide a model that will inspire others amounts to aggression.

The Cold War itself had important North-South dimensions. Soviet domains had in part been quasi-colonial dependencies of the West, which were removed from the Third World and pursued an independent path, no longer available "to complement the industrial economies of the West."[16] Furthermore, the Soviet Union offered a model of development that was not without appeal in the Third World, particularly in earlier years. Conventional practice is to contrast Eastern and Western Europe, which have not been similar in historical memory, but more realistic comparisons (for example, to Brazil or Guatemala) have led Third World commentators to rather different conclusions. Soviet power and brutality also offered a ready rationalization, however thin, for Third

14 John Foster Dulles telephone call to Allen Dulles, 19 June 1958, "Minutes of telephone conversations of John Foster Dulles and Christian Herter," Eisenhower Library, Abilene, Kansas.
15 John Lewis Gaddis, *The Long Peace: Inquiries into the History of the Cold War* (New York, 1987), 10.
16 Elliot, ed., *Political Economy*.

World intervention; Woodrow Wilson needed different pretexts when he sent marines to Hispaniola, just as Bush needs others today. Finally, the Soviet Union and its satellites interfered with Western exploitation and control over the South by supporting independent nationalist movements, and Soviet power had a deterrent effect, limiting the ability of the United States and its allies to exercise force for fear of confrontation with a dangerous enemy. These have been crucial features of the Cold War era. They help to explain Third World trepidations as the Cold War ends and provide certain guidelines for what may lie ahead.

One consequence of the collapse of the Soviet bloc is that much of it may undergo a kind of "Latin Americanization," reverting to the service role, with the ex-Nomenklatura perhaps taking on the role of the Third World elites linked to international business and financial interests. A second is that a new ideological framework is needed for intervention. The problem of the vanishing pretext arose through the 1980s, requiring a propaganda shift to international terrorists, Hispanic narcotraffickers, crazed Arabs, and other chimeras. A third consequence is the collapse of the Soviet deterrent, which "makes military power more useful as a United States foreign policy instrument . . . against those who contemplate challenging important American interests,"[17] an insight echoed by Elliott Abrams during the invasion of Panama and by commentators during the Gulf crisis, who noted that the United States could now send armed forces to the region without concern.

There are, however, several factors that are likely to inhibit the resort to force. Among them are America's past successes in crushing popular nationalist and reform tendencies, the elimination of the "Communist" appeal to those who hope to "plunder the rich," and the economic catastrophes of the last decade. In the light of these developments, limited forms of diversity and independence can be tolerated with less concern that they will lead to meaningful change. Control can be exercised by economic measures: structural adjustment, the IMF regimen, selective resort to free-trade measures, and so forth. Needless to say, the successful industrial powers do not accept these rules for themselves, and never have.

17 Dimitri K. Simes, "If the Cold War Is Over, Then What?" *New York Times*, 27 December 1988.

But for the purposes of domination and exploitation, there is great merit in imposing them on the weak: the Third World and its likely new members in the East.

Another inhibiting factor is that the domestic base for foreign adventures has eroded. A leaked fragment of an early Bush administration national security review observes that "much weaker enemies" must be defeated "decisively and rapidly"; any other outcome would be "embarrassing" and might "undercut political support."[18] The Reagan administration was forced to resort on an unprecedented scale to clandestine terror and proxy forces because political support for violent intervention was so thin. And it has been necessary to whip up impressive propaganda campaigns to portray "much weaker enemies" as threats to our very existence, so as to mobilize a frightened population to at least temporary support for decisive and rapid action.

Still another problem is that German-led Europe and Japan have their own interests, which may not conform to those of the United States, though there is a shared interest in subduing Third World independence, and the internationalization of capital gives competition among national states a different case than in earlier periods.

Yet another impediment is that the United States no longer has the economic base for intervention, a fact that has led to proposals that it take on "a more explicitly mercenary role than it has played in the past."[19] We must become "willing mercenaries," financial editor William Neikirk of the *Chicago Tribune* advises, using our "monopoly power" in the "security market" to maintain "our control over the world economic system," selling "protection" to other wealthy powers who will pay us a "war premium."[20] The profits of gulf oil production must also be available to help support the economies of the United States and its British associate, who will carry out the enforcer role. These developments were foreshadowed in British and American internal documents after

18   Maureen Dowd, "Bush Gamble: More War, Not Inconclusive Diplomacy," *New York Times*, 23 February 1991.
19   David Hale "How to pay for the global policeman," *Financial Times* (London), 21 November 1990.
20   William Neikirk, "We are the world's guardian angels," *Chicago Tribune*, 9 September 1990; "Supercost to be sole superpower," ibid., 27 January 1991.

the Iraqi military coup of 1958, which emphasized that Kuwaiti oil and investment had to remain available to prop up the ailing British economy.[21] By the 1970s, such concerns extended to the United States as well, a significant factor in Middle East policy.

Events of the recent past illustrate the interplay of these factors. As the South Commission observed, there were some gestures to Third World concerns in the 1970s, "undoubtedly spurred" by concern over "the newly found assertiveness of the South after the rise in oil prices in 1973." As the threat abated, the industrial societies lost interest and turned to "a new form of neocolonialism," monopolizing control over the world economy, undermining the more democratic elements of the United Nations, and in general proceeding to institutionalize "the South's second class status."[22] Japan and the EC recovered from the recession of the early 1980s, though they did not resume earlier growth rates. U.S. recovery involved massive state stimulation of the economy, mainly through the Pentagon-based public subsidy to high technology industry, along with a sharp increase in protectionist measures and a rise in interest rates. This contributed to the crisis of the South, as interest payments on the debt rose while investment and aid declined, and the wealthy classes invested their riches in the West. There was a huge capital flow from South to North, with effects that were generally catastrophic, apart from the NICs of East Asia, where the state is powerful enough to control capital flight and direct the economy efficiently.

The first years of the post-Cold War era reveal how little has changed, tactical adjustments aside. With Gorbachev's "new thinking" and the decline of the Russian deterrent, overt intervention became a more feasible option, but on condition that it be "decisive and rapid" and accompanied by massive propaganda campaigns of demonization. Immediately after the fall of the Berlin Wall, symbolically ending the Cold War, Bush inaugurated the new era by invading Panama, restoring the rule of the tiny white minority, and returning the security forces to U.S. control. The United States vetoed two Security Council condemnations, joined in one case by the United Kingdom and France. All of this is so

21   For a review of these see my *Deterring Democracy* (London, 1991), 183f.
22   *The Challenge to the South*, 216ff., 71f.

familiar as barely to merit a footnote in history, but there were some novelties. Even the most fertile imagination could not conjure up a Soviet threat, so new pretexts were needed. And, as noted, there was no concern over a Soviet response.

Reactions to the invasion north and south of the Rio Grande differed sharply. In the United States, opinion hailed "Operation Just Cause." In contrast, the Group of Eight Latin American democracies, which had suspended Panama because of Noriega's crimes, expelled it permanently as a country under military occupation. In August 1990, a Panamanian presidential commission called for an end to the "occupation of the State and its territory by U.S. troops" and the reestablishment of national sovereignty. A leading Honduran journal denounced the "international totalitarianism" of George Bush "in the guise of 'democracy'." Bush, it said, has "declared plainly to Latin America that for the North American government, there is no law—only its will—when imposing its designs on the hemisphere." "We live in a climate of aggression and disrespect," "hurt by our poverty, our weakness, our naked dependence, the absolute submission of our feeble nations to the service of an implacable superpower. Latin America is in pain."[23]

The second act of post-Cold War aggression was Iraq's invasion of Kuwait, shifting Saddam Hussein overnight from friend and favored trading partner to reincarnation of Attila the Hun, the familiar pattern when some murderous tyrant steps out of line. The United States and the United Kingdom moved quickly to bar the diplomatic track, for fear that peaceful means might "defuse the crisis" with "a few token gains" for their former friend, as the administration position was outlined by *Times* diplomatic correspondent Thomas Friedman.[24] The war policy was strongly opposed by the population in the region. The Iraqi democratic opposition, always rebuffed by Washington, opposed U.S. policy throughout: the pre-August 1990 support for the Iraqi dictator, the resort to war rather than peaceful means, and finally the tacit support for Saddam Hussein as he crushed the Shi'ite and Kurdish

23 Inter Press Service, *Latinamerica press* (Lima), 30 August 1990. *Tiempo* (Honduras), 5 January 1990.
24 Friedman, "Behind Bush's Hard Line," *New York Times*, 22 August 1991.

rebellions. One leading spokesman, banker Ahmad Chalabi, who described the outcome of the war as "the worst of all possible worlds" for the Iraqi people, attributed the U.S. stand to its traditional policy of "supporting dictatorships to maintain stability." In Egypt, the one Arab ally with a degree of internal freedom, the semi-official press wrote that the outcome demonstrated that the United States only wanted to cut Iraq down to size and thus to establish its own unchallenged hegemony, in "collusion with Saddam himself" if necessary, agreeing with the "savage beast" on the need to "block any progress and abort all hopes, however dim, for freedom or equality and for progress towards democracy."[25]

The United Nations suffered further blows. Since it fell "out of control" by the 1960s, the United States has been far in the lead in vetoing Security Council resolutions and hampering UN activities generally. The invasion of Kuwait was unusual in that the United States and the United Kingdom opposed an act of international violence, and thus did not block the usual condemnations and efforts to reverse the crime. But under U.S. pressure, the Security Council was compelled to wash its hands of the matter, radically violating the UN Charter by leaving individual states free to respond to the aggression as they chose. Further U.S. pressures prevented the council from responding to the call of member states for meetings, as stipulated by council rules that the United States had vigorously upheld when they served its interests. That Washington has little use for diplomatic means or institutions of world order, unless they can be used as instruments of its own power, has been dramatically illustrated in Southeast Asia, the Middle East, Central America, and elsewhere. Nothing is likely to change in this regard.

Hostility to meaningful democracy also continued without change. As the Berlin Wall fell, elections were held in Honduras in "an inspiring example of the democratic promise that today is spreading throughout the Americas," in George Bush's words.[26] The candidates represented large landowners and wealthy industrialists,

---

25 Ahmad Chalabi, "What the Iraqi Resistance Wants," *Wall Street Journal*, 8 April 1991; *Mideast Mirror* (London), 15 March 1991. Salaheddin Hafez, deputy editor, *al-Ahram*, 9 April 1991, quoted in *Mideast Mirror*, 10 April 1991.
26 Associated Press, 17 April 1990.

with close ties to the military, the effective rulers, under U.S. control. Their political programs were virtually identical, and the campaign was largely restricted to insults and entertainment. Human rights abuses by the security forces escalated before the election. Starvation and misery were rampant, having increased during the "decade of democracy," along with capital flight and the debt burden. But there was no major threat to order, or to investors.

At the same time, the electoral campaign opened in Nicaragua. Its 1984 elections do not exist in U.S. commentary, though they were favorably described by a host of observers, including Western government and parliamentary delegations and a study group of the Latin American Studies Association. The elections could not be controlled, and therefore are not an inspiring example of democracy. Taking no chances with the long-scheduled 1990 elections, Bush announced as the campaign opened that the embargo would be lifted if his candidate won. The White House and Congress renewed their support for the contra forces in violation of the agreement of the Central American presidents and the judgment of the World Court. Nicaraguans were thus informed that only a vote for the U.S. candidate would end the terror and illegal economic warfare. In Latin America, the electoral results were generally interpreted as a victory for George Bush, even by those who celebrated the outcome. In a typical reaction, a Guatemala City journal attributed the result to "ten years of economic and military aggressions waged by a government with unlimited resources." "It was a vote in search of peace by a people that, inevitably, were fed up with violence, . . . a vote from a hungry people that, more than any idea, need to eat." In the United States, in contrast, the result was hailed as a "Victory for U.S. Fair Play," with "Americans United in Joy," as *New York Times* headlines put it.[27]

Again expressing traditional attitudes, a Latin America Strategy

---

27 Guatemala City journal quoted in *Central America Report* (Guatemala City), 2 March 1990; David Shipler, "Nicaragua, Victory for U.S. Fair Play," op-ed, *New York Times*, 1 March 1990; Elaine Sciolino, "Americans United in Joy, But Divided over Policy," *New York Times*, 27 February 1990. For review of Latin American and U.S. reaction see Chomsky, *Deterring Democracy*, chap. 10.

Development Workshop at the Pentagon in September 1990 concluded that relations with the very conservative government in Mexico were "extraordinarily positive," untroubled by stolen elections, death squads, endemic torture, scandalous treatment of workers and peasants, and so forth. But "a 'democracy opening' in Mexico could test the special relationship by bringing into office a government more interested in challenging the U.S. on economic and nationalist grounds," the fundamental concern over many years.[28]

The first post-Cold War National Security Strategy report sent to Congress, in March 1990, recognized that military power must target the Third World, primarily the Middle East, where the "threats to our interests" that have required force "could not be laid at the Kremlin's door," a fact now acknowledged. Furthermore, the Soviet pretext for military spending having disappeared, the threat now becomes "the growing technological sophistication of Third World conflicts." The United States must therefore strengthen its "defense industrial base," with incentives "to invest in new facilities and equipment as well as in research and development," and develop further forward basing and counterinsurgency and low-intensity conflict capacities.[29] In brief, the prime concerns continued to be control of the South and support for high-tech industry at home, with the ideological framework adapted to new contingencies.

The use of force to control the Third World is a last resort. Economic weapons are far more efficient. Some of the newer mechanisms can be seen in the GATT negotiations. Western powers call for liberalization when it is in their interest, and for enhanced protection when that is in their interest. One major U.S. concern is the "new themes": guarantees for "intellectual property rights," such as patents and software, that will enable transnational corporations to monopolize new technology; and removal of constraints on services and investment, which will undermine national development programs in the Third World and effectively

28 *Latin America Strategy Development Workshop,* 26 and 27 September 1990, minutes, 3. Andrew Reding, "Mexico's Democratic Challenge," *World Policy Journal* (Spring 1991).
29 *National Security Strategy of the United States,* the White House, March 1990.

place investment decisions in the hands of TNCs and the financial institutions of the North. These are "issues of greater magnitude" than the more publicized conflict over agricultural subsidies, according to William Brock, head of the Multilateral Trade Negotiations Coalition of major U.S. corporations.[30] In general, the wealthy industrial powers advocate a mixture of liberalization and protectionism (such as the Multifiber Arrangement and its extensions, the U.S.-Japan semiconductor agreement, Voluntary Export Arrangements, etc.) designed for the interests of dominant domestic forces, and particularly for the TNCs that are to dominate the world economy. Third World proposals have been ignored.

The effects would be to reduce Third World governments to a police function, with the task of controlling their own working classes and superfluous population while TNCs gain free access to their resources and control new technology and global investment—and, of course, are granted the central planning and management functions denied to governments, which are unacceptable agents because they might fall under the influence of popular pressures reflecting domestic needs, what is referred to as "ultranationalism" in the internal planning record.

Meanwhile, the United States is establishing a regional bloc that will enable it to compete more effectively with the Japan-led region and the EC. Canada's role is to provide resources and some services and skilled labor, as it is absorbed more fully into the U.S. economy with the reduction of the welfare system, labor rights, and cultural independence. The Canadian Labour Congress reports the loss of over 225,000 jobs in the first two years of the Free Trade Agreement, along with a wave of takeovers of Canadian-based companies. Mexico, Central America, and the Caribbean are to supply cheap labor for assembly plants, as in the maquiladora industries of northern Mexico, where horrendous working conditions and wages and the absence of environmental controls offer highly profitable conditions for investors. These regions are also to provide export crops and markets for U.S. agribusiness. Mexico and Venezuela are also to provide oil, with U.S. corpora-

---

30 Quoted in Martin Khor Kok Peng, *The Uruguay Round and Third World Sovereignty* (Penang, 1990), 10. See also Chakravarthi Raghavan, *Recolonization: GATT, the Uruguay Round & the Third World* (Penang, 1990).

tions granted the right to take part in production, reversing efforts at domestic control of natural resources.

Such policies are likely to be extended to Latin America generally. And, crucially, the United States will attempt to maintain its dominant influence over Gulf oil production and the profits that derive from it. Other economic powers, of course, have their own ideas, and there are many potential sources of conflict. In general, prospects for the South, or for the domestic poor in an American society taking on certain Third World aspects, are not auspicious.

13

The End of the Cold War and the Middle East

NIKKI R. KEDDIE

The Middle East was arguably the first theater of the Cold War, which manifested itself in a number of dramatic regional developments in the four decades after 1946. In that year, Joseph Stalin's delay in removing Soviet troops on schedule from Iranian Azerbaijan and Kurdistan, where pro-Soviet autonomist regimes had been set up, brought U.S. counterpressure and a crisis that ended only with an Iranian-Soviet agreement that included the withdrawal of Soviet troops. The 1947 Truman Doctrine, arming Turkey and Greece, was the first of several U.S. military doctrines covering the Middle East and was aimed at the Soviets. Regional nationalizers of British assets in the 1950s, especially Mohammad Mosaddeq in Iran and Gamal Abdel Nasser in Egypt, were treated as dangerous and pro-Communist, and, in Mosaddeq's case, overthrown at U.S. instigation. U.S. backing for Israel was matched by Soviet backing for the Arab position and arming of favored Arab regimes, first Nasser's Egypt, and, more recently, Baathist Syria and Iraq. With the withdrawal of the British east of Suez, Saudi Arabia and especially Iran became the pillars and guardians of U.S. policy. These and other oil-rich states could afford to buy large quantities of advanced arms from the United States, while the strategic nonoil countries, Turkey, Israel, and Egypt, became three of the five largest recipients of U.S. aid, mostly military in nature. After the Soviet invasion of 1979, Afghanistan became a center for U.S.-Soviet military conflict.

Such concentration on the Middle East, which with regard to the Soviet Union was partly owing to proximity and shared borders, also grew out of American and Soviet concerns for the region's oil and strategic location. As Richard Cottam has demonstrated, however, the Soviets were nearly always far less aggressive than was depicted in U.S. writings—allowing the United States to overthrow Mosaddeq, for example, and to undertake other interventions without reacting.[1] Given the importance of the Middle East to the Cold War, we might suppose that the end of the Cold War would mean a notable decrease in such intervention, as well as a general decline in tensions in the region. But if we look at the actual results through 1991, we may be able to understand why no major decrease in regional tensions had occurred by then. Nor has there been a great decline in U.S. armaments aid or sales to this volatile area.

The impact of the end of the Cold War on the Middle East cannot be separated from the impact on the Third World of the crisis of communism, which became acute and worldwide in 1989. The combined impact may be discussed under several headings, although variations in wealth, ethnicity, and political orientation among Middle Eastern countries mean that there is not a single story line for the whole Middle East. First, there is the economic impact of the crisis of communism on Third World countries, notably the diversion of foreign concern and assistance from those countries to Eastern Europe. Second, there is the possible influence of democratization in Eastern Europe on the governments and populations of undemocratic Third World countries. Third, there is the influence on leftist or Communist movements and governments of the rapid abandonment of Communist economics and ideology by many Western leftists and Communists. Fourth, there is the end of superpower rivalry in most parts of the world, which made the Americans and the Russians, even before the demise of the Soviet Union, more willing than before to end their former unconditional support and armament of some Third World countries. Fifth, there is the willingness of the former "evil empire" to follow U.S. foreign policy leads, as in the Gulf war, which makes it impossible for Third World countries to counter the United States with Soviet backing.

1   Richard W. Cottam, "U.S. and Soviet Responses to Islamic Political Militancy," *Neither East Nor West: Iran, the Soviet Union, and the United States*, ed. Nikki R. Keddie and Mark J. Gasiorowski (New Haven, 1990).

The order of importance of the above headings varies in different parts of the Third World. For much of Africa and Latin America the first of these factors—the economic impact of the end of the Cold War and the crisis of communism—could be the most worrisome, as it could for all countries hitherto dependent on Soviet economic aid and now facing drastic cuts in such assistance. For much of the Middle East, however, questions of Soviet economic aid are less important than they are in many other parts of the Third World. The exceptions are a few countries formerly very dependent on the Soviet Union, such as Syria and South Yemen. The crisis of communism was a factor in South Yemen's decision to merge with North Yemen. Various Eastern and Western countries have vied as aid givers in North Yemen, and it may be that the end of the Cold War will put Yemen in a weaker position regarding aid than it was in the period of U.S.-Soviet-Chinese rivalries.

The economic impact of the end of the Cold War on the biggest recipients of U.S. aid is likely to be small, as this aid, although largely military, was less tied to a "Communist menace" than was claimed. The Middle East is valued chiefly for its oil, and secondarily for its central strategic location, and these factors have been little affected by the crisis of communism. Even before the Iraqi invasion of Kuwait, the United States had planned to keep military and economic aid at almost the same high levels to the three out of five top U.S. aid recipients that are in the Middle East—Israel, Egypt, and Turkey. A fourth, Pakistan, has been heavily involved in Afghanistan. With the Kuwait crisis, officials in Washington dropped all talk of reducing the U.S. aid program and forgave half of the Egyptian debt. These three countries thus seem unlikely, in the immediate future, to suffer major aid cuts. Of course, a number of Middle Eastern oil-rich countries were never dependent on aid from either the United States or the Soviet Union, and would therefore be unaffected by any reductions in foreign aid that might occur.

Besides countries like Syria that were closely tied to the Soviet Union, Iran has suffered some economically from the crisis of communism and the end of the Cold War. Whereas in earlier years the Soviets had used economic aid to gain political influence and to get a leg up on the United States in some countries, including Iran, this strategy is no longer possible. Even before the collapse of the USSR, Soviet officials had been reluctant to give Iran the generous terms for natural gas and other favorable advantages they might have given earlier. Nor can the new leadership in the former Soviet Union be a source of significant aid, however friendly Iran might be. It is hard to calculate how big a loss this will be for Iran. Because the two countries are neighbors between whom mutually profitable economic relations would not be hard to develop, it may be that Iran will not suffer much from a lack of preferential treatment.

On the other hand, a more pessimistic prognostication regarding the economic effects of the end of the Cold War in the Middle East is certainly defensible, especially because it is widely believed, based on performance, that the United States is only interested in shoring up rich oil states like Saudi Arabia and Kuwait, not in bettering the living standards of the majority of Middle Easterners who are poor.

Regarding the second factor noted above, the anticipated trend toward democratization, almost anything said today is speculative. While some journalists speak of a rise in democratic feeling in the Middle East, there is no evidence yet of a general trend toward democratic action. Those countries that have moved toward holding or expanding the importance and openness of elections— Algeria, Tunisia, Jordan, and Egypt—initiated this process before 1989 and apparently without important connections to developments in the Soviet Union and Eastern Europe. The promises by the ruler of Kuwait to restore that country's constitution were due to pressures unconnected to the crisis of European communism. There is also a negative factor in the Muslim world regarding the possible future growth of democracy: In the four countries mentioned as encouraging elections, Islamist parties had relative or absolute electoral success—in all cases running against essentially secular and Westernizing governments. This success was most dramatic in Algeria's elections, but was also apparent in Tunisia, Jordan, and Egypt. It has meant that the secular governments in those countries, while making certain concessions to Islamist feelings, have also dragged their feet on full-scale democratic elections and have not yet allowed parties to form and run on any platform. A related situation exists in parliamentary Turkey, where Islamism is strong and the government does not want to reverse the essential features of Ataturk's secularist system.

A country that will not worry about the Islamist prospect and may democratize more is Iran. Since the revolution, Iran has had frequent parliamentary elections in which some opposition and factional groups have participated, though not the most fundamentally oppositionist groups and individuals. This tendency toward moderation may lead to more democracy in Iran, but it is unclear how much this will owe to the crisis of communism and the end of the Cold War.

As to my third point, regarding the influence of the end of the Cold War on the Left, one may say that the decline of old-style communism, which began in the Middle East well before the crisis of European communism, has been accelerated by it. Even before the late 1980s the Soviet Union did far less to support the Communist movement abroad than was generally believed in the West. In the Middle East, as seen in Nasser's Egypt, Baathist Iraq and Syria, and Iran as recently as the 1980s, the Soviets had periodically abandoned local Communists when they found it in their interest to opt instead for good relations with a government that suppressed communism. After 1989, moreover, the old regimes in the Soviet Union and Eastern Europe were seen as good examples of how communism could ruin an economy. Under these circumstances, classical communism could hardly be a model for anyone.

Since 1989, leftists in the Middle East, as elsewhere, have been looking for another model. Some are turning to social democracy, some to the militant leftism of one of the schools not associated with the former Soviet Union, and some to populist Islamism. Non-Soviet leftisms, however, including both Islamic and secular varieties, were represented in the Middle East before the crisis of European communism. Iran in particular has known a variety of Islamic and secular leftisms, and these are less subject to annihilation because of association with the failures of the Soviets than is main-line communism. The physical destruction of the Left by the Islamic Republic, followed by the collapse of the (mostly Soviet-oriented) worldview of Iran's radical Left, has made many leftist intellectuals gravitate toward democratic and pluralistic, rather than dogmatic, interpretations of socialism. Many key activists of the Liberal to Social Democratic Iranian opposition in exile are ex-activists of the radical Left (this includes the left of Bakhtiar's and Reza Pahlavi's following).[2] Ultimately, in Iran and elsewhere in the Middle East where Communist parties were hobbled by attachment to a line that was often based on the needs of Soviet foreign policy, there could be a revival of a more independent Left, although there are not strong signs of this yet.

Regarding my fourth and fifth points, while the end of super-power rivalry has had an influence in the Middle East, it has not brought an outbreak of peace in the region. This influence was apparent before the collapse of the Soviet Union, when American and Soviet leaders cooperated in the UN sanctions against Iraq. For some weeks the Gulf crisis provided the Soviets with an opportunity to exercise world influence at the very time when their domestic problems appeared overwhelming. Foreign Minister Eduard Shevardnadze and his adviser, Evgeny Primakov, were active in talking with Saddam Hussein and others. While Shevardnadze generally backed U.S. policies, Primakov rather pushed the position, then popular in Europe and the Arab world, that the United States should not go to war but should join in a worldwide movement for collective security, patience, and serious negotiation. The weakness of the Soviet Union as compared to the United States was shown in the failure of these efforts and in Bush's ability to force through his war policy without Soviet opposition. The end of the Cold War made possible UN backing for a resolution taken as justifying military action against Iraq. A few years ago the Russians would have vetoed such a resolution. Hence, although the end of the Cold War was important, the expectation that it would be conducive to peace everywhere was belied, as in this case it rather strengthened the prowar forces.

Elsewhere in the Middle East, the foreign policies pursued by Moscow in the last days of the Soviet Union also dovetailed with American diplomacy. Soviet pressure helped to get the P.L.O. to

2 Interviews and dissertation research by Afshin Matin, UCLA.

moderate its position on Israel, for example. In addition, the Soviets were improving their relations with conservative Arab governments, with Israel, and with the United States. They were also cutting back on arms supplies to the more radical Iraqi and Syrian governments, and were alienating many Palestinians and other Arabs with their more relaxed policy regarding Jewish emigration. The flood of Soviet Jews into Israel increased Arab concerns and fears regarding Israeli settlements and expansion. Indeed, the most controversial part of the Soviet Union's new policy was its friendly relations with Israel, which many Arab nationalists, liberals, and leftists saw as harmful to the Arab states. At the same time, Arabs began to fear that the decline of the Soviet bloc would lead to the complete hegemony of the United States in the area, thereby making it difficult to get effective help in resolving the Arab-Israeli dispute without an American president and public opinion that were relatively friendly.

Perhaps the most important Soviet role that appeared under Gorbachev was that of international peacemaker, and this role was particularly important in the Middle East. Even with regard to the Arab-Israeli dispute the Soviets were not simply willing to move toward greater support for Israel. They also continued to emphasize the negotiation of differences, a policy that kept them politically closer to the dominant Arab position than to that of the government of Israel. At the same time, the Soviets decried terrorism and violent solutions. In the Iraqi-Kuwait conflict, for example, they were in the forefront of those trying to avoid a war.

The peaceful flexibility that characterized Soviet diplomacy in its last days also resulted in improved relations with Iran, minus the open rivalry with the United States that had characterized such improvements in the past. In Afghanistan, moreover, the withdrawal of Soviet troops was accompanied by attempts to negotiate an end to foreign intervention with the Americans, although Washington continued to arm the Mujahidin, despite evidence that they routinely attacked fellow Afghans and were predominantly reactionary Islamists, ineffective fighters, and heavily involved in drug traffic. Fortunately, it now seems that the U.S. position is changing.

As the Afghan story suggests, factors unconnected to Soviet policy have often militated against nonviolence and compromise in the Middle East—factors that should make us leary about the prospects for regional peace inherent in the end of the Cold War. In the Gulf war, to give another example, a divided P.L.O. saw no gains from its new policy of compromise and swung over to the pro-Iraqi side, while mixed signals from the United States played a part in Iraq's decision to attack Kuwait. In addition, Israel's refusal to negotiate a compromise regarding Palestinian territory has not met with effective counterpressure from the United States. On the other hand, it is true that the end of the Cold War made the Syrians more flexible about attending the Middle East peace conference, because they were no longer supported effectively by the Soviets and had to court U.S. aid. In addition, the end of the Cold War might encourage the United States to lessen its absolute support for Israel, which it no longer needs as a key Cold War ally. Regarding the Arab-Israeli conflict, although immediate dramatic results are unlikely, it may prove helpful to untie this most difficult dispute from the Cold War, and it is certainly better to talk than to shoot, whatever the immediate consequences might be. It is best not to be too optimistic, however. Popular feeling against many Israeli policies remains high in most Muslim countries, and the fact that weakened Arab governments or movements like the P.L.O. may now be willing to compromise does not end the possibility of mass pressures on Muslim governments against any compromise that does not involve Palestinian self-rule in the West Bank and Gaza.

And what of the other countries in the region? For Turkey, once among the most staunchly pro-Western, secular, and anti-Soviet countries, the end of the Cold War threatens its importance to Western Europe and to the United States. Turkey, like certain other countries, apparently does better as a serious international player in times of conflict than in times of peace, although the Iraqi-Kuwait crisis has, on the down side, caused Turkey economic and ethnic problems. In the special case of Yemen, where a country popularly identified as a unit was divided between a Communist-led South Yemen and a conservative North Yemen, the decline and collapse of the Soviet Union were major factors behind South

Yemen's decision to merge with the North essentially on northern terms in May 1990. This may bring problems, especially for the far more liberated women of South Yemen, who are faced with the more restrictive laws and customs of the North.

Let me close by summing up what I see as the probable results of the end of the Cold War for the Middle East. Looking at the current positive results, one may point to more cooperation between the major powers on important international issues and possibly the unification of Yemen, although many on the Left regret the disappearance of South Yemen, which in some ways, particularly regarding the mobilization and education of women, was a positive model. In addition, a number of Middle Easterners have voiced the expectation that democratization in Eastern Europe will speed democratization in the Middle East, but thus far this is no more than a hope, with those democratization tendencies that do exist in some countries owing almost nothing to Eastern European developments.

Looking at the more problematic results, one may note a Russian and East European tilt toward Israel, which may be seen as positive by most Israelis but not by the great majority of Arabs. The apparent lessening of Arab-Israeli hostility owes something to the end of the Cold War, but it is not certain that it will continue once the really difficult substantive questions have to be faced. Also, there has been a decline in Russian and Eastern European economic aid to the Middle East, and the West may be expected over time to give priority to Eastern Europe in its aid and investment decisions. The crisis of European communism is likely to further weaken the Middle Eastern Left, which will be seen as positive by nonleftists but not by leftists, and this crisis is one more encouragement to the Islamists in their attack on both Eastern and Western ways. Many Arabs also fear the growth of unilateral U.S. power in the area.

Although more long-term predictions are certainly speculative, it does seem possible that growing Great Power cooperation may lead to the solution, or at least to the dampening down, of some major Middle Eastern problems. On balance, however, it is important to note that the major trends in the Middle East in recent years have not been primarily owing to the end of the Cold War, but to more long-term indigenous factors. As noted, democratization and development began in several countries, especially in North Africa, independently of the crisis of European and Russian communism. Similarly, growing Islamist trends are independent of the crisis, although they may be encouraged by it. The Arab-Israeli dispute is largely independent, as is the Kuwait crisis and most smaller regional crises, including the growing ethnic and religious tensions. Hence, the various forces noted above that relate to the end of the Cold War and the crisis of communism are, to date, supplementary to existing indigenous forces.

On the whole, the end of the Cold War has brought less change to the Middle East than might have been expected. This is partly because U.S. policies in the region have not substantially changed. The U.S. desire to dominate the oil-rich and strategically important Middle East was formerly presented in anti-Soviet terms, but in fact after 1946 the Soviet Union was not the aggressive threat that the United States claimed.[3] The end of any plausible Soviet threat has not reduced U.S. efforts to dominate the region, as seen in the Gulf war, the continued and often increased arming of Middle Eastern "allies," the support of the Saudis and other autocratic states, and opposition to popular revolts in Iraq. Any gains for peace arising from the end of U.S.-Soviet maneuvering have thus far been outweighed by the loss of the Soviet bloc as a counterweight to overwhelming U.S. hegemony.

3 Compare with Keddie and Gasiorowski, eds., *Neither East Nor West*. There is considerable literature, primarily journalistic, on the subjects covered in this essay. Because this is not a research article, I have not tried to cite all of the items that I consulted. One useful collection is Micah L. Sifry and Christopher Cerf, eds., *The Gulf War Reader* (New York, 1991).

14

The End of the Cold War in the Near East: What It Means for Historians and Policy Planners

BRUCE R. KUNIHOLM

The primary concern of U.S. policy in the Near East during the Cold War was the potential Soviet threat to the sovereignty and territorial integrity of the Soviet Union's southern neighbors, and hence to Western interests in the region.[1] Although the U.S. role in the post-World War II Near East was unprecedented, the geopolitical factors involved were not. Since the nineteenth century, a rivalry between the expanding Russian and British empires had been played out in an arena that stretched from the Balkans to British India. The competition for influence in the buffer states between their empires was subsumed under various geographical focuses: the "Balkan Problem," the "Eastern Question," the "Persian Problem," and the "Great Game." In these regions the Great Powers attempted to carve out their respective spheres of influence. In order to survive, meanwhile, the so-called buffer states allied among themselves against threats from without, played one power off against the other, or looked to third powers, such as Germany, for assistance. After World War II, survival of the buffer states was threatened by the relative disparity between Soviet and British power and by the Soviet Union's policies toward its southern neighbors. Because Germany had been crushed, Iran and Turkey turned to the United States for assistance, and the United States responded.

In subsequent years, the United States attempted to replace a decreasing British presence with a series of commitments—articulated in presidential pronouncements, or "doctrines"—to the re-

1 Bruce R. Kuniholm, "Retrospect and Prospect: Forty Years of US Middle East Diplomacy," *Middle East Journal* 41 (Winter 1987): 7–25.

gion's defense against threats, both real and perceived, from the Soviet Union. In the process of containing the Soviet Union, the United States confronted the problem of limited resources by collaborating with the British, whose assistance was judged to be necessary, and in varying degrees supported British interests against those of emerging nationalist movements in the region. Anglo-American collaboration impeded better U.S. relations with the region's emerging nationalist forces, whose differences with Britain threatened to undermine the very policy that Anglo-American ties were designed to support. Nonetheless, during the early years of the Cold War, U.S. officials saw the threat posed by the Soviet Union as requiring that they collaborate with the British and risk the lesser threat to their interests posed by association with the vestiges of colonialism. As a result, most postwar presidential administrations were unable to respond constructively to the region's emerging nationalist and transnationalist forces, many of whose aspirations were thwarted by other American priorities and some of whom saw the increasing American role as little different from the earlier, imperial role played by Britain.

However one characterizes the post-World War II role of the United States in the Near East, it is clear that it helped to define and was defined by the Cold War. Just as the Cold War can be said to have begun in the Near East, and certainly it served as a forge for the emerging policy of containment, so it can be said to have begun its death throes there as well. By the 1970s and 1980s, both the United States (in Iran) and the Soviet Union (in Afghanistan) seem to have recognized the limits of their capacities to dominate the region—either by themselves or through surrogates.[2] They also seem to have understood that forswearing domination did not mean the abandonment of their interests. This is because it was always easier to counter, than it was to support successfully, those who aspired to regional hegemony. The Soviet invasion of Afghanistan, meanwhile, coupled with the international response to the Soviet occupation, served as a catalyst for developments within the Soviet Union, where the economic and political system was seen

2   See Bruce R. Kuniholm, "Rules of the Game: The Geopolitics of U.S. Policy Options in Southwest Asia," in *Neither East Nor West: Iran, the Soviet Union, and the United States,* ed. Nikki Keddie and Mark J. Gasiorowski (New Haven, 1990), 201–19.

as increasingly inadequate, and paved the way for a more cautious Soviet attitude toward Eastern Europe as the situation there began to unravel. Under President Mikhail Gorbachev's leadership, the stage was set for the end of the Cold War.

The end of the Cold War will have a profound effect on the judgments of future historians of American foreign relations who explain the post-World War II era in the Near East. It will also have a major influence on the assessments of policy planners who, in order to formulate government policies with a view to U.S. interests, attempt to anticipate the dynamics of relevant variables that will affect the future of the region. These assertions should come as a surprise to no one, although the reasons for them deserve brief discussion.

Diplomatic historians, who for the most part have had little experience in public affairs, in explaining the past tend to look beyond particular incidents and to focus on historical forces and general causes.[3] This is because the discipline is not an applied one that emphasizes practical action; rather, it puts a premium on creative and imaginative contributions to the profession—contributions that are generally judged not by diplomats, who have had the humbling experience of trying to ride the tides of history and shape them where possible, but by other historians who are more deeply invested in the historiographical exercise of myth making and myth breaking. Looking at the past from the perspective of the evolving present, historians will ask new questions and embark on investigations that result in new interpretations and judgments. This is because, as E. H. Carr has argued, history is a symbiotic relationship between interpretation and fact; an unending dialogue between the historian, grounded in the present, and the past.[4]

In the wake of the Cold War, revisionist scholars in the former Soviet Union, relatively unfettered by previous constraints, bene-

---

3 Alexis de Tocqueville notes: "I have come across men of letters who have written without taking part in public affairs, and politicians who have concerned themselves with producing events without thinking of them. I have observed that the first are always inclined to find general causes, whereas the second, living in the midst of disconnected daily facts, are prone to imagine that everything is attributable to particular incidents, and that the wires they pull are the same as those that move the world. It is to be presumed that both are equally deceived."

4 E. H. Carr, *What is History?* (New York, 1961).

fiting from new archival material, and informed by the current state of affairs in their country, will write histories of Soviet foreign policy that will be as harsh in their judgments of Stalin and most of his successors as were "traditionalist" historians of the Cold War in this country.[5] This development will undoubtedly send shudders through "revisionist" historians in the United States, who nonetheless will continue to raise questions about the Cold War's necessity and the extent to which Soviet policies were either justified by U.S. actions or exaggerated by U.S. officials, who then pursued policies the revisionists judge to have been counterproductive and even provocative.

Scholars in both the former Soviet Union and in the United States, meanwhile, regardless of their labels, will continue to argue that different Soviet and American policies at certain points might have made a real difference in the postwar Near East. Some Near East scholars, writing from a national point of view, will focus on the liberation of states that those with a geopolitical perspective once characterized as "buffer states" between imperial rivals. Other Near East scholars will write about the emergence of a particular sect, or tribe, or class, and the extent to which Great Power politics (or the power of regional states) inhibited (or facilitated) unity with their brethren (or independence from the domination of a particular state). Although most of us take our profession very seriously, we clearly need to have a sense of play about it and to recognize its grounding in the relationship between a particular historian's evolving focus and the past.

An abbreviated example should suffice to illuminate the manner in which historical judgments can (and should) evolve. In U.S. government circles, the Eisenhower administration's role in overthrowing Iran's Prime Minister Mohammed Mosaddeq and installing the shah in 1953 was seen for a time as a brilliant covert

---

5 See, for example, the controversy surrounding the first volume of the ten-volume "History of the Great Patriotic War" written by the Defense Ministry's Institute of Military History. "New Soviet History of World War II Rejected," *Christian Science Monitor*, 28 June 1991. For general discussion of the "traditionalist" and "revisionist" perspectives on the origins of the Cold War see John Lewis Gaddis, "The Emerging Post-Revisionist Synthesis on the Origins of the Cold War," *Diplomatic History* 7 (Summer 1983): 171–90, as well as the responses to it in the same volume.

operation that saved Iran from communism. In Iran, meanwhile, a number of Iranians who in 1953 had opposed U.S. interference in Iran's internal affairs, and who had become alienated from the government as the shah became more dictatorial, eventually were mobilized by the Ayatollah Khomeini. Their support for the ayatollah was due less perhaps to the religious ideas that he espoused than to his opposition to the shah, whose autocratic rule was attributable to the U.S.-supported coup in 1953—an event that was elevated to the level of a national catastrophe. Following the shah's overthrow in early 1979, a number of scholars (many of whom had supported his rule in varying degrees) came to see that rule as the explanation for Iran's plight and, in retrospect, judged the overthrow of Mosaddeq as having paved the way for subsequent excesses—whether under the shah or the ayatollah—by precluding the possibility of a viable liberal-democratic alternative to the shah.

As the Iranian revolution continued, and the hostage crisis evolved, a self-serving and selective account of the 1953 coup by a former CIA operative in 1979 found a ready audience.[6] Other scholars, informed not only by the excesses of the Iranian revolution but also by the developments that led up to the Soviet invasion of Afghanistan in late 1979 (which some depicted as the result of inaction on the part of the United States), asserted that what they foresaw in 1953 in Iran was more like what happened in Afghanistan between 1973 and 1980: the overthrow of a weak monarchy by nationalist forces, which were then overthrown by indigenous Communists, who were then overwhelmed by the Red Army. As a result, one scholar (a British MI6 operative in 1953) has argued that if the British could have foreseen the excesses of the shah, they would still have overthrown Mosaddeq but would have forestalled the consequences by keeping the shah on a more reasonable course.[7]

Another scholar, writing even more recently, argues that it is

---

6 Kermit Roosevelt, *Countercoup: The Struggle for Control in Iran* (New York, 1979). For a discussion of official misrepresentation of the U.S. role in overthrowing Mossadeq (through the selected release of documents in the *Foreign Relations of the United States*) see Bruce R. Kuniholm, "Foreign Relations, Public Relations, Accountability, and Understanding," *Perspectives* 28 (May/June 1990).
7 C. M. Woodhouse, *Something Ventured* (London, 1982).

overly optimistic to assume that if Mossadeq had remained in power the chances of democracy would have been enhanced. Accepting the logic of American policy in befriending the ruler of a client state, this scholar disputes instead the efficacy of American strategies in protecting a client.[8] I have no doubt that scholars in the future will take a more radical tack. Following the Soviet debacle in Afghanistan, the withdrawal of Soviet forces from the region, the end of the Cold War, and the disintegration of the Soviet Union, some scholars will argue that it was unnecessary to worry at all about the Soviet threat to the Near East. They will point out that Soviet expansion was unlikely (the Soviets, after all, *did* withdraw from Iran in 1946 and the threat perceived by U.S. officials in 1953 *was* overstated).[9] Alternatively, they will argue that if expansion had been attempted, we need not have worried; the Soviet Union would have been doomed to failure and would have been brought to its knees even sooner.

The difficulty with all of these interpretations, of course, is not only that they second-guess but also that they are virtually impossible to test—there is no control group to play out alternative scenarios. Policymakers at the time can be forgiven for not having followed their advice. One is reminded of more recent events in the Persian Gulf. Those in this country who supported going to war had their way, so the second-guessing was mostly by those who opposed the use of force. After the Gulf war, the latter criticized the administration for initiating a conflict that ultimately killed over one hundred thousand people and in addition brought enor-

8   Kuross A. Samii, *Involvement by Invitation: American Strategies of Containment in Iran* (University Park, PA, 1987).

9   The relationship between one's judgments of U.S. policy toward Iran in 1945 and 1946 and 1953 is an interesting one. The judgment of Eisenhower administration officials in 1953 (and one must distinguish these officials from a number of Truman administration officials who did not share their views) were, for the most part, colored by earlier understandings of what happened in 1945 and 1946: The Soviets had been up to no good in the early Cold War and they were seen by many as posing a similar problem in 1953. As a result, the Eisenhower administration saw Mosaddeq as a liability and decided to overthrow him. Most scholars, on the other hand, judged the administration harshly for its role in the coup, and perhaps for that reason, when they looked back at the period 1945–46, some have been more lenient in their judgments of Soviet motives and harsher in their assessments of U.S. policies. Subsequent developments, needless to say, also influence such judgments, as does, occasionally, a close reading of the events themselves.

mous misery to Iraq's Kurdish and Shiite population.[10] Few addressed the likelihood that Saddam would not have withdrawn from Kuwait very easily and that, over time, the embargo would have run into serious political difficulties. Forced to allocate scarce resources, Saddam might have chosen to starve his civilian population first. Public opinion in the West might well have reacted divisively; the international coalition might have begun to unravel. Saddam might have become a hero (and the coalition might have been villified) in an Arab world that admired him for toughing it out. He might have proceeded to develop even further his weapons of mass destruction—for example, he might have developed a capacity to carry chemical weapons in the SCUDS whose range he had increased. Such weapons used against Israel almost certainly would have provoked an Israeli retaliation; retaliation, in turn, might well have torn apart the coalition, and the United States and its allies might have been in a very difficult fix.

If the United States had pursued the embargo and the situation described above had come about, one can imagine the criticism coming from those advocating the use of force against Saddam. Instead, criticism comes now from opponents of the use of force. Their specific predictions about U.S. casualties, the outcome of the war, and the fallout in the Arab world may have been incorrect, but that is beside the point. When the Kurdish and Shiite rebellions caused the situation to deteriorate, those opposed to the use of force remembered their more general predictions of disaster. One is reminded of a remark that Isaac Deutscher, Trotsky's biographer, is supposed to have made to a student who questioned his assertion that Trotsky was an extremely far-sighted person. None of Trotsky's predictions, the student argued, had come true. "Not yet," Deutscher is said to have responded, "which shows you just how far-sighted he really was."

Just as with current policy debates, historical debates never end because the reference points are constantly changing. There is always some probability that one's judgments, however clouded by

10   It is interesting that the moral high ground in some of these debates is taken by those who argue that what we really need is an energy policy—a position that is unassailable by either hawks or doves but that no one seems to have the capacity to implement.

the passage of time, will periodically be vindicated. One way to facilitate meaningful debate when making judgments is to spell out what alternatives were available to decision makers, explore the feasibility of those alternatives in the context of the uncertainties that attended crucial decisions, and speculate on their efficacy in light of reasonable projections of what might have happened. Historians rarely do this.

Policy planners, like historians, are grounded in the evolving present, but unlike historians they conduct an unending dialogue with the future. Independent variables that have a bearing on emerging events constantly influence each other as well as the conceptions of the future held by policymakers—conceptions that must constantly evolve if they are to be useful. These conceptions, in turn, if bureaucracies begin to use them, can have a profound impact precisely on those variables whose dynamic interaction government policies are grappling to anticipate. The relationship between the policy planner and the future, between interpretation and emerging fact is, in short, very much like E. H. Carr's description of the relationship between the historian and the past, except that the outcome is open ended. The responsibilities of policy planners, moreover, are of a very different nature than those of historians; in foreign policy they often affect matters of life and death. As a result, policy planners struggle mightily simply to keep on top of and react to ongoing developments; even then, most detail is impossible to master and one's sense of control is extraordinarily limited. In this context, policy planners (who are responsible to elected officials, who in turn are responsible to their constituents) view imaginative conceptions of the future with caution and focus on developments that policy can manipulate.

For historians, imaginative conceptions of the past are easily assimilated as "contributions to the profession." Those responsible for grappling with current policy problems, however, second-guess assumptions that seem to be valid only with great difficulty and view imaginative conceptions of the future with skepticism. Gary Sick, a member of the National Security Council staff during the Carter administration, has written about how it was virtually impossible to question any aspect of U.S. policy toward Iran in the last years of the shah's reign.[11] One's inclination to espouse departures from accepted wisdom and embark on a risky course in the face of uncertainty (and a multitude of contingent variables that are beyond any one person's capacity to control) is probably inversely proportional to the level of responsibility that he or she bears. Unassisted by hindsight, burdened by responsibility, and constrained in the implementation of their ideas by a myriad of impediments, policy planners are most seriously impeded in their work by the immediate demands of day-to-day developments. It is no wonder that they have difficulty envisioning the larger questions that need to be asked about the future, questioning the assumptions that have undergirded their experience as public officials, breaking from the mold of earlier thinking that has shaped their vision of the world, and investing in the planning that historians always wish had been more extensive and well informed.

As we look to the future, what are the trends from the past to which we should be sensitive? To what extent can policy planners incorporate such insights into their thinking? To begin with, it is clear that an enormous sea change is under way in the Near East. This was suggested by events of the last decade and made clear by the Gulf war. The end of the Cold War means that Great Power rivalry will no longer inform developments to the extent that it has in the past. Iraq would not have attacked Kuwait (nor would the United States have attacked Iraq) if the United States and the Soviet Union had been rivals to the degree that they had been in previous years. Indeed, the Iraqi attack seems to have been based at least in part on Saddam's belief that, with the demise of the Soviet Union, U.S.-Israeli dominance of the region was certain unless he took such an initiative.

As we look to the future, the end of the Cold War will change the dynamics of regional interaction in fundamental ways. Up until the recent Gulf war, one could have hypothesized that rulers such as Saddam Hussein who were interested in regional hegemony might have been more tempted to realize their ambitions

11   Gary Sick, *All Fall Down: America's Tragic Encounter with Iran* (New York, 1985).

with the end of the Cold War, because there was no credible deterrent to them. The response of the United States and the allied coalition, on the other hand, has made an American/international commitment to oppose aggression in the region more credible, and allowed the United States to protect its interests in the context of international law. Aggressors (and those who would change the post-World War I boundaries by force) have been put on notice—at least where the vital interests of the Great Powers (and particularly the United States) are concerned.

One could go down a long laundry list of changes that will emerge in the aftermath of the Cold War. Syria, to cite one example, has been cut off from Egypt ever since the Camp David accords. Unable to count on Iraq, and now without the support of the Soviet Union, Hafiz al-Assad can no longer seek military parity with Israel or seriously contemplate military action against it. Instead, he will have to reorient his policies—a change of direction indicated by his decisions to support the allied coalition, come back to the Arab fold (which enabled him to get $2 billion from the Saudis and a free hand in Lebanon), and stand on an issue of principle in Kuwait (the inadmissibility of the acquisition of territory by war) that he intends to apply to the Golan. He must also confront the fact that the new political entities in the former Soviet Union will eventually normalize relations with Israel and that the influx of Russian Jews into Israel (two hundred thousand last year and as many as four hundred thousand in each of the next two years) will not only serve as an impetus to Israel's settlement policies but also seriously exacerbate the Palestinian question.[12]

Turkey, to cite another example, is casting about for a new role in world affairs. With the decline of its geopolitical importance in the context of U.S.-Soviet rivalry, and facing rejection by the European Community (EC), the Turks have begun to explore other alternatives: membership in an expanded EC, a free-trade agreement with the United States, membership in a Black Sea Region Economic Cooperative, membership in a Balkan Cooperative zone,

---

12 For a discussion of the complex issues involved in resolving this problem see Bruce R. Kuniholm, "The Palestinian Problem and U.S. Policy," in *Security in the Middle East: Regional Change and Great Power Strategies,* ed. Samuel F. Wells and Mark Bruzonsky, Jr. (Boulder, 1987), 184–214.

and several Middle East schemes, including the Economic Cooperation Organization (a revival of the RCD under CENTO).[13]

The House of Saud, to cite a final example, can no longer mobilize its resources in conjunction with the United States in a way
that does not challenge its legitimacy. The Gulf war required that
the Saudis make the tough choices they had long preferred not to
make.[14] In conjunction with the Gulf Cooperation Council, the
Saudis must rethink their relationships with the Arab and Islamic
worlds and differentiate between friend and foe—the latter category of which now includes Palestinians, Jordanians, and Yemenis. It also means a much closer relationship with the United
States (as the indispensable deterrent to regional aggression), rapprochement with the Iranians (who have a common interest in
containing Iraq as well as a need for Saudi credits), and a more
ambivalent relationship with Egypt and Syria than one might suppose.

These three examples suggest some of the problems that all of
the states in the region will have adjusting to the post-Cold War
era. But many of the problems that they will face are more complicated than accommodating to the end of U.S.-Soviet rivalry in
the region and positioning themselves geopolitically. Largely unrelated to the end of the Cold War, these problems are rooted in
the history of the region and could evolve in ways that are virtually
impossible to predict. In a region whose boundaries have been established largely by imperial powers, with little more than passing
reference to their internal logic, it is only natural that existential
questions will be central to future developments. How do the Le-
banese define themselves? By religion, by sect, by class, by one's
allies? How do Iraqis define themselves? By tribal affiliation, by
religion, by ideology, by one's allies, by one's allegiance to pan-
Arabism? These questions will be answered differently in every
state in the region. In each case, people will assign priority to one
or another element of their identity, a priority that can change as
circumstances change.

---

13 See Bruce R. Kuniholm, "Turkey and the West," *Foreign Affairs* 70 (Spring 1991):
    34–48.
14 Bruce R. Kuniholm, "What the Saudis Really Want: A Primer for the Reagan Admin-
    istration," *ORBIS* 25 (Spring 1981): 107–21.

Circumstances are impossible to predict, as are the forces that particular circumstances set in motion. Pan-Arabism, for example, while ascendant after the 1956 Arab-Israeli war, was dealt a blow by the 1967 Arab-Israeli war. Islamic fundamentalism (however one wants to define it) was encouraged by the advent of the Ayatollah Khomeini in the Iranian revolution of 1978–79. No one, except in retrospect, could have predicted the events in question or the forces they set in motion. As individuals define themselves, so do groups whose cohesion is dependent on the saliency of the elements that bind them. There are forces in the region (such as Islam, pan-Arabism, and class-based ideologies) whose adherents aspire to unity in one form or another, often beyond national borders. There are also forces (sometimes the same ones, but particularly tribal and religious forces) whose separatist tendencies could cause the disintegration of the states within which their adherents reside. Such forces will have their own dynamic.

From a U.S. point of view, formulating a policy toward the region in the post-Cold War/post-Gulf war era is not easy. Although recognizing the necessity of paying close attention to the forces described above, it is fatuous to assume that one can manage them. What is not fatuous is to assume that the United States and the republics of the former Soviet Union now have common interests and that a code of conduct between them would facilitate both peace and prosperity in the region.

A starting point for U.S. policy toward the Persian Gulf region would probably include the following guidelines: promote a balance of power in the region; explore shared security arrangements; limit spending on arms sufficient to provide for an adequate defense of particularly vulnerable countries; seek an international understanding on conventional arms sales to the region; control the proliferation of weapons of mass destruction and delivery systems; support democratization and human rights while guaranteeing the territorial integrity and sovereignty of the states in the region; undergird that guarantee with a credible deterrent; encourage the development of mechanisms for peaceful change; and take advantage of opportunities for peace and stability in the region. These imperatives in fact appear to be the thrust of U.S. policy, which includes the notion of "a new world order . . . where the United

Nations—freed from Cold War stalemate—is poised to fulfill the historic vision of its founders."[15]

Forces described in the previous paragraphs, however, work against such notions and necessarily involve policymakers in profound contradictions. Reasons of state, of course, are well understood. Why support the Kurds beyond a certain point, risking the disintegration of Iraq, destabilizing the region, and incurring the wrath of Turkey, Iran, Iraq, and Syria? Borders worked out in the aftermath of World War I are problematic, but they cannot be changed without enormous effort, risk, and cost. To do so would also create more problems than it would solve.

There are other problems. Most of the regimes in the region, for example, need to create better structures for political participation. To recognize the need and to accommodate it are two very different issues. The gap between the "haves" and the "have-nots," to cite another example, is enormous; it would be desirable for the haves to develop a sense of responsibility for closing that gap both within their countries and throughout the region. But there is no agreement on the responsibility of the haves. Palestinians, Yemenis, and Maghribis have very different views (and historical perspectives) from Gulf Arabs.[16] The point is that blueprints rarely resolve such problems. What one can do when it comes to a policy is to have a sense of the past, a sense of direction, an agreement on the international ground rules one is prepared to accept, and a capacity to respond flexibly to problems as they arise.

15 See, for example, Secretary of State Baker's statement to the House Foreign Affairs Committee on 6 February 1991, "Opportunities to Build a New World Order," *US Department of State Dispatch,* 11 February 1991, 81–85; and President Bush's address before a joint session of Congress on 6 March 1991, "The World after the Persian Gulf," ibid., 11 March 1991, 161–63.
16 See the discussion by James E. Akins, "The New Arabia," *Foreign Affairs* 70 (Summer 1991): 36–49.

15

After the Cold War: The United States, Germany, and European Security

HERMANN-JOSEF RUPIEPER

The onset of the Cold War was, at least in part, caused by the struggle over how to incorporate Germany into the postwar order. Despite total military defeat, the devastation of its economic base, and the loss of its political sovereignty, Germany remained a potentially important European power. If its economic and military potential could be controlled by either the United States or the Soviet Union, it might well determine which side emerged victorious in the Cold War. Today, as Europe, the republics of the former Soviet Union, and the United States begin to fashion a new European order, Germany will again play a pivitol role. Indeed, many of the ideas and concerns that governed the thinking of policymakers during the postwar era, as to how to end the division of Germany and still maintain the stability and security of Europe, will reemerge as contemporary leaders try to forge a post Cold War order on the Continent.

Two interconnected concepts shaped American foreign policy toward Europe in the 1940s and 1950s, and continued to play a role until recent events led to revolutionary changes in Eastern Europe and "solved" the German question in a way that most policymakers would earlier not have believed possible. These two concepts, "the containment of the Soviet Union" and "security for and from Germany," complemented each other. Together they meant that there would be no return to "fortress America" or to the political isolation that had characterized the interwar years. They also implied that neither the neutralization of Germany, nor the creation of a power vacuum in Central Europe, would be tolerated.

All of the other developments of the postwar era, including the creation of NATO and the move toward European integration, were determined by these two basic concepts. The Western European system, which developed over time and in which the United States became an important pillar, functioned under the assumption that the people of West Germany would accept the division of their country and an alliance with the West until the East-West conflict had been resolved. Collaboration with the West would guarantee freedom, liberty, and security as well as economic prosperity, not only for West Germany but also for Western Europe as a whole, and would thus serve to effectively block Soviet expansionism.

Cooperation with the West during the postwar era effectively ended any fears that Germany might return to the Rapallo policy of the interwar years and attempt to play off East against West. As West Germany continued its association with the Western democracies, fears that West German democracy was somehow different and less stable than other European democracies abated. By the mid-1950s, it was clear that the political culture of the Federal Republic belonged to the mainstream of Western civilization and that a return to National Socialism had been decisively rejected by the German people. Thus, by the middle of the postwar era, "security from Germany" was no longer a concern, and one of the barriers to reunification had thus been removed.

In addition to providing a military umbrella for Western Europe and supporting its economic recovery, the United States also sought to reinvigorate the free-market ideology among the Western Europeans, a task made especially difficult by European suspicions that capitalism had been responsible for the rise of fascism and National Socialism. Nevertheless, with the successful economic recovery of Western Europe, the American liberal and political order was eventually embraced by the majority of the European political, industrial, and trade-union elites, as well as by the general public.

Thus was created the postwar order in Europe. From the very start, as Michael J. Hogan has shown, those involved assumed that if prosperity and democracy were to flourish in the Western half of a divided Europe then the Western Europeans, with American aid and protection, would have to move toward an integrated political, military, and economic system. European integration was also seen as the necessary precondition for solving the tangled German problem. The American presence in Western Europe was viewed as an essential element binding the West Europeans together. It made possible the Franco-German rapprochement and eliminated the fear that Germany would dominate any European security system.[1] While the Soviet Union did everything it could to prevent West German integration into the NATO alliance, in the long run the continued American presence in Germany probably reassured the Soviet Union as to the ultimate implications of German rearmament.

Although "containment" of the Soviet Union and "security for and from Germany" marked the initial framework for American policy in Europe during the Cold War, by the early 1950s ideas were being put forward as to how the division of Germany and Europe might be ended. These ideas always sought to maintain peace in Europe by insisting that any new order there would have to be based on the principle of self-determination and that all disputes between states would have to be resolved peacefully on the basis of the UN Charter. Any new order that ended the division of Europe required that tensions between East and West be dramatically reduced, that extensive disarmament be accepted, and that any new European security system include the United States. Whether these ideas could be implemented and the division of Germany ended required to a large extent that the Soviet Union change both its foreign and domestic policies. These early ideas now seem to be fulfilled, nearly fifty years after the start of the Cold War.

When the policy of Soviet Premier Mikhail Gorbachev combined with an unexpected grassroots revolution in East Germany to begin the process of German reunification in 1990, the postwar era came to an abrupt end. German Chancellor Helmut Kohl, seizing the moment, surprised both his NATO allies and the Soviet leadership by presenting proposals for a negotiated reunification of Germany and for establishing the role of a united Germany

1 Michael J. Hogan, *The Marshall Plan: America, Britain, and the Reconstruction of Western Europe, 1947–1952* (New York, 1987).

within Europe. Remarkably, politicians in both the East and the West, including many who doubted the wisdom and pace of the proposed reunification, quickly fell in line and agreed thereby to bring the postwar era to a close.

Kohl's plans for the reunification of Germany came at an opportune moment. Europe was ready to reexamine its own past and future and to assign to a united Germany a new role in Europe, for which no specific model existed. Now that Germany was no longer the central battleground of the Cold War, the Kohl government was able to become the driving force behind a settlement that was graciously accepted by the United States and, after some initial hesitation, by the other powers as well. Several factors explain why the reunification occurred so smoothly. Germany's acceptance of the structures of peace that had been developed in stages since the late 1940s, the promise of a continued American presence in Europe after reunification, and the apparent willingness of Gorbachev to permit further change in Eastern Europe all served to reassure Germany's neighbors and made possible a peaceful settlement. Equally important, the Soviet Union, which clearly faced extraordinary internal problems, refrained from trying to lure a united Germany away from NATO. Furthermore, the Kohl government left no doubt that a united Germany would remain a staunch supporter of NATO as a political and military alliance. Despite these factors, however, a reunification settlement might not have been possible had it not also fulfilled, at least in its broad outlines, the ideas for a European settlement that had already been laid down by Western policy planners in the 1950s, during their preparations for that era's four power conferences.

Throughout the postwar era, from the creation of the Federal Republic to the General Treaty of 1952, from plans for Western European integration to the closely knit European community, and from German entry into NATO to the "Treaty on the Final Settlement with Respect to Germany" of 12 September 1990, there was a remarkable degree of continuity in American foreign policy and in the peace-making process with Germany. Although not formally a peace treaty in the traditional sense, the Four-Plus-Two Agreement solved the postwar dilemma of reconciling Germany's reunification with the requirements of European security. It finally overcame the antagonism between East and West and laid a foundation for the development of broad cooperation among all of the states of Europe. It solved the problem of the German-Polish frontier and thereby ensured stability and a German-Polish rapprochement. The freely negotiated Polish-German Agreement that was subsequently signed should serve as a model for further cooperation in rebuilding Eastern Europe. The Four-Plus-Two Agreement also reinforced European security by incorporating arms control, disarmament, and confidence-building measures. In addition, while maintaining German membership in NATO, the treaty established a nuclear-free zone in East Germany, an idea first proposed in the 1950s, but rejected as unfeasible at the height of the Cold War.

The implications of the agreement in terms of its effect on Europe's security structures has not been fully recognized up to now. In fact, the agreement prevents NATO from advancing beyond the Elbe River. Thus, even though the Soviet Union no longer exists, the old Soviet defensive perimeter, created after 1945 in order to ensure that the traumatic experience of the 1941 German invasion and the subsequent devastation of Soviet territory would never happen again, actually remains intact and will continue to enhance Eastern Europe's sense of security, and that of Russia and the other republics of the former Soviet Union.

The treaty also guaranteed that reunification would take place on the basis of self-determination; that is, that the Western model of democracy would be implemented in all of Germany, a demand that had shaped both West German and Western policy from the very beginning of the Cold War. In short, although reunification came about in circumstances that had not been anticipated in the postwar era, the reunification agreement itself successfully incorporated all of the requirements that had been laid down by both the East and the West. The treaty also resolved the Berlin problem, asserted Germany's commitment to the UN Charter, and reaffirmed earlier German decisions to renounce the acquisition of nuclear, biological, or chemical weapons. The question as to what economic system would be adopted by a united Germany, an issue of great significance in the 1950s, was not even discussed in 1990. The economic success of the Federal Republic and the total failure of the Soviet Socialist model spoke for themselves. Finally, with the end of the Cold War, a settlement was possible that reconciled the requirements of European security with the reunification of Germany.

The reunification of Germany abolished once and for all the political structures that had been built up after World War II and during the Cold War. There has not yet appeared, however, a new European order in its place, although the "Treaty on the Final Settlement with Respect to Germany" is indicative of the form that the new order will take. In this new order, a united Germany, the EC, and the United States will be jointly responsible for the stabilization of Eastern Europe and for the economic reconstruction of that region, as well as for the creation of a new European security system that now must also include Russia and perhaps other republics of the former Soviet Union.

For Germany, the new order imposes special requirements. Germany must redefine its role within the European political framework and be willing to play a greater part. Although the past policies of the Federal Republic within the framework of Western Europe have significantly contributed to the stabilization of Europe, German policy toward Eastern Europe, haunted by the legacies of National Socialism and the Holocaust, needs to be redefined. There is a chance that competition and a traditional system of alliances between European powers might well emerge again and upset European security if Germany does not take a more active political role. At the same time, failure on the part of Germany to assist in the stabilization and reconstruction of the East may well help to intensify the ethnic strife in the region, with a concomitant impact upon European security. Fortunately, there are signs, in the Yugoslav crisis, for example, that Germany is prepared to play an active and positive part in cooperation with its allies.

The rebuilding of Eastern Europe after forty years of political suppression and economic mismanagement will be quite a challenge for the countries of the North Atlantic community. It will require a combination of both cooperation and competition among the states involved. The economic reconstruction of Eastern Europe has already begun, and while the contributions of the EC and of Germany are significant, the amounts committed so far barely begin to address what will undoubtedly be a gargantuan task. It surpasses the rebuilding of Western Europe after 1945, a feat that was only made possible by extensive supranational cooperation.

A debate will undoubtedly ensue as to whether or not investment in Eastern Europe, and especially in the former Soviet Union, should be made dependent upon further democratization of the region's societies. On this issue, the Cold War teaches the very important lesson that bringing about change through a policy of force is far more difficult than through a policy of cooperation. The problems involved in the rebuilding of Eastern Europe impose a special responsibility on Germany, a responsibility that the government in Bonn has already accepted. So far Germany has committed billions of deutsche marks to the economic reconstruction of the former Soviet Union, and additional billions to the countries of Eastern Europe, with at least half of the total earmarked for Poland. These funds, like the Marshall Plan expenditures of 1948–1952, will not only contribute to economic reconstruction but will also help to sustain the peace and security of Europe. This is especially true of investment in the new Länder of the old East Germany. If the former GDR can be rebuilt quickly, it will serve as a model for the economic reconstruction of Eastern Europe as a whole, and its success will contribute to a successful economic recovery in the East. If the reconstruction of Eastern Europe is too slow, however, and if the economic misery of the region is prolonged, the introduction of democracy may well prove abortive. The failure of economic and democratic reform might then lead to a massive wave of emigration from the East, which in turn could create major political and economic problems for the EC as well.

Both the United States and the EC must also play a significant role in rebuilding eastern Germany, Eastern Europe, and the former Soviet Union. The task of rebuilding eastern Germany cannot be carried out by Germany alone, nor should it be. The problems of Eastern Europe and the former Soviet Union are even more formidable, and can only be overcome if all of the EC countries as well as the United States are willing to make significant contributions to the region's recovery. If the EC and the United States cooperate in rebuilding the East, they will help to prevent the development of friction that might otherwise occur between American trade interests and European efforts to create an integrated Western European market. Because American leadership has been instrumental in guiding Europe through much of the postwar period, it will be difficult for Washington to accept a united European bloc as an equal partner and to respect its decisions on trade and defense policies. It is imperative that the EC not become a rival to the United States in relations with Eastern Europe. If a rivalry develops the economic recovery of the East will be delayed, to the detriment of the peoples of both the East and the West.

The postwar era has shown that Europe thrives best if an overarching political, economic, and security system provides a basic framework for the general development of the region. The political and economic institutions of the EC might well develop into such a system for the new order by incorporating the countries of Eastern Europe, beginning perhaps with Poland, Hungary, and Czechoslovakia. But this would only be a partial solution. The markets of Russia and the other former Soviet republics must also be made available to the countries of Eastern Europe and, as in the 1950s, the United States will have to open its markets to European products. Clearly, the reconstruction of Eastern Europe and the creation of a viable new order in Europe require a combination of cooperation and competition among the states involved in order to succeed.

The creation of a viable European security system will be even harder than the reconstruction of Eastern Europe, especially because the final outcome of the changes occurring in the former Soviet Union is as yet unclear. Although it has asked to join NATO, Russia as well as the other republics could turn their backs on cooperation with the West if their efforts to introduce political and economic reforms fail. Such a failure could even result in the creation of dictatorships or lead to military rule. It is thus only prudent to keep the Western defensive alliance intact, even if the level of armaments is scaled back. The American presence in Europe should be maintained. During the Cold War the American presence not only provided an umbrella against the perceived Soviet threat but it also made possible the Franco-German rapprochement and contributed to American security by immunizing Western Europe against Soviet pressure. Although one of the major problems of the postwar era has been solved with the reunification of Germany, the other major obstacle to the stabilization of the Continent—the restructuring of the former Soviet system—is still in progress and the outcome uncertain. If this restructuring fails, Europe will be filled with anxiety for years to come, a situation not at all conducive to the creation of mutual trust and security.

Of the existing security organizations, NATO and the Conference on Security and Cooperation in Europe (CSCE), only NATO can play an effective role in stabilizing Europe under current conditions. The role of the CSCE in creating a European security system will have to be further defined, although it is already useful insofar as it is the only structure that enables all of the European states, as well as the United States, to conduct joint discussions on European security. The CSCE might also be useful if it adopted a role similar to that of the United Nations Security Council and willingly discussed the problems of ethnic and nationality conflicts in Europe, such as those in Northern Ireland, Spain, Yugoslavia, and the Baltics. As long as the internal situation in the former Soviet Union remains unstable, however, and as long as the EC avoids developing its own security structures, NATO and a continuing American presence in Europe remain the only barriers against the failure of reform in the East. For the foreseeable future, NATO, despite the partial French withdrawal, is the only functioning military and political alliance in Europe. Although indispensable to the framework of peace in the region, the 1991 Gulf war showed that NATO cannot serve as an adequate organization to coordinate European involvement in external conflicts, even when European action is sanctioned by UN resolutions. This will not change in the future. Despite German preparations to make constitutional changes so that Germany can participate in UN efforts to enforce peace and security in the world, the German people will not sanction the sending of German troops under NATO command outside of the NATO area. Thus, although NATO is the only viable option currently available for maintaining peace in the Old World, there is no chance that the passing of the postwar era presages an expanded role for either Germany or NATO outside of the European area.

16

The End of the Cold War: A Skeptical View

DENISE ARTAUD

Less than two years after the fall of the Berlin Wall, which led almost automatically to the reunification of Germany, one thing is certain: The division of Europe, for forty-five years the symbol of the Cold War, has come to an end. Beyond this not much can be said. Because of the swift succession of events, the most enticing assumptions about the future very quickly lose their credibility. This has been true of recent predictions by Paul Kennedy and Francis Fukuyama. Kennedy argues that "imperial overstretch" has led to a relative decline of American power and hence to a shift in the balance of global economic power. To his way of thinking, the United States should seek to redress the balance by reducing its excessive overseas commitments, spending less on defense, and devoting more of its resources to social and educational programs and to industrial investments.[1] In an essay published in June 1990, Fukuyama presented an even bolder assessment of the past and prescription for the future. He asserted that the demise of fascism and Marxism-Leninism had brought about "the end of history," a growing "Common marketization" of international relations, and a diminution of the likelihood of large-scale conflict between states.[2] Subsequent developments have not been kind to these prescriptions.

In the wake of the Gulf war and the demise of the Soviet Union, the situation appears more complicated than either Kennedy or

---

1 Paul Kennedy, *The Rise and Fall of the Great Powers: Economic Change and Military Conflict from 1500 to 2000* (New York, 1987).
2 Francis Fukuyama, "The End of History?" *The National Interest* 16 (Summer 1989): 18.

Fukuyama anticipated. The United States has obviously emerged as the only superpower, a development that challenges the credibility of the declinist theory. Moreover, a number of countries—Pakistan, India, Israel, Argentina, and Brazil, to name a few—are now capable of equipping themselves with nuclear armaments or of purchasing sophisticated long-range missiles. These nations could pose a real threat to the security of their neighbors, not to mention the interests of the major powers. Until arms sales are controlled more effectively, war is not likely to be eradicated. What is more, it may be premature to envision a new era of cooperation between American policymakers and the new leadership of the former Soviet Union, a development supposedly presaged by Soviet-American collaboration in the Gulf crisis. Even during that crisis, it should be remembered, the media often hinted that the Soviets were not complying fully with the UN embargo against Iraq. Under these circumstances, perhaps it would be better to await the opening of archives in Moscow before jumping to the conclusion that the two sides had perfectly identical goals, as was suggested at the time by Eduard Shevardnadze.[3]

The Gulf crisis, the danger of nuclear proliferation, and other developments thus raise doubts about a New World Order of everlasting peace, and also about the real unthinkability of a return of East-West tensions. Despite the recent celebrations over the end of the Cold War, will we one day lament "the end of the end of the Cold War"? This proposition may appear so paradoxical as to preclude discussion. But it remains to be seen if Russia's challenge to the West is truly over, or for that matter the challenges raised by Marxism or some other brand of authoritarianism. Beyond these issues, moreover, we must ask about the future of European unification and of American leadership.

To the question of whether the challenge of Marxism is a thing of the past, the obvious answer is "yes," if one considers only the economic aspects of Marxism. *Perestroika* was triggered by the bankrupt state of the Soviet economy, and market economics is now the name of the game not only in countries newly freed from communism but throughout the world. In France, for example, the

3   Eduard Shevardnadze, *L'avenir s'écrit Liberté* (Paris, 1991).

Socialist government seeks to promote private investments, although it does not command a majority in Parliament and therefore depends on the tacit agreement of the Communist party in order to carry out its policies. The privatization of state-owned firms is also making considerable headway in Latin America, where the seduction of Marxism had combined with a mercantilist tradition to produce large public sectors (so large that in some cases the percentage of GNP generated through the public sector was higher than in most of the Eastern European countries). The pope himself, in *Centesimus Annus,* his latest encyclical, no longer puts capitalism and Marxism on an equal basis, and has openly pronounced himself in favor of market economics and free enterprise.[4]

On the other hand, even in late 1991 there was still much reluctance in what used to be the Soviet Union to adopt all of the reforms that are essential to a liberal order. The difficulties stemmed in part from the fact that Marxism has always been more than an economic system. It has been a form of totalitarianism, which, unlike democracy, is beyond the reach of law. It has also been a revolutionary praxis that gave its supporters a useful tool in wielding power and acquiring privileges long-embodied in the *nomenklatura.* Marxism created a society based not on merit and competence but on growing bureaucratization and ideological loss of faith, a society where initiative and responsibility did not exist, where values and virtues were corrupted. In this way, Marxism contributed to family breakups, declining health conditions, galloping alcoholism, and the proliferation of gangs. In effect, to quote a French scholar, Marxism-Leninism brought about "a general decapitalization" of Soviet society. More to the point, it set in motion a swift and irreversible process that blocked the creation of values as well as products, of knowledge and know-how, of information of all sorts, and of modernity.[5]

In other words, the difficulties with which the former Soviet Union is now struggling stem from the bankrupt state not only of its economy but also of its society and political system. Assuredly,

---

4 *Centesimus Annus* (Vatican City, 1991).
5 Illios Yannakakis, foreword to Thieryy Mallerer and Murielle Delaporte, *L'armée rouge face à la Perestroika* (Brussels, 1991), xviii.

there are liberal elements that can help in solving many problems, but they are loosely structured and have little grassroots support, especially outside of the large cities. They must also deal with former Communist party members who have not renounced their ideology and who continue to exercise a degree of influence in certain quarters of the armed forces and the military-industrial complex. To be sure, Boris Yeltsin's success may be one step forward on the road to democracy. We should not overlook the authoritarianism of the Russian president, however, or the fact that he cannot rely on a well-developed and democratic political or party structure to thwart the advocates of authoritarianism who are surely waiting in the wings. Nor should we forget that Russia and the other republics still possess substantial conventional and nuclear weapons and that these still remain a potential threat to peace in general and to the global interests of the West in particular.

Regarding the potential threat to Western interests around the world, it might be instructive to remind ourselves of the Soviet Union's foreign policy in the last year of its existence. Although many commentators celebrated the "new thinking" of policymakers in Moscow, the reality was not quite so rosy. The Soviets, it is true, did reduce their aid to Vietnam and Laos and apparently terminated their assistance to several African countries, including Ethiopia, Angola, and Mozambique. They also hammered out a rapprochement with Israel and stopped meddling in the Angolan civil war. At the same time, however, the Soviets managed to maintain their economic aid to Cuba, sent spare parts to the Sandinista-controlled Nicaraguan army, and continued to prop up Afghanistan's Communist government. As these commitments demonstrate, even Moscow's own precarious economic situation did not prevent it from supporting client states whose policies deviated in large measure from the "new thinking" propounded by Shevardnadze. Clearly there existed a sharp contrast between the swift retreat that Soviet leaders were forced to accept in Eastern Europe and Moscow's efforts to retain some links to its clients in the Third World. This contrast, as Charles Fairbanks noted at the time, conjured up the image of a doughnut-shaped empire with a hole in the middle.[6] Fairbanks may have exaggerated the extent to

6 Charles H. Fairbanks, Jr., "Gorbachev's Global Doughnut," *The National Interest* 19 (Spring 1990): 21–33.

which the Soviet Union still wielded power overseas. But he was right to warn that Moscow continued to pose a threat at the end of the Cold War, a warning that might also apply one day to Russia and some of the other republics of the former Soviet Union. However weakened, they have interests of their own and retain substantial real and potential military power.

Even in Europe it is legitimate to ask if the strategic retreat that moved the Soviet frontier from the Oder River to Brest Litovsk marks the start of a postimperial era in Eastern Europe. German reunification is a fait accompli, and it is unlikely that the former Soviet Union will regain its sway over Poland, Hungary, or Czechoslovakia. The situation in the Balkans is less stable or predictable, as evinced by what happened in Yugoslavia. In 1914 the Sarajevo incident was the spark that ignited World War I. Is it possible that at some time in the future the struggle between different national or ethnic groups might lead to regional conflict? Is it possible that such a struggle might encourage the Russians to extend their influence into the Balkans? Or perhaps the Germans will become diplomatically more aggressive, as they have been in the Yugoslav case. And if so, will Germany's initiatives reveal serious differences with France or within the European Community—differences that the Russians could play upon?

This leads to the issue of European unity, for only a united Europe can countervail potential problems. On an economic level, hopes for European unity have been high in the last few years, because of the transition to a single European market in 1993. Recent talks on monetary union made progress, although there is still evidence of British reservations that could spell trouble in the future. Talks between the EC and Japan also provide evidence of differences between the British, who see the post 1992 European Community as a genuinely open market, and the French, who prefer a more regulated economy. On a political level, the community has even greater problems. During the Gulf crisis, despite its GNP, the size of its population, and its military forces, the EC proved unable to reach a common decision on overseas intervention, and François Mitterrand's diplomatic initiatives failed to conceal the fact that the community had to seek shelter under American foreign policy. Things could not have been otherwise, because the EC has no truly democratic and efficient institutions. In most cases, the Council of Ministers must make its decisions by unanimous vote. The Brussels bureaucracy is largely an irresponsible technocracy. The Strasbourg Parliament, which has no real links to its constituents, is more concerned with ideology than with solving practical problems and more prone to increase the burden of community expenses without much concern for the taxpayers.

Another reason why the EC is stalled is that many see it as only an interim solution before real reorganization of the Continent following the collapse of the Berlin Wall and the Warsaw Pact. In effect, the geographical space held by the EC seems small when compared to the cultural legacy of Ancient Rome, Christendom, and the Enlightenment. Because Europe is too imbued with its spiritual heritage to be only a technocratic entity, some are inclined to object to a community born of the Treaty of Rome and to call instead for "a Europe based on hope," in the words of Georges Bidault, a Europe that might encompass not only a reunited Germany but also Poland and all of the countries of the former Austro-Hungarian Empire.[7] Indeed, all of those countries share a common heritage of rationality, humanism, skepticism, and tolerance.

On the other hand, while the cultural and educational life of Central Europe still sports many intellectuals, it has been dreadfully weakened by forty years of communism. It is no wonder under these circumstances that the churches represent the strongest element in Central Europe and that religious conviction played such an important part in the political revolution of 1989. The political revolution was preceded by a moral and cultural revolution, one of whose ignition points was the "most fantastic pilgrimage in the history of contemporary Europe"—the visit of the newly elected pope, John Paul II, to his homeland in March 1979. The church also helped to shape the "Velvet Revolution" in Czechoslovakia and in the late, unlamented, German Democratic Republic, where the Lutheran *Evangelischekirche* provided an organizing ground for civic opposition to the Communist regime throughout the 1980s. This opposition first formed around the issue of conscientious objection to conscription and took its inspiration from

7 Quoted in Alain-Gerard Selma, "L'Europe des rendez-vous manqués," *Politique Internationale* 51 (Spring 1991): 331–32.

the life and death of the theologian Dietrich Bonhoeffer, a martyr to Nazi tyranny. The Catholic Church also retained its force in those countries. It emerged, in the words of James Kurth, as "the most significant multi-national institution operating in Central Europe,"[8] and was a powerful force in Germany as well, although after reunification the number of German Catholics dropped from 50 to 40 percent of the population.

Religious forces are likely to become a leading factor in the political life of the new Europe and may even serve as a basis for democracy, which, as suggested above, decays unless nourished by the politically sensible and morally virtuous behavior of its citizens. To quote Plato: "The best is for everyone to be ruled by a wise and godlike power, if possible seated in his own heart; if not, let it act upon him from without." In other words, if the state is to be denied control of economic and social life (contrary to what existed in the whole of Soviet Europe), each citizen must accept a check on his or her passions so as not to encroach on the freedom of others. Along that path, religion is no doubt one of best guides, as the Pole Adam Michinik, a former Communist, declared as early as 1979.[9]

The buoyant religious forces currently at work and the related evolution of Catholic social doctrine lead some to think that Europe will be able to chart a middle course between American capitalism and Communist statism. Such a trend would point to a major victory for the Christian Democratic parties, especially for the CDU in Germany. Should the Social Democrats emerge victorious at the polls, however, the results will not be significantly different. Their platform remains moderate: They adhere to the principles of civil society, social-market economy, and electoral democracy. Outside of Central Europe, notably in France, socialism is very different. It still bears the mark of the Marxist tradition and remains bent on state intervention. It is also nonreligious and even deeply anticlerical. Thus, when François Mitterrand in his October 1989 Valladolid speech implored the Central European countries not to sacrifice their Socialist inspiration to their hatred

8 James Kurth, "The Shape of the New World Order," *The National Interest* 24 (Summer 1991): 7.
9 Adam Michinik, *L'église et la gauche: le dialogue polonais* (Paris, 1979).

of the Soviet system, the project he meant to promote was worlds apart from those of Helmut Kohl, Lech Walesa, or Vaclav Havel. In other words, no single project comparable to that of the American Founding Fathers has yet taken shape in the Old World. Hence the pessimism of someone like Ralph Dahrendorf, for whom Europe "will always be a patchwork of languages and cultures in everyday life, politics and the economy."[10]

In the future such a patchwork could provide Russia and some of the other republics of the old Soviet Union with a means of exerting greater influence in Europe than might be expected. And so far as these republics are concerned, we cannot predict whether they will be democratic, Fascist, or Communist ten or twenty years from now. But one thing is certain: Authoritarianism, perhaps even Marxism-Leninism, cannot be whisked away as if by magic. It is too deeply rooted in the mind of an old elite and takes its strength from those in society who shrink from risks and who prefer the status quo to change. At the same time, there are those in Eastern and Central Europe, as well as in the Socialist countries of Western Europe, who still prefer the welfare state to the risks and responsibilities of a free society, even if that entails stagnation in their standards of living. There is a possibility, however remote today, that the Russians and the Europeans might come to an understanding on this basis, at least so far as certain issues are concerned. This eventuality could be reinforced by centuries of historical links and by the fact that the former Soviet Union, whatever its regime (except in the extreme case of a civil war), will always enjoy the status of a major power because of its size, population, economic potential, and armaments.

Bearing all of this in mind, the question remains: What role can the United States play in Europe? Much has been said on this issue, most of it discouraging. Some have asserted that a growing imbalance between the legislative and executive branches prevents the American government from "acting strategically" in Europe. Some have said that economic problems in the United States, the resurgence of neo-isolationist sentiment, and the demise of a clear Soviet threat will continue to prompt cuts in American military

10   Ralph Dahrendorf, *Réflexions sur la révolution en Europe, 1989–1990* (Paris, 1991), 137.

spending in Europe. But so long as Europe lacks a common defense policy and so long as there is even a remote threat from the East, a complete American pullout would be unwise. Above all, we must keep in mind that while the Soviet Union fades into history, there is always a danger that its successor will emerge eventually with interests, influence, and ambitions similar to those of tsarist Russia around 1914. In that case, we might indeed wonder who had won the Cold War.

17

The End of the Cold War, the New Role for Europe, and the Decline of the United States

GEIR LUNDESTAD

In this short piece I shall briefly address two rather large points. First, I shall discuss the question of whether, if the Cold War is over, this is likely to result in a more peaceful world. The role of Eastern Europe will be of particular interest in this context. Second, I shall comment on the effects the end of the Cold War will have on that apparently most burning of political questions, certainly in the United States but not only there: Will the United States remain Number One in the post-Cold War era? U.S.-(Western) European relations will be crucial here.

If the Cold War is defined as a very antagonistic relationship between two blocs, East and West, where the antagonism is at least in part based on irreconcilable ideological differences, then it is surely over. The basic change took place in the mid-1980s. In the course of a few years, Ronald Reagan went from denunciations of "the evil empire" to walking hand in hand with Mikhail Gorbachev in Red Square. The Soviet leader was pronounced the statesman not only of the year but also of the decade. The shift in American attitudes was only surpassed by that of the other side. Under the old system, Reagan had been described in the crudest of terms; under Gorbachev the Soviet caricature of the American president changed from "Rambo to Mister Rogers." The euphoria is now gone, but so is the old antagonism.[1]

Second, with the Communist party and economic planning now

---

1 I have discussed the changing American and Soviet attitudes in "Uniqueness and Pendulum Swings in US Foreign Policy" in my *The American "Empire" and Other Studies of US Foreign Policy in a Comparative Perspective* (Oxford-Oslo, 1990), 122–27, 131–34.

discredited and democracy and the market rapidly advancing in the former Soviet Union, the ideological chasm has also been greatly reduced. Even during détente in the 1970s, Brezhnev had proclaimed that "detente does not in the slightest way abolish and cannot abolish or change the laws of the class struggle. We do not conceal the fact that we see detente as a way to create more favorable conditions for peaceful socialist and communist construction." Gorbachev's favorite image, on the other hand, was one where the countries of the world are bound together by a single rope in trying to reach the top of the mountain: "Either we reach the top together or we fall into the abyss together."[2]

Third, the bloc system has been greatly changed. More specifically, while the triangular relationship between the United States, Western Europe, and Japan has to be defined anew, the Eastern bloc has collapsed entirely. The Cold War started over Eastern Europe. Western definitions of "democracy" could not be reconciled with Soviet definitions of "security." While we may not see flourishing democracy in all of the East European countries, the Soviet definition of security had to be totally altered. This was the premise for the East European revolutions of 1989, when, in the half-year between the elections in Poland in June and the fall of Ceaucescu in Romania in December, the old order was swept aside.

Naturally, the end of the Cold War has had a beneficial influence on the overall international climate, particularly that between East and West. What effects will the end of the Cold War have on the many regional and local conflicts around the world? No simple answer along the lines of "the end of history" argument can be given to this question.[3] At least three different developments can be seen. First, some regional conflicts have been solved apparently at least in part because of the new climate. Angola-Namibia is probably the most clear-cut example. Cambodia could possibly become another. Second, in Afghanistan and the Middle East the end of the Cold War has certainly modified the conflicts, although

2 Soviet developments are analyzed in my *East, West, North, South: Major Developments in International Politics, 1945–1990* (Oxford-Oslo, 1991), chaps. 5, 6.
3 Francis Fukuyama, "The End of History?" *The National Interest* 16 (Summer 1989): 3–18. For Fukuyama's response to some of the attention his article attracted see his "A Reply to My Critics," ibid. 18 (Winter 1989/90): 21–28.

the fundamental issues are still unresolved and are basically un connected to the old East-West struggle. Other regional conflicts, such as that between India and Pakistan, are even less related to the Cold War and thus less likely to be affected by its end.[4]

Third, some conflicts will probably be exacerbated by the new climate. It can possibly be argued that the Iraq-Kuwait war falls into this category. The more obvious example, however, is Eastern Europe. The dissolution of the Soviet Union and of Yugoslavia is complete. Tension is likely to increase not only inside states but in some cases also between states. This has conjured up memories of Sarajevo and the First World War, but the major powers have neither the kind of interests in the area nor the overall security problems that they had in the earlier period. Northern Ireland provides the opposite Western European parallel in that the rest of the world has been happy to stay out of that conflict and leave the fighting to the locals and the political maneuvering to London and Dublin.

Yet, it appears highly unlikely that, for instance, the disintegration of Yugoslavia, while far from providing another Sarajevo, can be localized to the extent that the Irish situation has been. The biggest question of all is of course what will happen in the former Soviet Union and whether its breakup will be peaceful (highly unlikely, I would guess) or result in local violence (most likely) or even international violence of some sort (hopefully and probably contained to the region). Empires do not tend to dissolve peacefully. Both the British (Ireland) and the French experience (Algeria) underline the special problems involved in giving up territories close to the core areas.

The end of Pax Sovietica has undoubtedly created a more just order, but probably also a less stable one, at least temporarily. In Eastern Europe the conflict between justice and stability has been more or less permanent. The Austro-Hungarian order before 1914 and particularly the Soviet order after 1945 were unjust, but for decades fairly stable, while the interwar order was considerably more just, but also much more unstable. Michael Doyle has ar-

---

4 Patrick Brogan, *The Fighting Never Stopped: A Comprehensive Guide to World Conflict since 1945* (New York, 1990), gives a good, factual survey of regional and local conflicts.

ight at first sight appear to be almost the opposite
alysis, a just order, at least in the form of democra-
e in that democracies are inherently peaceful toward
ard totalitarian regimes and toward their own
y have proved far less peaceful.) Even threats of war
en regarded as illegitimate in relations among democratic
ountries.[5]

Most of the democracies of the world have traditionally been found in Western Europe (and North America). It can be argued that after 1945 peace in Western Europe hinged in part on American leadership, while in Eastern Europe it was based on Soviet suppression. With the Cold War over, the influence of the superpowers will recede in Europe. What will then emerge? Will it be a new, integrated, and cooperating Europe dominated by the European Community or will it be the old, fragmented, and feuding Europe that resulted in two world wars and, eventually, American and Soviet supremacy?[6]

History never repeats itself. (Historians do, but that is a different matter.) It seems a safe guess, therefore, that in Europe we will see both integration and fragmentation. Most likely the Continent will come to represent a unique mixture of supranationalism, in the form of the EC, and nationalism, even "localism," in Eastern Europe. (The Irish example in particular, not to mention developments in Spain and Belgium's old problems, shows how the two elements can be found side by side even in Western Europe.)

Yet, in discussing the relationship between stability, justice, and democracy, it is important to remember that neither Austria-Hungary before 1914 nor the Soviet Union after 1945 solved Eastern Europe's many national problems. At best they just postponed them, at worst they made them even worse. And although the interwar order was relatively just in the ethnic-national sense, only Czechoslovakia among the countries in Eastern Europe had a

5 Michael Doyle, "Kant, Liberal Legacies, and Foreign Affairs," *Philosophy and Public Affairs* 12 (Summer/Fall 1983): 205–35, 323–35. See also Samuel P. Huntington, "No Exit: The Errors of Endism," *The National Interest* 17 (Fall 1989): 3–11.
6 The conflict between integration and fragmentation is dealt with on a more general level in John Lewis Gaddis, "Toward the Post-Cold War World," *Foreign Affairs* 70 (Spring 1991): 102–22.

democratic record to speak of. Again, in a long-term perspective it may be argued that only a truly just order will really prove stable. With the number of democracies now increasing we shall have a chance to find out more about the extent to which the peaceful record of democracies is based on accident and/or logic. The test of the alleged connection between democracy and peace will be tougher in Eastern Europe than has so far been the case in any other region in history. And it will be complicated by the probability that more authoritarian structures will survive in parts of the region. Serbia, Albania, Romania, and Bulgaria are the most likely areas in this respect.

In conclusion, there always has been and most likely there will continue to be Great Power rivalry, although the intensity of the conflicts has varied greatly. Even with the old antagonism gone, the United States and Russia, not to mention the other republics of the former Soviet Union, will still have different interests in many respects. Some old challenges to stability have reemerged in the new shapes of religious, particularly Islamic, fundamentalism and economic nationalism. In the many different regions of the world there also will undoubtedly continue to be lots of combustible material around. So, while the threat of an East-West nuclear holocaust has diminished vastly, the fighting apparently never stops.

If the Cold War is over, what then will the implications be for the United States? The end of the Cold War will probably mean a relative reduction in its global role. The leadership of the United States, not to mention the Soviet Union, had been most pronounced in the military field. In recent years, the two were military superpowers more than anything else. Together they had 95 percent of the world's nuclear weapons and were responsible for 60 percent of the world's military expenditures and more than 50 percent of the world's arms exports.

The end of the Cold War will reduce these percentages and, even more important, will mean a reduction in the importance of the military dimension as such. In times of Great Power tension the military aspect is quite important. In more peaceful times the currency of power will be measured more in economic and political terms. The Gulf war in early 1991 provides ample warning against seeing this transition as a very abrupt and clear-cut one. But it would not seem to obviate the phenomenon as such, and we should be careful not to make too much of a conflict that will probably prove rather special in a long-term perspective. After all, Saddam Hussein and his actions were near perfect from the point of view of the Bush administration getting broad support for its actions both internationally and nationally. For the United States to use about 75 percent of its tactical aircraft and 40 percent of its tanks to defeat a country with the gross national product (GNP) of Portugal will also have to be a rare event.[7] With modern weapons technology, smaller states than Iraq, even small groups inside states, as events in Afghanistan and Lebanon have illustrated, can do substantial damage to a superpower, and that will probably continue to deter Great Power involvement in most ordinary cases.

On the economic side, the Soviet Union was never a true superpower. In terms of living standards, it was always quite far down on the world list. In terms of gross national product, it had been surpassed by Japan, a country with a population less than half that of the Soviet Union. Although the discrepancy between military and economic power is much smaller on the American side, the United States too has become stronger militarily than economically. There can be little doubt that the United States has been suffering a relative economic decline compared with its position in the first two decades after the Second World War.[8] In 1945 it produced almost 50 percent of the world's total production, a percentage far surpassing that of any earlier Great Power. This percentage was bound to go down as the rest of the world recovered from the ravages of war. In 1960 the percentage stood around 30. The decline continued, however, and today the U.S. GNP constitutes around 23 percent of world GNP.

It is true that in the 1980s the United States held its own in terms of this percentage of world GNP, but the economic slippage has continued in other rather significant fields. Thus, in the course of four years under President Reagan the country went from still being the world's largest creditor to becoming its largest debtor. All ten of the world's largest banks are now Japanese, and West Ger-

7 *Economist*, 9 March 1991.
8 My analysis of the rise and fall of the United States is found in *The American "Empire"*, 31–115. Most of the analysis in the following paragraphs is based on that account.

many's exports are as high as those of the United States. Traditionally an oil exporter, the United States is now importing almost half of the oil it consumes. America's lead was long the greatest where it counted the most, in the technologically advanced fields. But this is not so evident any more. The United States probably still holds an overall lead in inventions and patents, but the so-called patent balance became negative with West Germany in the mid-1960s and with Japan in the mid-1970s. In the 1980s, Japan's share of the world's semiconductor market nearly doubled, to 49 percent, while that of the United States declined from 55 to 39 percent.

From the tone and range of the debate about America's decline, it has been difficult to detect that there is actually agreement on one very basic point: America has indeed been declining compared to its heyday in the 1950s. Those opposed to the "declinists" have simply argued that the basis of comparison should not be the 1950s and 1960s, because America's position then had been "artificially high."[9] It may, of course, be comforting to know that America's position has not declined compared with the 1930s, but in studying America's contemporary world role it is strange indeed simply to write off the fifties and sixties as "artificially high."

In the flurry of optimism after the Gulf war, an optimism that would appear to have declined considerably already, one should not forget the rather unique fact, at least in recent centuries, that a Great Power's warfare was to a large extent financed by others. With a great deal of exaggeration but still a kernel of truth, America can be seen as the mercenary of the two oil states primarily affected, Saudi Arabia and Kuwait, and its two industrialized creditors, Japan and Germany.

On the political side, the American starting point is quite good. Since the Civil War, and certainly in this century, the United States has been a well-functioning political unit. That is no little thing in the world of today. Most large states have very serious problems in maintaining their territorial integrity. The Soviet Union has col-

---

9   See particularly Joseph S. Nye, "Understating U.S. Strength," *Foreign Policy* 72 (Fall 1988): 105–29; idem, *Bound to Lead: The Changing Nature of American Power* (New York, 1990); and Samuel P. Huntington, "The U.S.—Decline or Renewal," *Foreign Affairs* 67 (Winter 1988/89): 76–96.

lapsed, and problems can also be seen in ethnically mixed India and even in China, where the Han constitute 94 percent of the population. Canada's situation is the counterargument to those who think that the market alone can solve this problem too. The European Community has not even reached the level of integration found in the Articles of Confederation.

To a large extent, America's role depends on the attitudes found inside the United States. After all, the United States has been the world's economic leader since the Civil War, but it chose to exercise political and military leadership only after the Second World War. Isolationism in the historical sense is dead and will not return, despite the support the far Right has recently given to the far Left's slogan of the 1970s: "Come home, America."[10] In the new post-Cold War period the pessimism of Vietnam and the initial optimism after the Gulf war will perhaps blend into a still quite active role for the United States, but one, I would guess, reduced compared to America's heyday in the 1950s and 1960s, and particularly reduced in a now stable area like Western Europe.

With the Cold War over, public interest in foreign affairs would seem likely to diminish and interest in domestic matters to increase. In addition to the budget and trade deficits, America is bound to be affected also by what we might call a "social deficit." For too long it appears that the United States has neglected its economic and moral infrastructure. On the economic side, considerable problems exist with regard to savings and investment, bridges and roads, among other things; on the moral side, drugs and crime, racism, and the environment represent great challenges. The same United States that pioneered democracy and mass education and celebrated the "common man" seems to be increasingly content to develop two separate sectors, a private one that is in most fields still the best in the world and a public one that is all too often rather mediocre. It is not only immoral but probably also an economic waste of talent to let a large part of the population fall behind in health, in education, in jobs.

Supplementing these more or less traditional state dimensions, there is the world's rapidly growing interdependence, which of

10 Interesting examples of conservative positions are found in the Winter, Spring, Summer, and Fall 1990 issues of *The National Interest*.

course affects all states, but which may well be more difficult to cope with politically and emotionally for a traditionally self-sufficient country such as the United States than for the already more interdependent countries of Western Europe. International finance provides an illustration from one important field of the quantum leaps we are talking about. During a serious exchange crisis in 1961, $0.3 billion was converted into Swiss francs during a four-day period; in the 1973 currency crisis, $3 billion was converted into European currencies in one day; in 1986 the foreign exchange volume on the London, New York, and Tokyo markets alone reached nearly $200 billion per day.[11]

America's supreme role after 1945 has to a considerable degree rested on its unique relationship with Western Europe and Japan. The American "empire," if we can call it that, involved key areas strategically and economically and to a large extent it has been an empire "by invitation."[12] With the end of the Cold War, what will happen to America's role in Western Europe? The fear of the Soviet Union was undoubtedly the single most important factor behind the European invitations issued to the United States. At least since the 1960s, with that fear reduced, the invitations became rather ambiguous. The Europeans still wanted a strong American presence, but they wanted fewer strings attached to that presence and also a much larger European influence than in the early years of the Atlantic alliance. Now, with the fear of attack from the East virtually gone, even united Germany's new role will not be sufficient to prevent a further weakening of the invitations.

Germany's role was the most burning question in Great Power politics in the long years from 1870 to 1945. The country's unification, its economic strength, and its geographical position in the heart of Europe are bound to make it a central actor. Most likely its full independence will now result in pressure to reduce the Western military presence. Fears of the new united Germany can easily be exaggerated, however. Its economy is the strongest in Europe, but it is still quite a bit smaller than those of Britain and

---

11 Robert D. Putnam and Nicholas Bayne, *Hanging Together: Cooperation and Conflict in the Seven-Power Summits* (Cambridge, MA, 1987), 14.
12 I have dealt with the concept of empire by invitation on several occasions, most recently in *The American "Empire"*, 54–62, 100–104.

France combined. In relative Great Power terms the new Germany is weaker than that of the 1870–1945 period. It has been integrated into both NATO and the EC, with America providing the ultimate counterweight. Attitudes in Germany are quite different from what they were in the earlier period. In fact, national feelings are surprisingly weak, squeezed as they have been between European integrationist sentiment and strong Länder attachment. To integrate the five East German Länder with the eleven Western ones will take considerable time, and Germany will probably continue to represent an interesting mixture of European, national, and local loyalties at one and the same time.

Most likely, the passing of the Cold War, America's problems, and new attitudes in Western Europe in general, and in Germany in particular, will come to have dramatic consequences for the U.S. role in Europe. The need for America's strategic deterrence will decline and the American troop commitment will be cut at least in half, a two thirds reduction is probably most likely. These changes are bound to reduce America's influence in Europe and thereby push America's decline further along.

In historical perspective, America's "empire" was special also in that its prime economic rivals represented the core of its imperial system. With the reduced importance of the security dimension, it would appear likely that economic disputes between the United States, Western Europe, and Japan will become both more prominent and more numerous. This tendency has already become quite striking vis-à-vis the Japanese and has contributed to a significant shift in popular attitudes in the two countries.

In relations with Western Europe, the United States in the 1940s and 1950s not only gave substantial economic aid but also pushed for economic and political integration in Western Europe. In a way this was a policy of decline by design, a strange position indeed for an imperial power and one to be understood primarily in light of the overriding common purpose, the containment of the Soviet Union. Now the United States is clearly worried about the effects that the European Community's integrated market of 1992–93 will have on American economic interests. Economic considerations will no longer have to be subordinated to those of foreign policy.

It is thus becoming increasingly clear that the assumption that traditionally undergirded America's pro-integrationist stance vis-à-vis Western Europe—that the two continents had the most basic interests in common—is no longer self-evident. Now Washington is increasingly worried that the European defense pillar it promoted for more than four decades is actually about to be realized through the European Community and the Western European Union. Then warnings against alliances within the NATO alliance are heard. There is to be no more decline by design.

In the late 1940s and early 1950s, when the basic structure of the American-Western European relationship was established, the Soviet threat was seen as clear and present and the United States was far stronger in every respect than Western Europe, which was economically weak and politically divided. Now the Soviet threat is gone. Not only is the population of the EC larger than that of both the former Soviet Union and the United States, but the GNP of the EC is about the same as that of the United States and the conventional military strength of the EC members is quite a bit larger than that of the United States in Europe.[13]

To establish a more balanced relationship will undoubtedly be difficult for the Europeans, but probably even more so for the Americans. The United States has never really had a balanced relationship with Europe. Before the Second World War, isolationism meant military-political isolation primarily toward Europe. After the war the United States was so strong and the European invitations so unambiguous that there was little danger of America's interests being compromised and its values corrupted. Instead, the United States was free to spread its influence over Western Europe. Now, for the first time, there will have to be much more give and take on both sides.

In America, to illustrate a cultural difference, you are always supposed to end on an optimistic note. Let me therefore conclude that although the United States has undoubtedly been suffering a relative decline, and will most likely continue to do so in certain important respects, at the moment no country is really able to

13   I have analyzed the American-European relationship in the Reagan era in "The United States and Western Europe under Ronald Reagan," in *Reagan and the World*, ed. David E. Kyvig (New York, 1990), 39–66.

challenge the United States for the Number One position as such. Even Japan and Europe will not seriously threaten this position, at least not in the foreseeable future. Japan has only a few of the dimensions of a superpower. Western Europe still lacks a great deal of the political organization and also some of the military strength necessary to become a superpower. Thus, as even Paul Kennedy admits, "the United States is at present still in a class of its own economically and perhaps even militarily."[14] Whether the United States will always remain Number One, and thus reverse the cycles of all previous supreme powers, is really for each and every one of the world's citizens to decide, not for historians, who can only claim special competence in making predictions about the past, not the future.

14   Paul Kennedy, *The Rise and Fall of the Great Powers. Economic Change and Military Conflict from 1500 to 2000* (New York, 1987), 514.

18

The Fading of the Cold War— and the Demystification of Twentieth-Century Issues

GAR ALPEROVITZ AND KAI BIRD

By now it is a commonplace that the "Cold War" is over, or at least radically altered. General Colin Powell, chairman of the Joint Chiefs of Staff, recently put it bluntly: "We have seen our implacable enemy of 40 years vaporize before our eyes."[1] The implications of the shattering events in the Soviet Union, however, are regularly misconstrued. The end of the Cold War is neither the great triumph that the Bush administration trumpets ("we have won") nor the minor event that some on the Left suggest ("the old pattern of intervention will continue unchanged"). It is nevertheless extraordinarily important in three quite specific senses.

First, the collapse of the Soviet-American military stand-off clearly represents a significant, though still limited, coming to terms with the thermonuclear threat. The idea that nuclear weapons are useful (and moral) elements in a nation's international strategy, an idea born at Hiroshima, continues to persist, but there is a reasonable chance—give or take a decade, give or take a major scare— of moving toward a new wisdom that will relegate such weapons to something like the restricted status of poison gas. They exist, but they are less and less likely to be used, less and less "thinkable."

This is not the same, of course, as establishing a "new world order." As Paul Kennedy has suggested in *The Rise and Fall of the Great Powers,* we may simply see the emergence of a five-way balance-of-power system rotating around the United States, Eu-

---

1 Testimony before the Senate Armed Services Committee, 27 September 1991, as reported by R. Jeffrey Smith, "Initiative Affects Least Useful Weapons," *Washington Post,* 28 September 1991.

rope, Japan, China, and what remains of the Soviet Union.[2] If so, we will have to cope with all of the inherent instabilities that such systems entail. Or, as Henry Kissinger has argued from time to time, we may witness the development of a regional spheres-of-influence system.[3] The proposal for a U.S. free-trade zone with Canada and Mexico points in this direction, as do Japan's efforts to build a new "Co-Prosperity Sphere" throughout the Pacific. The United Nations (with at some point an expanded Security Council including Japan and Germany) would then likely serve as a newly empowered cover for the domination of smaller states by larger ones. We are a long way from establishing a more equitable system based on the rule of law and greater international sharing.

Second, the end of the Cold War may radically reduce, if not eliminate, the kind of large, limited wars of intervention that the United States fought in Korea and Vietnam. Although covert wars, so-called surgical strikes (Grenada, Panama), and air power engagements like the one in the Persian Gulf are likely to continue, it is difficult to rationalize major troop commitments if Third World wars are no longer defined as Cold War proxy contests.

Third—and perhaps ultimately most important—the shift in the nuclear threat and the reduced likelihood of large limited wars may mean that the Cold War will no longer dominate domestic political discourse in the United States. If this is the case—if the Cold War no longer overhangs the American economy and American politics—fundamental issues that have been obscured for more than four decades are likely to resurface. From the 1940s onward, the Cold War played an important role in at least three fundamental areas: It provided the rationale for major, economy-stimulating arms spending, thereby concealing deeper problems in the economic system; it repeatedly occupied center stage in America's media-dominated politics, thereby preempting other important domestic political debates; and it distorted our understanding of the real choices available to developing Third World countries. If the Cold War fades, the shroud of misconceptions, political hys-

---

2   Paul Kennedy, *The Rise and Fall of the Great Powers: Economic Change and Military Conflict from 1500 to 2000* (New York, 1987), 536–40.
3   Henry Kissinger, "What Kind of New World Order?" *Washington Post*, 3 December 1991.

teria, and war fears that has prevented serious discussion of these critical issues is likely to be slowly lifted.

From World War II until very recent times, the United States has not had to wrestle with many crucial problems of overall economic management because of the Cold War. Though the stimulative economic effects of military spending can easily be exaggerated, it is nonetheless true that after World War II the U.S. economy was boosted by successive waves of military spending made possible by the Cold War. Initially, such spending jumped from roughly 4 percent of GNP in the period 1946–1948 to a Korean War peak of 13–14 percent of GNP. In the post-Korea environment of international tension, the United States maintained military expenditures at roughly 9–10 percent of GNP for two decades. In the Kennedy era, the missile gap and McNamara's flexible response provided justifications for expenditures above those of the Eisenhower administration. Thereafter, the Vietnam War offered a new rationale for large military budgets.

After Vietnam, the fading likelihood of large limited wars of intervention laid the groundwork for a slow rollback of military spending as a major economic stimulus. The Pentagon budget dropped to an average of 6 percent of GNP during the 1970s and 1980s, including the Reagan buildup. Even before the collapse of the Soviet Union—and not allowing for further, likely cuts—military spending was projected to decline to under 4 percent of GNP by 1996. Given the changes in the former Soviet Union, these percentages are likely to fall even further.

Though many issues are involved (including renewed global economic competition), there is a rough relationship between reduced military spending and such large macroeconomic problems as declining productivity and rising unemployment. The average level of unemployment, for instance, has been growing steadily over time, from 4.5 percent in the 1950s, to 4.8 percent in the 1960s, to 6.2 percent in the 1970s, to 7.8 percent in the 1980s. The Reagan administration was temporarily able to put off the full economic impact of declining military spending in three ways: First, it simply raised such spending (thereby stabilizing the average for the 1980s). Second, it effectively devalued the dollar in an attempt to stimulate exports. Third, it used tax cuts and radical Keynesian deficits to stimulate the economy (in the process generating a trillion dollars of public debt).

All of these major economic cards have now been played; politically, none is available in significant scale to the Bush administration. Although further, and perhaps continued, easing by the Federal Reserve Board is possible, the remaining policy option of low interest rates is very weak medicine for a very sick economy. The most likely result, as military spending declines, is continued stagnation and decay of the U.S. economy—*with no major policy response* by a political system that is profoundly stalemated in its approach to economic problems.

It is often forgotten that unlike Germany or Japan, the United States in the twentieth century has never demonstrated a capacity to resolve major economic problems in a peacetime context. Defense spending in World War I, World War II, and the Korean War, not to mention Vietnam and the Cold War in general, stabilized the U.S. economy at crucial moments in each of the first three quarters of the century. Many of the problems of the current final quarter simply reflect the decline of such spending. Indeed, save for a brief period in the 1920s, which saw the genesis of problems that resulted in the Great Depression, the U.S. economy has not prospered for an extended period during this century except in time of war, postwar boom, or Cold War.[4]

Perhaps equally significant is that political and media attention devoted to Cold War issues, and especially to Korea and Vietnam, relegated to a secondary role a wide range of domestic issues. At the same time, the politics of anticommunism at home and abroad contributed to the destruction of the Left (such as it was) in the United States, first through the Truman administration's loyalty and security programs, then through the red-baiting of Henry Wallace in the 1948 campaign, and most dramatically through the McCarthyism of the 1950s, which built upon both. The decline of the Left in turn made it easier for the media to ignore domestic problems. Above all, a series of dramatic Cold War crises stretching over forty years tended to push economic and social issues off the front page. This was the case with the Berlin airlift of 1948—

4   For a convenient review see Richard B. Du Boff, *Accumulation and Power: An Economic History of the United States* (Armonk, 1989).

49; with the Korean War that began in 1950; with the so-called bomber and missile gaps later in the decade; with the Berlin and Cuban crises between 1959 and 1962; and with the large number of U.S. interventions in the Third World, culminating in the Vietnam War—not to mention the events of the 1970s and 1980s.

What course might domestic politics be expected to take once U.S. media and culture are no longer dominated by the repeated spectacle and drama of such Cold War events? Some progressives expect to see a resurgence of a significant progressive politics. What is more likely, however, is that the weakness of the American economy and the stalemated policy process, so far masked by the warfare state, will now be revealed and current problems will deepen. The United States already has the highest child poverty rate of eight recently studied Western democracies—two to three times higher than the other nations reviewed. During the 1980s, tax and transfer policies ended the poverty of more than 60 percent of the poor in the Netherlands, 46 percent in the United Kingdom, and nearly 44 percent in Sweden. In the United States, by contrast, tax and welfare transfers during the 1980s lifted virtually no households out of poverty.[5] Indeed, not only has U.S. economic policy been hobbled but there is also very little evidence that state action has moved the American system toward greater economic equality in any noncrisis period of the twentieth century. Again, only in time of war, postwar boom, or full economic collapse has there been any sustained positive improvement in the distribution of income, and such improvement has repeatedly faded when such periods have ended.[6]

A recent Congressional Budget Office study showed that at the end of the last decade the top 5 percent of American families received almost as much income as the entire bottom 60 percent of American society put together—roughly 150 million people. The top one fifth of American society now receives approximately 50

---

5 For comparative international studies see Timothy Smeeding, Barbara Boyle Torrey, and Martin Rein, "Patterns of Income and Poverty: The Economic Status of Children and the Elderly in Eight Countries," in *The Vulnerable*, ed. John L. Palmer, Timothy Smeeding, and Barbara Boyle Torrey (Washington, 1988). See also Katherine McFate, *Poverty, Inequality and the Crisis of Social Policy* (Washington, 1991).

6 For a more extended discussion see Gar Alperovitz, "Building a Living Democracy," *Sojourners* (July 1990).

percent of all income (including interest, rent, and dividends). Just about the same number of human beings (fifty million) among the bottom one fifth make do on less than 3.5 percent of such income. Income is, in fact, more unevenly divided today than at any time since the end of World War II. In 1989 the share of national income going to the wealthiest quintile of families was larger than in any other year since the Census Bureau began collecting such data in 1947. The share going to the bottom fifth was as low or lower than in any year since 1954.

The current trend is also clear. Average after-tax income of the richest 1 percent of American households rose 75 percent from 1980 to 1990. Such income increased from $313,206 in 1980 to $548,970 in 1990. At the same time, young male high school graduates actually earned less per week in 1987 than their counterparts did twenty-four years earlier in 1963.[7]

In addition to obscuring the extraordinary domestic economic and political problems in this country, the Cold War distorted the debate over political-economic development in the Third World. For decades now, any form of noncapitalist development has been officially condemned in Washington. If international rivalries decline—and the fog of competing Cold War ideologies lifts—it may also be possible slowly to begin to reassess the real problems and options facing many Third World nations. And these problems are enormous.

Two thirds of developing countries suffered a decline in per capita income from 1980 to 1989.[8] The World Bank estimates that as many as 950 million of the world's 5.2 billion people are "chronically malnourished"—more than twice as many as a decade ago. In Africa, per capita food production has declined every year for the past thirty years. Although India is now a food exporter, throughout widespread rural areas, per capita caloric intake has declined since 1964. In Bolivia, El Salvador, the Ivory Coast, the

---

7 For a convenient review of income distribution and related data see Isaac Shapiro and Robert Greenstein, *Selective Prosperity: Increasing Income Disparities since 1977* (Washington, 1991). See also Lawrence Mishel and David M. Frankel, *The State of Working America* (Armonk, 1991).
8 *World Economic Survey 1990* (New York, 1990), 157.

Sudan, Zambia, Peru, and a half dozen other developing countries, GDP has plummeted by one third during the past decade.

Although the United States urges free-market policies as a general answer to all development problems, such an approach faces increasing difficulties in many nations. A study for the United Nations Children's Fund, for instance, found that during the 1980s, average incomes in most of Latin America fell by 10 percent—and by over 20 percent in Sub-Saharan Africa. In many urban areas, real minimum wages declined by as much as 50 percent.

Even where free market strategies appear to have had some success, such as Chile in some recent years, the social and environmental costs have been staggering. Nearly half of all households live below the poverty line, double the percentage in the decade before General Augusto Pinochet came to power. The poorest 40 percent make do today with half of what they had in 1970, while the richest 10 percent have captured 47 percent of national income. Unregulated exploitation of timber and fishing resources threatens to destroy the country's ecosystem. Most revealing is that GNP per capita in 1989 was 6 percent less than in 1972.[9]

The former Soviet Union and Eastern Europe are also beginning to learn just how difficult the free-market "path" is—and it is by no means obvious that the initial direction urged in former "bloc" nations will continue. Even the celebrated export-led economies of newly industrialized countries in East Asia are beginning to run aground on the shoals of environmental damage. In addition, violent labor disputes have exploded as free-market "structural adjustment" policies have been accompanied by increasing social pain.

The Cold War has also distorted critical understanding of traditional socialism. Although available statistics leave much to be desired, many economists judge, for instance, that despite enormous waste, economic growth in the Soviet bloc between 1950 and the mid-1980s was better on average than that of the United States.[10] Economic development in China has also been impres-

9 Joseph Collins, *Draft Report on Visit to Chile* (San Francisco, 1990). See also "Chileans Pay Dearly for Economic Growth," *New York Times*, 10 November 1991.
10 See Central Intelligence Agency, *Handbook of Economic Statistics, 1985: A Reference Aid*, CPAS 85-10001 (Directorate of Intelligence, September 1985), 39; Joint Eco-

sive, with annual GDP growth rates in the 8 percent range in many years. The related assumption that all forms of public enterprise and economic planning are inefficient begs additional questions. The Soviet space program, to give one example, looked very impressive compared to NASA. And in the West, there are numerous public industries, from energy utilities to European airlines and auto producers, that are just as efficient as similar private firms.

In 1989, the U.N. Economic Commission for Africa concluded that those countries in Africa that had pursued aggressively free-market structural adjustment policies had lower rates of growth than countries that continued to rely on the public sector and government subsidies for basic human needs.[11] The current rush to privatize public enterprises will no doubt eliminate many uneconomic plants and introduce greater efficiency in some companies. But environmental factors and labor conditions may easily force the pendulum to swing back as consumers demand better regulation of the marketplace.

The public sector's record might have been even better had the Cold War not served to cripple several experiments in public sector development. With the United States financing counterrevolutionaries and intervening directly in the name of Soviet-American rivalries, the difficulties facing any left-leaning economic regime were extraordinary. Fear of U.S. intervention also gave ample reason for would-be dictators to rationalize what some may have wanted to do anyway.

None of the above is intended to excuse the brutal authoritarianism of Communist systems or the irrationalities of the dreary, state-socialist command economies; nor is it to contend against the utility of market mechanisms in future development alternatives. But most conventional accounts have so lost perspective that we need to jolt ourselves out of media-induced nodding if we are

nomic Committee, *USSR: Measures of Economic Growth and Development, 1950–1980,* 97th Cong., 2d sess., 1982, 64–67; and U.S. Department of Commerce, Bureau of the Census, *Statistical Abstract of the United States, 1985,* 105th ed. (Washington, 1984), 434. See also UNCTAD, *Handbook of International Trade and Development Statistics* (New York, 1984), 386.
11 Nancy E. Wright, "Disastrous Decade: Africa's Experience with Structural Adjustment," *Multinational Monitor,* April 1990.

to make rational judgments about the real world options that the Third World faces.

The United States could contribute to the exploration of such options if it were simply to back away from more extreme forms of intervention. What might have happened had the United States been more open to the moderate regime of Mohammed Mosaddeq in Iran in the early 1950s? What might the Allende government in Chile have accomplished had it not been overthrown in part because of U.S. Cold War fears? What of the Guatemalan possibility of a social democratic Jacobo Arbenz? The fading of the Cold War might also slowly bring about a significant reduction in the huge sums that the United States has contributed to building an institutional base for military groups in many Third World nations. The weakening of such groups, in turn, might ultimately both shift resources to productive uses and open new political possibilities for reform. (The emerging U.S. posture in El Salvador appears to be a small step in this less extreme direction.)

If U.S. policy were less straight-jacketed by Cold War assumptions, new experimental "mixes" of policies might also be possible. As Robin Broad, John Cavanagh, and Walden Bello have recently emphasized, decentralized, local, cooperative forms of economic activity, focused on such "micro" institutions as transportation collectives, farmer co-ops, and tiny business credit committees, are presently being explored in tandem with public sector enterprises in many parts of the Third World.[12]

Even allowing for a slow demystification of development problems, however, the long record of twentieth-century interventionism provides little reason to be sanguine about an abrupt shift in U.S. manipulation of the Third World. And what is not likely is that significant Western resources will be readily forthcoming, as urged by the Brandt Commission and others.

If such forecasts are even partly correct, one of the most important consequences of the fading of the Cold War could be a fun-

---

12 Various data on development in the above is drawn from Robin Broad, John Cavanagh, and Walden Bello, "Development: The Market is Not Enough," *Foreign Policy* 81 (Winter 1990–91); Graham Hancock, *Lords of Poverty* (New York 1989), 191–93; and Kennedy, *Rise and Fall of the Great Powers*, 420.

damental alteration of basic "system" stereotypes. We have been forced to come to terms with the incapacity of the traditional Socialist system to resolve important political-economic problems. But if the emerging economic trends and social decay in the United States are accurate indicators, we may also be forced to confront the profound weaknesses of the American political-economic system as well. In connection with Third World development, *none* of the traditional models may make sense.

In sum, we may be forced to rethink many of the basic assumptions that have set the terms of reference for much debate, East and West, for most of the twentieth century. Put another way, the fading of the Cold War could become the first stage in a delegitimization process at home and abroad—thereby laying the groundwork for a much more open dialogue about the systemic requirements of a successful domestic and international order in the new century ahead.

19

The U.S. Government, a Legacy of the Cold War

ERNEST R. MAY

In Westminster, the houses of Parliament and Buckingham Palace—both structures of the Victorian era—and the Georgian and Regency offices along Whitehall are buildings for a seat of empire, not for the capital of a middle-ranking member of the European Community. The drab, modest government office blocks of Tokyo and Bonn seem equally ill-suited, given that they serve the second and third ranking powers of the economic world. None of these capitals vies with Vienna, where the magnificent Hofburg is the seat of government for a republic smaller than Indiana, but in all of them form and function seem mismatched.

Before long, if not already, Washington, DC, may also seem a capital where form and function are not in kilter. A tour of today's action centers starts at the White House. One sees the West Wing and the Old Executive Office Building next door, the quarters of the president's National Security Council (NSC). The tour goes on to the squat, plain New State Department building on Twenty-first Street, where the building directory lists numerous bureaus and subbureaus for politico-military affairs. It also lists the autonomous Arms Control and Disarmament Agency.

Across the Potomac, a visitor sees the Pentagon. With a daytime population of twenty-five thousand, it is the crest of a mountainous defense establishment, which employs almost two thirds of the nearly five million persons who work for the U.S. government. Farther out in Virginia, at Langley, the Central Intelligence Agency (CIA) has more office acreage than the Pentagon. At Fort Meade in Maryland sits the even larger, more mysterious, and more expensive National Security Agency, engaged in encrypting and de-crypting signals.

If the trip from Langley to Fort Meade follows a straight line, the guide will point to the Department of Energy, noting that it grows out of the former Atomic Energy Commission and is pri-marily manager of the nation's nuclear weapons programs. If the tour is roundabout, following the Beltway, the tourist sees build-ing after building housing contractors who do research primarily for the military establishment.

On Capitol Hill, many of the recognizable faces are members and staffers attached to the committees that oversee the diplo-matic, military, and intelligence establishments or the correspond-ing Appropriations subcommittees. In warrens housing the Wash-ington bureaus of the news media, the recognizable stars are similarly men and women whose beats include national security affairs.

One of those sage, naïve Orientals favored by the philosophes could return from a visit to Washington, writing, "Yes, a city. But, at heart, a military headquarters, like the Rome of the Flavians or the Berlin of the Hohenzollerns." Washington is a headquarters for what was a global diplomatic-military contest with a hostile, secretive, heavily armed rival superpower. Though the contest seems to be over, and no new military rival is evident, the capital is likely to remain as it is for a long time to come. The American national government may prove one of the longer-lasting artifacts of the Cold War.

Sixty years ago, the American government had a very different shape. As of the mid-1930s, it seemed designed primarily to pro-vide modest help to people within the continental limits—chiefly business managers and farm owners but also, in some degree, con-sumers, nature lovers, and the elderly. The principal foreign affairs agencies—the State, War, and Navy departments—were cooped up in what is now the Old Executive Office Building. The Treasury Department, on the other side of the White House, had almost equivalent space. The other grand structures of the city were the neoclassical piles along Fourteenth Street and Constitution Ave-nue that housed the Departments of Commerce, Labor, Agricul-ture, and Justice.

The Cincinnatian capital of the 1930s could not have survived

World War II. Most Americans took from that war the lesson that the United States should not again be isolationist. Hence, the postwar State Department was bound to be a busier organization. Many Americans also took from the war the lesson that military unpreparedness was dangerous. Hence, there was likely to be a larger military establishment, differently organized. Memories of Pearl Harbor also made likely more attention to secret intelligence. And there had to be new machinery to govern nuclear weapons and nuclear energy. Supposed lessons of the 1930s did not, however, dictate the exact character of a postwar government. They certainly did not dictate that it become essentially a military headquarters.

As of 1945, at least three futures seemed almost equally plausible. The government could have become more international in orientation but still been primarily a manager of internal affairs. The State Department and the military establishment would have been larger. The most prominent and powerful agencies would nevertheless have been, as in the 1930s, the Departments of the Treasury, Agriculture, Labor, the Interior, and Commerce. Domestic concerns would have dominated the executive and legislative agenda and media reportage with Washington datelines.

A second possibility was a government organized to manage chiefly international economic affairs. The State or Treasury Department would have gained a paramount role. In other departments and agencies, international affairs branches would have dominated exclusively domestic branches. Questions concerning international trade and investment, exchange rates, and political conditions affecting economic conditions would have led the agenda for Congress and the news media.

A postwar government looking like the wartime government, with the military establishment transcendent and military-security concerns dominant, was only a third possibility.

During the first eighteen months after World War II, it became increasingly unlikely that the government would regain a primarily domestic focus. The 1946 congressional elections effected a near revolution. Republican minorities of 38 to 56 and 190 to 242 in the Senate and House turned into Republican *majorities* of 51 to 45 and 245 to 188. This augured a period of partisan posturing at both ends of Pennsylvania Avenue. At least for a time, those big neoclassical rectangles on Fourteenth Street were sure to be hives in which little happened.

In the early postwar years, however, the new American government seemed almost equally unlikely to emphasize military security. From 1945 to 1947, the services wrangled about unification. Their squabbles were mean, often petty, and always public. The compromise National Security Act of 1947 settled little. Open antagonism continued. Meanwhile, President Truman made it plain that he meant, if possible, to prune military spending back toward levels of about 1938.[1]

Part of the 1947 compromise had involved establishment of the NSC. Truman had seen this council—accurately—as a device with two purposes. One was to give the military services a voice in diplomacy, something that they had sought since before World War I. The second was to surround the amateur, "political" president with professional, "nonpolitical" advisers. Truman initially cottoned to neither purpose. He convened the council sparingly and gave it minimal staff. He delegated foreign affairs to his successive secretaries of state.

As a further element in the 1947 compromise, Truman had accepted the appointment of a secretary of defense to preside over the service secretaries. As first holder of that office he chose the most adroit opponent of service unification, former Secretary of the Navy James V. Forrestal. When elected president in his own right in 1948, Truman fired Forrestal and put in his place an ambitious politician, Louis Johnson, who took it as his mandate to keep the military out of foreign policy.[2]

For the first five years after World War II, the new American government looked as if it would concentrate on the international economy. The State Department had a much stronger position than prior to the war. This became even more the case after the elections of 1946, for Republican leaders in the Senate were prepared

---

1 I have recently described this in some detail in "Cold War and Defense," in *The Cold War and Defense*, ed. Keith Nelson and Ronald G. Haycock (New York, 1990), 7–73.

2 Anna K. Nelson, "President Truman and the Evolution of the National Security Council," *Journal of American History* 72 (September 1985): 360–78. John Prados, *Keepers of the Keys: A History of the National Security Council from Truman to Bush* (New York, 1991), 29–39, is the most recent survey.

to work with Truman's new secretary of state, General George C. Marshall, so that foreign relations would not be paralyzed by the partisan split between the presidency and Congress; and Marshall and Republican congressional leaders agreed that priority should go to European economic recovery. Not until 1949 did the government become one organized primarily to cope with supposed military threats.[3] The most important factors accounting for this shift were: (1) evidence of a Soviet military buildup; (2) the U.S. 1948 election; (3) "McCarthyism"; (4) the Truman-MacArthur confrontation; and, above all, (5) nuclear weapons.

Evidence of a big Soviet military buildup steadily accumulated after 1945. By 1950 the best intelligence possessed by the U.S. government indicated that the Soviets had 175 divisions, very large and rapidly improving tactical air forces, several hundred bombers on the model of the U.S. B-29, able to fly missions against the British Isles or any part of the Mediterranean, and over three hundred submarines, many of which were either former German craft or copies, capable of extended underwater operation in the Atlantic.

Some of the estimates of Soviet military forces seemed later to have been too high. Scholars have charged that the American military deliberately exaggerated Soviet capabilities so as to improve chances of getting money. These charges do not withstand scrutiny. The estimates faithfully reflected the evidence sent to Washington from the field. What seems most likely is that the Soviets planted some of this evidence, hoping thereby to deter or intimidate Western nations.[4]

The evidence frightened Europeans. They communicated their alarm to Americans interested in Europe. Here, the U.S. 1948 elec-

---

3 Michael J. Hogan, *The Marshall Plan. America, Britain, and the Reconstruction of Western Europe, 1947–1952* (New York, 1987), 380–427; and Robert J. Pollard, "The National Security State Reconsidered: Truman and Economic Containment, 1945–1950," in *The Truman Presidency*, ed. Michael J. Lacey (New York, 1989), 205–34, develop this point in detail.

4 Matthew Evangelista, "Stalin's Postwar Army Reappraised," *International Security* 7 (Winter 1982–83): 110–38, makes the case for deliberate overstatement. A detailed and careful reconstruction of field intelligence for the period is being prepared by Philip Karber of the BDM Corporation. Karber's data will be released, probably during 1992, through the multinational Nuclear History Program based in the United States at the Center for International Security Studies of the School of Public Affairs of the University of Maryland.

tion played its part, for Europeans and their American friends had expected a Republican victory and hence a president and Congress who would cooperate in concentrating on the international economy. Instead, they saw an ebullient Truman talking of concentrating on a domestic "Fair Deal." They also saw resentful Republicans sounding increasingly like isolationists or "Asia-firsters." Pointing to the evidence of growing Soviet military might, Europeans and their American friends warned loudly that Europe might not achieve economic recovery unless the United States showed more capability and willingness to prevent the Red Army from moving west.

The logic was best worked out in NSC-68, the now famous twenty-six-thousand-word paper composed by Paul H. Nitze as chief of the Policy Planning Staff for Marshall's successor, Dean Acheson. NSC-68 argued that by the mid-1950s the United States "must have substantially increased general air, ground, and sea strength, atomic capabilities, and air and civilian defenses to deter war and to provide reasonable assurance, in the event of war, that it could survive the initial blow and go on to the eventual attainment of its objectives."[5]

The Korean conflict turned most doubters into believers. Truman not only ordered the rescue of South Korea but also directed that NSC-68 be fulfilled to the letter. Congressional leaders, Republican as well as Democratic, went along with Truman's recommendations for massively increasing the permanent military establishment and gearing the United States for an indefinite "period of acute danger."[6]

"McCarthyism" then accelerated these changes and made them harder to reverse. Many prominent figures who had earlier shown sympathy or even tolerance for Communists suffered harassment, often with front-page publicity. This made it difficult for anyone in public life to question the need for a virtual state of war. To do so involved the risk of being labeled "soft" or even "pink."

The Truman-MacArthur confrontation had the effect of giving the professional military great domestic political influence. Tru-

5 NSC-68, 14 April 1950, U.S. Department of State, *Foreign Relations of the United States, 1950* (Washington, 1977), 1:237–92 (hereafter *FRUS,* with year and volume).
6 NSC-114/1, 8 August 1951, *FRUS, 1951* (Washington, 1979), 1:127–57.

man survived—and MacArthur faded away—because a parade of other military men backed him. These included Marshall, now secretary of defense; every one of the Joint Chiefs; Eisenhower, again in uniform as supreme commander for NATO; and a number of others. Though many contemporaries celebrated the outcome as a victory for civilian control, the reality was that Congress and the public had followed one set of military leaders instead of another.

In combination with "McCarthyism," the MacArthur affair left deep marks on the men who were to lead America from the 1950s to the 1970s. Though Eisenhower had the advantage of being himself a professional soldier, even he could not dictate to the military as presidents traditionally had, and as Truman had done before 1950. Especially in the period of the "missile gap" debate, Eisenhower had to bend to the military and its supporters in Congress and the country. John F. Kennedy, Lyndon B. Johnson, and Richard M. Nixon had all been on Capitol Hill during the MacArthur hearings. Each showed himself loath, as president, to have a confrontation with any service chief. From 1951 until at least the aftermath of Watergate, presidents exercised control over the professional military principally by manipulation and artifice. The potential political power of the professional military contributed to giving military force its centrality in the evolving national government.

It is hard to imagine this having happened—or NSC-68 having been implemented or McCarthyism having run rampant—absent nuclear weapons. Indeed, it is hard to imagine these developments absent the history of nuclear weapons specific to the period 1945–1955. The bombs dropped on Hiroshima and Nagasaki had inspired horrified musings, the most notable of which were Bernard Brodie's in *The Absolute Weapon*. As Paul Boyer and Spencer Weart have shown, the first atomic bombs also seized the public imagination. Ancient myths about the perils of tampering with nature coiled themselves around the image of the mushroom cloud.[7]

---

7 Paul Boyer, *By the Bomb's Early Light: American Thought and Culture at the Dawn of the Atomic Age* (New York, 1985); Spencer Weart, *Nuclear Fear: A History of Images* (Cambridge, MA, 1988). Analyses of the implications of nuclear weaponry, including Brodie's, are well summarized in Lawrence Freedman, *The Evolution of Nuclear Strategy* (New York, 1983); and Fred Kaplan, *The Wizards of Armageddon* (New York, 1983).

The practical people who managed the American government were not as much affected. Manhattan Project insiders knew how hard it was to handcraft a bomb. Though the actual meagerness of the stockpile was kept secret, anyone with a modest grasp of the relevant physics and engineering could estimate that the potential number of bombs was small. From publicity about the Bikini tests of 1946, the world learned that these bombs were exceedingly hard to target. One had missed an island by miles! Senior military officers privy to the test results became aware of the bomb's wretched ballistic characteristics. At the time when the American government seemed to be evolving toward a focus on international economic affairs, officials knew that a future war might involve other Hiroshimas and Nagasakis, but few of them envisioned nuclear war.

In 1948 this began to change. Premium prices had produced new finds of uranium. A new series of tests at Eniwetok demonstrated the feasibility of massproducing nuclear weapons, greatly widening the range of yields, and so reducing yield-weight ratios that a bomb twenty-five times more powerful than the Hiroshima bomb could be put in the casing of a World War II "blockbuster." These tests showed the technical feasibility of actual nuclear war.[8]

Coincidentally, both diplomats and military leaders began to think of nuclear weapons as potential solutions to problems otherwise seemingly insoluble. During the Berlin crisis of 1948, Truman, Marshall, and their advisers were acutely conscious of how little the West could do if the Soviets seized Berlin or otherwise used their military forces. One expedient had been a move of B-29s intended as a signal that the United States might respond with atomic bombs. Though the press noticed and reported that the B-29s were not equipped to deliver atomic bombs, Marshall and his aides calculated that the signal might nevertheless be effective. From then on, the trend within the State Department was toward dependence on the nuclear threat as the deterrent to any Soviet exploitation of superior conventional military power.[9]

---

8 The fundamental study is David Alan Rosenberg, "The Origins of Overkill: Nuclear Weapons and American Strategy, 1945–60," *International Security* 7 (Spring 1983): 3–71.
9 Gregg Herken, *The Winning Weapon: The Atomic Bomb in the Cold War* (New York, 1981), 256–80.

In the Pentagon, the crucial problem was Truman's budget ceiling. By exploiting fear of nuclear war, the new air force found a way of inducing Congress to give it more money. The other services soon followed suit, with the navy advertising the potential for carrier-borne nuclear attack and the army packaging programs under the label "continental defense."

The Soviet nuclear test of 1949 made the possibility of actual nuclear war seem much more real. It was a key argument of NSC-68 that the U.S. nuclear stockpile was a wasting asset.[10] By the mid-1950s, NSC-68 contended, the Soviets would have neutralized the U.S. nuclear advantage. It was for this reason that the United States would by then need large, ready conventional forces. But, on a premise that the advantage might be continued, Truman meanwhile approved development of a hydrogen bomb and a large expansion in nuclear weapons production capacity. Once the reactors and gaseous diffusion plants authorized in the period 1949–1951 came on line, the "overkill" of the 1960s became something that was going to materialize unless halted by a positive decision to curtail weapons output.

The Soviet bomb and related developments almost certainly contributed to the surge of "McCarthyism." Betrayal of atomic secrets was a constant theme in congressional witch hunts. The extent of fear was evident in the Oppenheimer affair. The MacArthur controversy is a different matter, for it is not clear that the existence of nuclear weapons had more than marginal bearing on the conflict between the president and the general. Without what was happening in the nuclear realm, however, it is plausible that the effects of the controversy would have worn off much more quickly.

The transformation in the American government occurred rapidly. In Fiscal 1950 (July 1949 to June 1950), the military budget represented less than one third of government expenditures and less than 5 percent of GNP, with much of that due to obligations left over from World War II. By Fiscal 1953, the military accounted for more than 60 percent of government outlays and more than 12 percent of GNP. Because military spending did not continue to rise at the same relative rate, the subsequent trend was

---

10   See Marc Trachtenberg, *History and Strategy* (Princeton, 1991), 100–52.

downward. In absolute terms, however, the military establishment created in the early 1950s lived on. It was nearly always the dominant consumer of the federal government's discretionary funds. Defense and defense-related agencies accounted steadily for 60 to 70 percent of all federal personnel.

In the 1950s, the intelligence community mushroomed as essentially an auxiliary of the military establishment. The wartime Office of Strategic Services had been disbanded in 1945. Its remnants had been partially reaggregated after passage of the 1947 National Security Act. A small clandestine service had organized special operations such as transfers of funds to the Christian Democrats during the Italian elections of 1948 and transfers of weapons to Tito after the Yugoslav break with the Soviet Union. After 1950 the CIA multiplied in size. The same period saw even greater growth in the National Security Agency and, after the late 1950s, of the National Reconnaissance Office (NRO), both of which were directly managed by the military establishment.[11]

Though it is hard to distinguish among the missions of the intelligence community, it seems clear that a substantial part of its expansion was geared to measuring the Soviet nuclear threat, providing warning of nuclear attack, and locating targets for a U.S. nuclear offensive. The National Intelligence Estimate 11-8 series, estimating Soviet strategic forces, became the prime product of the community's analysts. NSA and the NRO invested unstintingly in capacity to monitor Soviet weapons complexes. And the first question asked of any defector by the CIA's case officers had to do with knowledge of Soviet war plans.[12]

Diplomacy shifted after 1950 to a heavy emphasis on issues of military security. For 1949, only 7 percent of the more than ten thousand pages of *Foreign Relations of the United States* are in sections with the words "security" or "military" in their titles. For

---

11 John Ranelagh, *The Agency: The Rise and Decline of the CIA* (New York, 1986); James Bamford, *Puzzle Palace: A Report on NSA, America's Most Secret Agency* (Boston, 1982); and William E. Burrows, *Deep Black: Space Espionage and National Security* (New York, 1986), are journalistic accounts that seem largely reliable. Jeffrey T. Richelson, *The U.S. Intelligence Community* (Cambridge, MA, 1985), is an encyclopedic compilation of every datum that has leaked into the press.
12 John Prados, *The Soviet Estimate: U.S. Intelligence Analysis and Soviet Strategic Forces* (Princeton, 1982); William Hood, *Mole* (New York, 1982), 135.

1951, with thirteen thousand pages, the corresponding figure is 28 percent. From 1950 onward, secretaries of state spent most of their time on questions having to do with troop levels in military alliances; levels of military aid to client states; arrangements concerning American military forces abroad; and, increasingly, arrangements governing nuclear weapons and/or nuclear arms control.

The White House organized itself to give precedence to politico-military issues. From being merely one part of the executive office of the president, not as large or as busy as the Council of Economic Advisors, the NSC became the government's main steering mechanism, almost as central as the Cabinet in Britain or the Politburo in the Leninist-Stalinist Soviet Union.

From Eisenhower's time to George Bush's, real decision making always involved the aides who managed the NSC for the president. Except for the president, the only other invariable presence was some person or persons from the Pentagon. In the Nixon and Carter years alike, presidential NSC assistants sometimes shouldered aside the secretary of state. Decision making sometimes involved the director of central intelligence, but this was more variable.

From 1950 to the 1990s, in any event, the serious hours of presidents were mostly occupied with issues brought to them through the NSC system. Although their calendars included many other activities, most were either ceremonial or routine. Even concerning the budget, the hardest issues frequently had to do with defense. As manifested in all of those buildings in and around the District of Columbia, the main business of the U.S. government had become the development, maintenance, positioning, exploitation, and regulation of military forces.

One need not look back on this history with regret. The militarization of the American government during the Cold War can be seen as a creative response to a challenge. Given Soviet militarism, insecurities in so many countries, and dizzying developments in nuclear and other military technologies, the world might have been much worse off if the United States had not organized itself to deal primarily with military issues. The fact that it was so organized may have made a contribution to international stability rivaling the contribution of nuclear weapons themselves. After all, how credible a buttress for NATO or the East Asian security system would have been a United States organized to give priority to domestic or to international economic affairs?[13]

The Cold War has nevertheless left the United States with a government that seems ill-suited for the future. The NSC is an odd mechanism for framing policy options regarding trade, resources, the environment, population, hunger, or disease. Even if the defense and intelligence establishments contract and undergo shuddering reorganization, they will still be equipped primarily for military or quasi-military missions.

It will be difficult, to say no more, to design new institutions for the new era. At the beginning of the Cold War, the United States had so little machinery for dealing with international affairs that it could build anew. Many men and women were willing to work for low pay with little or no recognition in the interest of national security. There is now no comparable void in Washington. There probably is no comparable pool of available talent.

Nor is it easy to imagine a resurgence of the departments and agencies that manage domestic affairs. The Departments of Agriculture, Commerce, the Interior, and Labor are largely moribund. Except for the Department of Energy, which is not much more than a reclothed Atomic Energy Commission, the other domestic departments are upgraded spinoffs from New Deal agencies. When reporters for the *National Journal* looked into the Veterans Administration just before it became the Department of Veterans Affairs, they were reminded of the film *Journey to the Center of the Earth*. They described it as "entirely self-contained, complete with dinosaurs and prehistoric men."[14] The open question is whether, before long, all of Washington will seem such a scene.

---

13 John Lewis Gaddis, *The Long Peace: Inquiries into the History of the Cold War* (New York, 1987), develops in detail the argument for the stabilizing influence of nuclear weapons. John E. Mueller, *Retreat from Doomsday: The Obsolescence of Major War* (New York, 1989), makes the best case to the contrary.
14 *National Journal* 20 (12 March 1988): 671.

20

Foreign Policy, Partisan Politics, and the End of the Cold War

MICHAEL J. HOGAN

Does the end of the Cold War mean the end of the Cold War consensus? Since 1950, at the latest, the nation's foreign policy has taken shape within the framework of a basic political consensus. There were notable instances of dissent, to be sure, but the major political parties and their constituencies generally supported the policy of containment and the diplomatic and military initiatives it seemed to dictate. Will foreign policy become a matter of partisan conflict in the new era that is dawning? If so, what might be the sources of that conflict and how can it be contained? The answer to these and related questions must be speculative, of course, and must be informed by what we know about American history. With this in mind, let me begin by reviewing the historical record and then speculate about the likely influence of partisan politics on foreign policy in the time ahead.

If history is any guide, some such influence is inevitable. Since the founding of the Republic, foreign policy and partisan politics have been linked inextricably. The first political parties emerged in part because of partisan differences over the direction of American diplomacy. The War of 1812 brought these differences to a head, at one point threatening the very survival of the Union, and there were similar differences during the war with Mexico in 1848 and the Spanish-American War a half-century later. Woodrow Wilson's war to make the world safe for democracy also led to a bitter partisan battle over Senate ratification of the Versailles treaty. So great were the differences, so intense the animosity, that Wilson's strongest opponents were known as the "irreconcilables," the "bitter-enders," and the "battalion of death."[1]

As this overview suggests, partisan conflicts have usually been party conflicts. Jeffersonian Republicans and Hamiltonian Federalists battled for control of the nation's foreign policy from the 1790s through the War of 1812. By the time of the Civil War, party labels had changed. The Democratic party had emerged as the champion of territorial expansion; the Whigs and later the Republicans were more likely to see this course as an aid to slavery and to support commercial expansion instead. In the twentieth century the partisan debate over foreign policy became in large part a debate between internationalists and nationalists, with each group increasingly identified with a particular political party. During the struggle over the Treaty of Versailles, the Democrats under Wilson began to emerge as the champions of internationalism. Republicans were more likely to be ardent nationalists, basically unilateralists, whose views on foreign policy made them vulnerable to charges of isolationism. Although not always accurate in the case of particular politicians, these labels continued to cling to both political parties over the next three decades.

Some of Wilson's Republican critics reprised their roles in the 1930s, forming an isolationist vanguard in opposition to any attempt by the Roosevelt administration to embroil the United States in another world war. Similar critics took much the same position in the early Cold War. By that time the Republican party had split into nationalist and internationalist factions. It was the nationalist wing, led by former President Herbert Hoover and Ohio Senator Robert A. Taft, that raised the most serious reservations against the North Atlantic Treaty and other collective security arrangements; against military conscription, universal military training, burgeoning defense budgets, and the rising influence of the military establishment; against the British loan, the Marshall Plan, and the liberal design for a multilateral system of world trade. Defeat did not entirely silence this wing of the Republican party, although

---

1 Alexander DeConde, *A History of American Foreign Policy*, 2d ed. (New York, 1971), 479; Selig Adler, *The Isolationist Impulse: Its Twentieth-Century Reaction* (London and New York, 1957), 102–5.

its voice thereafter would be muffled within the Cold War consensus that stretched over the next forty years.

If the partisan battle over foreign policy has been drawn along party lines, other considerations also influenced the struggle and its outcome. This has been the case throughout American history. For example, historians have long been aware of a regional influence on foreign policy, dating back to the early years of the Republic. The split between the Jeffersonian Republicans and the Hamiltonian Federalists was in part a split between the south and the west, on the one hand, the northeast, on the other. In the era of Manifest Destiny, to cite another example, the debate over expansion became to a large extent a debate over slavery that followed sectional lines. The same point can be made about other debates in other times, including the struggle for the soul of American foreign policy on the eve of Pearl Harbor and in the early Cold War. In both cases, as historians have noted, internationalist sentiment was especially strong in the northeast, while nationalist or isolationist opinion was greatest in the conservative Republican strongholds of the midwest and west.

In addition to party and regional characteristics, the partisan struggle over foreign policy has long displayed an economic dimension. I am not speaking here in Marxist terms. While it would be a mistake to ignore social-class divisions entirely, the most interesting economic dimension historically has to do with function rather than class. The struggle between the Republicans and the Federalists in the early period was in part a struggle between the farmers and planters of the south and west and the commercial and mercantile interests of the northeast. The first group had a natural interest in territorial expansion across the continent and was largely hostile toward Great Britain; the second group gave highest priority to commercial expansion, especially within the framework of the British Empire, and was generally pro-British. In the era of Manifest Destiny, as suggested earlier, the issue of expansion increasingly pitted southern planters, on the one hand, against western farmers and northern merchants, on the other. The imperial debate at the turn of the century had an economic dimension as well, with export-driven agriculture and its allies in the business and banking communities taking a prominent place among those groups supporting the outward thrust of the American empire.

Historians disagree over the part played by functional economic considerations in the modern shift toward internationalism and over when that shift occurred. Those who still subscribe to an older, more conventional interpretation see the Cold War as the critical turning point on the road from isolationism to internationalism. They admit that Roosevelt had earlier brought the nation into World War II on the Allied side. But to their way of thinking the permanent transformation came in the postwar period, when the United States finally began to accept the peacetime political and military responsibilities it had shunned in the 1920s. If the shift toward internationalism came with the Cold War, its causes, according to these historians, were almost wholly external to American politics and the American economy. They were rooted instead in the postwar international system, basically a bipolar system in which the Soviet Union menaced the security and well-being of the United States and its allies. Confronted with this menace, policymakers in Washington thought it prudent to expand American influence into the power vacuums created by the war and to bolster friends and allies with economic aid, military assistance, and defense commitments—all backed by a substantial arsenal of conventional and nuclear weapons.[2]

Another group of historians sees the shift toward internationalism beginning in the 1930s, and attributes this shift not only to changes in the international system but also to the changing structure of American politics and the American economy.[3] The eco-

2   This argument is implicit in the works of postrevisionist scholars. See, for example, John Lewis Gaddis, *The United States and the Origins of the Cold War, 1941–1947* (New York, 1972); idem, *Strategies of Containment: A Critical Appraisal of Postwar American National Security Policy* (New York, 1982); and Melvyn P. Leffler, *A Preponderance of Power: National Security, the Truman Administration, and the Cold War* (Stanford, 1992).

3   I have developed this line of argument in *The Marshall Plan: America, Britain, and the Reconstruction of Western Europe, 1947–1952* (New York, 1987). My argument borrows from Thomas Ferguson, "From Normalcy to New Deal: Industrial Structure, Party Competition, and American Public Policy in the Great Depression," *International Organization* 38 (Winter 1984): 41–94. For a similar, more recent argument, also see Bruce Cumings, *The Origins of the Korean War*, vol. 2, *The Roaring of the Cataract, 1947–1950* (Princeton, 1990), 3–32.

nomic changes, basically changes in the industrial structure, had to do with the emergence of a powerful bloc of large, capital-intensive firms with a growing stake in the global economy. These firms challenged the influence over public policy of a larger bloc of small, labor-intensive companies that were interested primarily in national rather than international markets. Their rivalry ruptured the Republican party, which increasingly became the party of small business, and created the New Deal coalition, which included organized labor, the large, capital-intensive firms, and their allies among investment bankers. Changes in the industrial structure thus led to a fundamental political realignment that made possible the New Deal at home and the turn toward internationalism abroad.

Under the New Deal, in other words, policymakers in Washington abandoned the economic nationalism that had marked American diplomacy in the early years of the Great Depression. They threw their weight behind the Reciprocal Trade Agreements Act of 1934, the tripartite currency accord that came later in the decade, and other measures of economic internationalism. To be sure, the road to internationalism was not smooth. The nationalist bloc, which remained strong in the Republican party, waged a determined defense of the home market, denounced the interventionist thrust of Roosevelt's foreign policy after 1939, and resisted the globalization of American commitments in the early years of the Cold War. Concessions to their point of view often resulted in an imperfect internationalism. Nevertheless, the shift toward internationalism was unmistakable, already in the 1930s, and was as much a response to changes in the country's industrial structure and party alignment as it was to external developments. Had the old guard of the Republican party remained dominant in the 1940s, as it had been in the 1920s, it would have met the Soviet challenge of the early Cold War by substituting Hoover's vision of Fortress America for the global commitments undertaken by the Truman administration.

The preceding summary notwithstanding, the partisan battles over foreign policy involved more than a clash of regional, economic, and party interests. Ideology played a part as well. Involved, in other words, were fundamental disagreements over the

meaning of America. This was clearly the case with the bitter fighting between Republicans and Federalists during the early Republic—over the Jay Treaty, for example, or the War of 1812. Each
side was driven by a different ideology, a different vision of America: The Federalists looked to a strong central government, commercial expansion, and rapprochement with England; the Republicans favored states' rights, territorial expansion, and friendly
relations with revolutionary France. Other examples abound. The
era of Manifest Destiny came to an end in part because southerners and northerners, slave holders and abolitionists, no longer shared
the same vision of America. Southerners wanted to expand the
empire of slavery; northerners envisioned an empire of free labor,
free men. Ideology also colored the debate following the war with
Spain in 1898, especially the decision to acquire the Philippines.
The advocates of acquisition were often self-conscious imperialists
who sought to emulate the European system of colonialism. To
the anti-imperialists, on the other hand, a policy of military conquest and imperial grandeur would corrupt Republican virtue and
depart from the simple principles of the Founding Fathers.

The Cold War itself was as much an ideological battle at home
as abroad, and the vocabulary of this battle often echoed the language of an earlier day. Taft, Hoover, and other nationalists drew
on an older Republican ideology to attack the internationalist thrust
of American foreign policy. They warned against a large standing
army that might imperil the supremacy of civilian leadership. They
denounced universal military training as a European device that
would corrupt the institutions on which American democracy rested,
especially the family and the school. They also argued that national security policy was accelerating the dangerous trend, begun
during the New Deal, toward a centralization of authority in
Washington, particularly in the executive branch. If left unchecked, they said, this trend would destroy the balance of power
between different branches of the federal establishment and between federal and state governments. In addition, Taft, Hoover,
and their allies warned that excessive defense spending was debas-
ing the currency, bankrupting the treasury, imposing an undue
burden on the taxpayer, and leading to permanent government

controls over the economy. It was creating a "garrison state," in Taft's words, without private incentive and economic liberties.[4]

As this overview points out, partisanship has always played a role in the history of American foreign policy and has often been rooted in party affiliation, region, economic function, and ideology. By reconfiguring our discussion thus far, it is also possible to anticipate how factors like these might influence the debates over foreign policy in the post-Cold War era. The past, in other words, remains our guide to the future. If we think of the Cold War, as John Mueller does, as the rough equivalent of world war three, then the partisan struggles that lie ahead might be similar to those in the wake of previous conflicts.[5] The aftermath of World War I, World War II, and the Korean War can stand as examples about which we have a good deal of published research and settled opinion.

The aftermath of each of these conflicts witnessed a great popular demand for relief from the burdens of war, especially the economic burden, which led in part to the retrenchment or redesign of the country's commitments and strategy abroad. Following the First World War, industry and agriculture demanded an end to wartime controls and people everywhere wanted to reduce taxes and trim the budget. The Republican party gave voice to these expectations. Its victory at the polls in 1920 accelerated the pace of industrial demobilization and set the stage for budget cuts, especially cuts in the defense budget made possible in part through a large-scale program of naval disarmament. These cuts then paved the way to the peace dividend that Secretary of the Treasury Andrew Mellon distributed in the form of lower taxes. Although popular with the American people, this return to "normalcy," as Warren Harding called it, robbed government of the resources needed to deal with some of the major international problems of the day. It lacked the military power to enforce the terms of the peace treaty. It could not forgive the war debts that Allied countries owed the

---

4   Taft, "Constructive Criticism of Foreign Policy is Essential to the Safety of the Nation," 5 January 1951, *Congressional Record*, 97, pt. 1:54–61.

5   See Mueller's contribution to this volume, "Quiet Cataclysm: Some Afterthoughts on World War III."

American treasury, which in turn made it difficult for these countries to reduce the value of Germany's reparations. Nor could the American government play a financial role in reconstructing the European economy. Instead, the Republicans designed a foreign policy that relied on economic rather than military strategies to guarantee the peace and on private rather than public funds to rebuild Europe.

A similar story unfolded after the Second World War. Once again, the Republican party in particular vented popular demands for rapid military and industrial demobilization. Although the Truman administration sympathized, these demands usually exceeded what policymakers had in mind. Economic controls were scaled back over Truman's opposition and despite inflationary pressures. The military establishment also shrank dramatically, notwithstanding complaints from the army and the navy. Liberals, mainly Democrats, and conservatives, mainly Republicans, squabbled over how to spend the second peace dividend of the century. The outcome was another Republican victory: In 1948 Congress passed a major Republican tax cut that put a lid on domestic spending and forced even deeper reductions in a modest defense budget. The Republican desire to cut taxes combined with Truman's hope for a balanced budget to shape a foreign policy that limited the nation's commitments abroad, largely to Europe, and that again relied primarily on economic rather than military instruments. The program of aid to Greece and Turkey and the Marshall Plan for Western Europe encapsulated both aspects of this policy, which remained the dominant policy until the outbreak of the Korean War in 1950. At that point, Truman approved NSC-68, vastly expanded the nation's commitments abroad, turned toward military rather than economic instruments of containment, and greatly increased defense spending.

In 1952 the Republican party again gave voice to widespread discontent with wartime economic controls, high wartime taxes, and mounting budget deficits. Dwight D. Eisenhower promised in his presidential campaign that year to cut federal spending by forty billion dollars over several years. It was this promise, as much as his pledge to "go to Korea," that led to Eisenhower's victory at the polls. Once in office, moreover, the new president brought the

Korean War to a conclusion and began to dismantle the wartime
system of economic controls, burgeoning budgets, and high taxes.
As in the first and second postwar periods, the Republicans deliv-
ered a peace dividend in the form of lower taxes made possible
through budget reductions. For all practical purposes, these reductions came in the area of national security expenditures—which
never returned to prewar levels, to be sure, but which shrank by
about ten billion dollars between fiscal years 1953 and 1956.

Eisenhower's military strategy facilitated his budget and tax cuts,
although it might be more accurate to argue that these reductions
dictated the president's military strategy. Something similar could
be said of the Truman administration. The Republican tax cut of
1948, together with Truman's own plans for balancing the budget,
had led to a military strategy prior to the Korean War that relied
largely on atomic weapons to deter Soviet aggression.[6] Eisenhower
adopted a similar strategy to accommodate what were fundamentally economic rather than national security imperatives. The result was the New Look, basically a capital-intensive strategy of
containment based on nuclear weapons, the B-52 bomber, and
ballistic missiles. This strategy enabled Eisenhower to control the
size of the navy and drastically curtail the army, which together
accounted for most of the military savings.

What does this historical survey suggest about the connection
between foreign policy and partisanship in the post-Cold War era?
Already it is clear that a partisan conflict is emerging along familiar lines.[7] Sometimes viewed as a by-product of "divided government," the current clash is less one between an imperial presidency
and an imperial Congress than between Republicans and Democrats, with the former controlling the executive and the latter the
legislative branch of government. Like previous struggles, in other

6 The Truman administration had plans to return to much the same strategy after the
   Korean War. For this and the similarity between Truman's strategy and Eisenhower's
   New Look see the contribution to this volume by Samuel F. Wells, Jr., "Nuclear Weapons and European Security during the Cold War." See also Samuel F. Wells, Jr., "The
   Origins of Massive Retaliation," *Political Science Quarterly* 96 (Spring 1981): 31–52.
7 For recent views on this subject see Robert A. Pastor, "Congress and U.S. Foreign Policy: Comparative Advantage or Disadvantage?" and Jay Winik, "The Quest for Bipartisanship: A New Beginning for a New World Order," both in *The Washington Quarterly* 14 (Autumn 1991): 101–14, 115–30. See also Aaron L. Friedberg, "Is the United
   States Capable of Acting Strategically," ibid. (Winter 1991): 5–23.

words, the new conflict over foreign policy has a party dimension. It is also likely to have regional and functional dimensions, already apparent in the growing strength of the Republican party in the south, southwest, and west and in the tendency of Democrats, most noticeably in debates over trade and tariff policy, to speak for organized labor and other economic groups that are increasingly identified as neo-isolationists.

Nor is the foreign policy debate currently emerging without a powerful ideological content, similar to that of past disputes. For this reason, it is useful to think of the debate as one between liberals and conservatives, not Democrats and Republicans, even though it is drawn largely along party lines. As Jay Winik has noted, the ideological differences between these two sides have been apparent in wrangling over a host of foreign policy and national security issues, including the Strategic Defense Initiative, most-favored-nation treatment for China, aid to El Salvador, and the Gulf war.[8] At the center of these differences are competing liberal and conservative visions of America's role in world affairs: the one stressing human rights, support for democratic reforms, opposition to an interventionist diplomacy, and suspicion of military instruments; the other emphasizing geopolitical considerations, global management by collaborating national elites, a willingness to intervene abroad, and a related reliance on military force.

These competing visions also imply different domestic priorities that influence foreign policy. Democrats will often accuse their Republican rivals, especially in the White House, of being indifferent to domestic social and economic issues, of being more concerned with Arabs in the Middle East than with Americans in the midwest. However useful as campaign sloganeering, accusations like this do not help us to understand the nature of the new partisanship. The choice is not between a Republican emphasis on foreign policy and a Democratic emphasis on domestic policy. In both areas the two parties have different priorities, the one party driven by its conservative wing and the other by its liberal wing, so that their ideological differences become more apparent. For our pur-

8   Winik, "The Quest for Bipartisanship," 124–25.

poses, the important point to note is how the dispute over domestic priorities is likely to influence foreign policy.

Here again, the battle lines are clear already and involve what historians will see as a familiar issue—the peace dividend. For some time now, Democrats have been using the collapse of the Soviet empire to demand substantial cuts in the defense budget. The Pentagon and its allies have been reluctant to go along. They have stressed the new threats to American interests and security, such as international terrorism, the proliferation of sophisticated military technologies, and the danger of Third World dictators, while many Democrats have countered by pointing to the country's economic decline. They see this decline as the greatest danger in an era when economic rather than military competition promises to dominate, and they seek to address the danger by transferring resources from military to economic and social programs. The Republicans have responded to this challenge by trying to preempt it, reducing military expenditures in an effort to prevent even deeper cuts. As in the past, moreover, they have sought to outflank the Democrats by tying the peace dividend to their own plan for economic revival at home. Much like the Republican leadership after the First and Second World Wars, and after Korea as well, they want the peace dividend used primarily to reduce the deficit and lower taxes, including the capital gains tax.

There is no reason to believe that these and other partisan differences will be less intense in the years ahead than they have been in the past, regardless of which party captures the White House. If the Republicans retain the White House, however, while the Democrats control Congress, it might be appropriate to suggest a Republican model of how partisan conflict could be moderated. Even though the Democrats controlled Congress for most of his presidency, Eisenhower pursued a coherent foreign policy that enjoyed widespread support on both sides of Capitol Hill and in both political parties. To be sure, Eisenhower was careful to avoid foreign adventures that might provoke domestic controversy and disrupt bipartisanship. This much is well known. But equally important, if less noted, was Eisenhower's success in coopting criticism by tailoring national security strategy to a reduced level of expenditure and by using the savings to underwrite social programs, as well as to lower taxes.

Eisenhower came to office convinced that domestic and national security priorities were seriously out of whack, an argument often heard today. During the 1952 campaign and in the years thereafter, he complained repeatedly that national security expenditures absorbed more than half of the government's annual budget and contributed billions of dollars each year to the Gross National Product. He worried about a defense establishment that owned more than a hundred billion dollars in goods and property, employed millions of workers directly or indirectly, drove up the price of scientific talent, and siphoned both money and talent from productive civilian investment. Still worse, defense spending created what Eisenhower saw as a complex of military and industrial interests with a vested stake in the arms race. If left unchecked, he warned, these interests would dominate and distort the American economy, bankrupt the treasury, and lead to both the decline of American power and the withering of private enterprise. This was the danger of the garrison state that Taft had foretold.

It was this danger that Eisenhower tried to preclude, and with a measure of success. Through the New Look, Eisenhower aimed to reduce the military burden on the budget and thereby protect the economic foundations on which military strength ultimately rested. As noted earlier, he reduced government spending by approximately ten billion dollars in the first years of his administration, with almost all of the savings coming from the defense budget. What is more, while defense spending increased in fiscal years 1957 through 1959, largely in an effort to bridge the bomber and missile gaps, it leveled off again during Eisenhower's last couple of years in office. In addition, increases in military pay and rising costs probably resulted in less rather than more bang for the buck over the eight years of Eisenhower's presidency. Nor is that the most important point. By allocating a smaller portion of the budget to national security, Eisenhower was able to hold the line on tax hikes, as well as budget deficits, and to shift national resources from defense to nondefense programs. While national security expenditures declined as a percentage of the budget during the Eisenhower years, the share going to other programs increased.

In this sense, the New Look helped Eisenhower to achieve what he saw as a better balance between domestic and national security priorities. Because his policy amounted to a middle course, moreover, it also tended to dampen the partisan battle. Conservatives, mainly in the president's own party, disliked his brand of Modern Republicanism, with its emphasis on social programs, but were delighted with his success in reducing taxes and shrinking the deficit. And while Democrats complained that Eisenhower's New Look left the country unprepared for local wars of aggression, they were reluctant to offset new defense spending with cuts in domestic programs, which they supported, or to pay for both through higher taxes, which the voters opposed. So long as defense spending seemed to involve such tradeoffs, the Democrats were not in a strong position to stoke the fires of partisanship successfully.

Eisenhower's political strategy provides an example of how damaging partisan battles might be avoided if the era of divided government continues. Although divided government lends itself to ideological and political warfare, Eisenhower generally believed that the politics of confrontation did more harm than good. A Republican president with a Democratic Congress, he pursued a middle way that compromised ideological differences and permitted a degree of progress acceptable to all sides. At a time when genuine consensus is missing, as it is today, when a single party lacks firm control over the levers of power, it might be wise to adopt the Eisenhower paradigm as a reasonable alternative to the kind of regional, party, economic, and ideological conflict that has marked so much of American history.

There is considerable evidence that President George Bush has adopted such a strategy and will continue to pursue it. In a fashion reminiscent of Eisenhower, he has been willing to trim the defense budget and use the savings to cut taxes and minimize both the budget deficit and reductions in social spending. Eisenhower's experience allows us to anticipate the results of this policy. Besides considerable resistance from defense contractors and allied congressional interests, it seems likely to produce the usual interservice battles over how to divide a shrinking Pentagon budget. It will also lead to considerable debate, signs of which are already apparent, over a new strategic doctrine that dovetails with lower spending levels and new threat perceptions. Running parallel to this debate will be another over the scale and scope of America's commitments abroad, as well as its foreign aid program. While these debates are likely to smolder for several years, so far the president seems anxious to avoid confrontation, foresake ideology for pragmatic politics, and seek compromise.

Although this strategy may have permitted progress on both the domestic and diplomatic fronts in the 1950s, there is no reason to believe that a Republican president could sustain it in the years ahead or that such a strategy is even desirable. Eisenhower, after all, headed a Republican party dominated by its liberal, internationalist wing rather than its conservative, isolationist wing. That made it easier for the president to negotiate and compromise with the Democratic leadership in Congress. Today, conservatives and neo-isolationists like Pat Buchanan are more active in the party and less inclined to compromise. This suggests that the post-Cold War era might see a sustained and powerful resurgence of ideological struggle over domestic and foreign policy alike. What is more, the initiative in such a struggle need not come solely from the right wing of the Republican party. With the threat of international communism behind us, it is possible to imagine the emergence of a Democratic left every bit as aggressive as the Republican right.

Although the left has never flourished in American politics, its biggest handicap in recent years was the tendency of critics and voters to associate it with un-Americanism and with the Soviet threat to national security. The end of the Cold War may enable the left to break these old associations and to stand on its own agenda, which should be very appealing to voters who are rightly concerned with such old-fashioned, bread-and-butter problems as unemployment, health care, education, industrial efficiency, and the maldistribution of income and taxes. By linking success in managing these problems to the nation's ability to compete in global markets, the Democratic left has an opportunity to discredit the Republican party in the area of foreign affairs, where it has long appeared to be invulnerable. It can claim with a good deal of justification that the geostrategic and military prowess so touted by Republican leaders from Nixon to Bush is now less important to the nation's global standing than the economic strength they failed to build.

The end of the Cold War, in short, may bring a return to the economic, partisan, and ideological conflict that characterized other postwar periods. This conflict could exacerbate the difficulties already apparent in the system of divided government and make these difficulties less amenable to the solutions proposed by Eisenhower. One thing is certain, however. The kind of foreign policy and national security problems that were central to the politics of the Cold War are bound to become less salient in the years ahead. Foreign policy and national security will increasingly enter the political arena as issues of economic rather than military power. This will focus political debate on the domestic sources of national greatness and thus on familiar economic and social issues that often involve basic principles of equity. Whatever the short-term electoral results, these issues are likely to be at the center of politics for many years to come, and they are issues on which the Democrats and the left have done well in the past.

21

Beyond Bipolarity in Space and Time

DAVID REYNOLDS

In November 1990, George Bush made it official. "The Cold War is over," the president proclaimed in Paris, finally echoing what had been Mikhail Gorbachev's refrain for more than a year.[1] From a historical perspective, one might question the now-pervasive use of the term "Cold War" to embrace the whole post-1945 era. It is perhaps more correct to talk about alternating phases of Cold War and détente within an overall Soviet-American antagonism—hence, for instance, the growing use of the term "the First Cold War" to refer to the period from roughly 1947 to 1953.[2]

Despite these caveats, it seems reasonable to claim that what might be labeled "the era of Cold Wars" has come to an end. Unlike previous phases of détente, such as the early 1970s, there has of late been a fundamental shift in the structure of international relations. Particularly notable has been the dismantling of the Soviet bloc in Eastern Europe, the collapse of communism in this area, and the demise of the Soviet Union. These are changes that would require nothing less than another war to reverse. At the same time, the unification of Germany has redrawn the map of Europe and clearly marks the end of an era.

I am grateful for various helpful comments from John A. Thompson, Barry Supple, Timothy Breen, and Bernard Bailyn.

1 *New York Times*, 22 November 1990.
2 For examples of different attempts at periodization see D. C. Watt, "Rethinking the Cold War: A Letter to a British Historian," *Political Quarterly* 49 (1978): 450; Fred Halliday, *The Making of the Second Cold War*, 2d ed. (London, 1986), chap. 1; and Stanley Hoffmann, *Dead Ends: American Foreign Policy in the New Cold War* (Cambridge, MA, 1983). For an attempt to use such periodization see Anne Deighton, ed., *Britain and the First Cold War* (London, 1990).

The reemergence of Germany suggests immediately one probable consequence of the new international situation for our understanding of the history of American foreign policy. The impetus
toward "depolarization" of the origins of the Cold War will surely
be intensified.[3] That means taking seriously the way in which the
patterns of Cold War confrontation arose not simply from the imperatives of Soviet and American policy (ideological, economic,
domestic political, and so on) but also from the interaction of these
new "superpowers" within the context of the regional problems
of Europe, Asia, and the Middle East. At its heart, in Europe, the
Cold War of the 1940s was a struggle for mastery of Germany,
for control of the resources of the Continent's strongest power,
whose economy was the locomotive of Europe's prosperity but
also the potential engine of European war making, as it had been
in 1870, 1914, and 1939.[4] (Analogously, we are now encouraged
to see the Korean War of 1950 as having its genesis not so much
in global bipolarity but in the regional power struggles of the
peninsula and of East Asia.[5]) Recent research on the 1940s and
1950s suggests that often the superpower puppet masters were not
pulling the strings but being pulled themselves. All of this will surely
stimulate the current methodological debate among historians as
to whether American foreign relations should be studied as "international history."[6]

The vitality of these regional quarrels points us to a deeper

3 Bert Zeeman, "Britain and the Cold War: An Alternative Approach—The Treaty of
   Dunkirk Example," *European History Quarterly* 16 (July 1986): 346. Compare this
   with Robert M. Hathaway's earlier call to "depolarize these years" in *Ambiguous Partnership: Britain and America, 1944–1947* (New York, 1981), 2.
4 David Reynolds, "The 'Big Three' and the Division of Europe, 1945–8: An Overview,"
   Diplomacy and Statecraft 1 (1990): 132. Essays exploring the European dimension of
   the Cold War can be found in Josef Becker and Franz Knipping, eds., *Power in Europe?:
   Great Britain, France, Italy and Germany in a Postwar World, 1945–1950* (New York,
   1986); and in David Reynolds, ed., *The Origins of the Cold War in Europe: International Perspectives* (forthcoming).
5 Bruce Cumings, *The Origins of the Korean War*, 2 vols. (Princeton, 1981, 1990); John
   Merrill, *Korea: The Peninsular Origins of the War* (Newark, DE, 1989). For a contrast-
   ing view, emphasizing the international angle, see William Stueck, "The Korean War as
   International History," *Diplomatic History* 10 (1986): 291–309.
6 For a recent discussion see the symposium "Writing the History of U.S. Foreign Relations," and the presidential address by Michael H. Hunt, "Internationalizing U.S. Diplomatic History: A Practical Agenda," *Diplomatic History* 14 (Fall 1990): 553–605,
   and 15 (Winter 1991): 1–11, respectively.

problem—the previous tendency to treat 1945 as "year zero," "nullpunkt," a blank slate on which the two new superpowers could scribble as they pleased. Hans Morgenthau claimed in 1954 that "the international situation is reduced to the primitive spectacle of two giants eying each other with watchful suspicion."[7] Today, however, the argument that a multipolar European states system had given way during World War II to a bipolar global one—and given way irrevocably—no longer seems tenable.[8] The classic Cold Wars may be over, but what abides is the German question (and, in Asia, the Japanese question) around which those Cold Wars took shape. Despite changes in the forms of German and Japanese power, from military to economic, in the 1990s as in the 1930s we are still asking what should be the place of these two great states in the international order?

More generally, we should see the Cold War as rooted in the problems of the Second World War—problems underlying the war and also those created by it. For that war was a conjunction of various regional quarrels, especially those caused by the revisionist aims of Germany and Japan, but also the unresolved issue of the post-Habsburg succession in eastern and southeastern Europe. All of these problems were fused into a global inferno as a result of Hitler's astonishing victories of 1940 and Japan's equally remarkable successes in the winter of 1941–42. The eventual defeat of the Axis did more than leave power vacuums in Central Europe and East Asia that superpower rivalry sought to fill. In the Middle East and Southeast Asia it also accelerated the nationalist reaction to Western colonialism, opening up new arenas for Soviet-American rivalry as the British, French, and Dutch first struggled to retain and then eventually relinquished their imperial possessions, of which Indochina gradually became the principal battleground. It has taken fifty years for Germany and Japan to begin to

7 Hans J. Morgenthau, *Politics among Nations: The Struggle for Power and Peace*, 2d ed. (New York, 1954), 339. See also, for example, John Lukacs, *1945: Year Zero* (New York, 1978), 13; John L. Gaddis, *Russia, the Soviet Union, and the United States: An Interpretive History* (New York, 1978), 180; and Thomas G. Paterson, *On Every Front: The Making of the Cold War* (New York, 1979), 22–23.

8 A classic statement of this argument can be found in A. W. DePorte, *Europe between the Superpowers: The Enduring Balance* (New Haven, 1979), preface, esp. ix, where DePorte sees the postwar bipolar order as offering a lasting "resolution of the German problem."

regain some kind of place within the international system. And we are still coping with the consequences of often abrupt Western decolonization and the absence of viable indigenous state structures on Western models. Arguably, the era of Cold Wars has been a gradual coming to terms with the legacies of world war. The termination of that era may allow us to see World War II in its full and unique enormity rather than as almost a prelude to bipolarity.[9]

One might push the argument further. The form and degree of bipolarity were themselves a product of World War II. To update the British statesman of the 1820s, George Canning, it could be said that the superpowers came into existence to redress the balance of the world.[10] Power, after all, is relative. What made the United States and the Soviet Union seem so strong in 1945 was not merely their intrinsic resources of manpower and matériel but also the weakness of their rivals and allies. The gradual recovery of Germany and Japan and, more generally, the emergence of Western Europe and the Pacific Rim, have readjusted the balance of economic and political power (if not of nuclear weaponry).[11] The *extent* of bipolarity was clearly artificial.

Of the two, the Soviet Union's decline was obviously more precipitous and dramatic. It was always recognized in the West that the Soviet Union was in some senses an "incomplete superpower," flawed by its economic backwardness. But the full extent of those deficiencies became apparent only at the end of the Cold War. Official CIA statistics, estimating that the Soviet Union by the 1980s was spending 50 percent more in real terms on defense than the

9   This remains a virtue of Gabriel Kolko, *The Politics of War: The World and United States Foreign Policy, 1943–1945*, highlighted in the preface to the new edition (New York, 1990). More recently, it is also the approach of Thomas J. McCormick, *America's Half-Century: United States Foreign Policy in the Cold War* (Baltimore, 1989). See also David Reynolds, "1940: Fulcrum of the Twentieth Century?" *International Affairs* 66 (1990): 325–50.

10   The term "superpowers" was probably coined by William T. R. Fox in his book *The Super-Powers: The United States, Britain, and the Soviet Union—Their Responsibility for Peace* (New York, 1944).

11   As a crude economic indicator of this pattern, the United States produced 49 percent of world manufacturing output in 1946, but by 1980 its share had fallen to 31.5 percent—virtually the same proportion as in 1938 (31.4 percent). See Paul Bairoch, "International Industrialization Levels from 1750 to 1980," *Journal of European Economic History* 11 (Fall 1982): 301, 304.

United States, with an economy about half the size of America's, may prove to be *underestimates*.[12] In retrospect, Soviet power seems to have rested on two pillars. One was a command economy, which, through the dominance of the Communist party, could divert a massive proportion of national resources to the military-industrial sector. In an authoritarian, nonmarket society, economic consequences and consumer protests could be ignored for a remarkably long time. Gorbachev destroyed this old system, but without successfully creating an efficient market alternative.

Underlying the command military-industrial complex, and constituting the second pillar of Soviet power, was the fact that the Soviet Union was the world's last great empire—a point familiar to historians of colonialism but only recently made transparent.[13] In the First World War the multiethnic Habsburg and Ottoman empires, long crumbling, finally collapsed in bloody chaos. The Romanov empire survived, however, albeit in truncated form and under new Bolshevik leadership, and this constituted the resource base to compensate for the inefficiencies of Soviet economic organization. After the Second World War the Russification policies of the last tsars were resumed and Gorbachev's new openness allowed the simmering ethnic rivalries to boil over anew, within what was officially acknowledged to be a country with 140 different national groups. What is more, this occurred at a time when the Russian proportion of the Soviet population had declined from nearly three quarters at the time of the Bolshevik revolution to a bare majority.[14]

The limits of Soviet *superpotentia* therefore became particularly apparent as a result of the Gorbachev era. By comparison, as the Persian Gulf war reminded us, the United States is in a different league, exhibiting "great power plus great mobility of power"— the criteria of William Fox's classic definition of superpower status.[15] But if the United States is, for the foreseeable future, "bound

---

12 Paul Dibb, *The Soviet Union: The Incomplete Superpower*, 2d ed. (London, 1988), 80–89.
13 D. K. Fieldhouse, *The Colonial Empires: A Comparative Survey from the Eighteenth Century*, 2d ed. (London, 1982), 334–41.
14 Graham Smith, ed., *The Nationalities Question in the Soviet Union* (London, 1990), esp. v, 363–64.
15 Fox, *Super-Powers*, 21.

to lead," to quote Joseph Nye, it also faces the problems of "Number One in relative decline," in the words of Paul Kennedy.[16] The underlying problems of relative economic decline internationally and fiscal crisis throughout the federal system have not disappeared. Indeed, recent projections abroad of American power have depended on foreign investors, notably from Japan but also from Britain, the Netherlands, and elsewhere, who have been willing to finance a budget deficit that shows little sign of significant diminution.

The end of the era of Cold Wars therefore highlights both the extent *and* the limits of American power. To grapple with this duality we need to break away from the bipolar criteria that the Cold Wars imposed—what Thomas J. McCormick has called "our myopic preoccupation with Soviet-American relations."[17] Across the board since World War II the power of the Soviet Union and the ideology of revolutionary communism have been the focuses not only of American politics and culture but also of the historiography of American foreign relations, nurtured by the Cold War, McCarthyism, and Vietnam. Whether or not "orthodoxy," "revisionism," and "postrevisionism" exist outside the field of diplomatic history, the intensity with which their existence has been debated is one indication of the centrality of the Cold War to the metaphysics of Americanism. Another is the sheer popularity of the first Cold War as a topic for research. In 1983, John Lewis Gaddis calculated that one in five U.S. doctoral dissertations in diplomatic history completed in the previous four years dealt with some aspect of the period 1945–1950.[18] As the archives have become open, the creeping barrage of publications has moved on to the 1950s, but the narrowness of its targeting remains. This is not to be excessively critical. Cold War in the nuclear age was, literally, a life and death issue for Americans; attention to it was un-

---

16 Joseph S. Nye, Jr., *Bound to Lead: The Changing Nature of American Power* (New York, 1990); Paul Kennedy, *The Rise and Fall of the Great Powers: Economic Change and Military Conflict from 1500 to 2000* (London, 1988), 514.

17 Thomas J. McCormick, "World Systems," in the Round Table "Explaining the History of American Foreign Relations," *Journal of American History* 77 (June 1990): 132.

18 John Lewis Gaddis, "The Emerging Post-Revisionist Synthesis on the Origins of the Cold War," *Diplomatic History* 7 (Summer 1983): 171.

derstandable, indeed desirable. What I am really noting is the vulnerability of the study of recent history to the perspectives and passions of current affairs. The Cold War might almost be said to have frozen historiography as well as politics.

The end of the era of Cold Wars makes it possible to examine the nature of U.S. power in a broader framework, to break out of the prism (prison?) of Soviet-American relations and the confines of the period after 1945 or even 1917. A provocative invitation may be found in economic historian Gavin Wright's recent contribution to the debate about why the United States has lost its competitive edge. Michael J. Hogan and other historians of American "corporatism" have given us a far richer understanding of the 1920s, in the process correcting simplistic conceptions of American interwar "isolationism" that derived from World War II polemics.[19] Yet, in consequence, they have not always discouraged us from taking 1920s "boosterism" at face value. Wright's essay suggests that American industrial prowess at the beginning of this century did not rest on skills that have now, mysteriously, been lost—entrepreneurship, organization, education, research and development, and so on. Rather, it was the consequence of abundant natural resources (both food and raw materials) that were exploited earlier and more aggressively than elsewhere and were harnessed to a highly effective system of mass production within the context of a vast, continentwide common market. This was the base from which America achieved a remarkable dominance of world output in the first half of the twentieth century. In 1913 the United States produced 65 percent of the world's petroleum, 56 percent of its copper, 39 percent of its coal, 37 percent of its bauxite, and 36 percent of its iron ore. The industrial technologies in which America excelled—such as steel, automobiles, and farm machinery—were closely associated with these raw materials. But in the second half of the century, Wright argues, other countries have belatedly exploited their geological endowment. At the same time, new mass markets have been created elsewhere and, most important, manu-

---

19 See, for example, Michael J. Hogan, *Informal Entente: The Private Structure of Cooperation in Anglo-American Economic Diplomacy, 1918–1928* (Columbia, MO, 1977); and Frank Costigliola, *Awkward Dominion: American Political, Economic, and Cultural Relations with Europe, 1919–1933* (Ithaca, 1984).

facturing has freed itself from resource dependence through the electronic and computer revolutions. In this new situation, America's resource-intensive technology is a liability.[20]

Wright offers his essay as the beginning of a debate rather than as a conclusion. It is certain to stimulate lively controversy among specialists in economic history. But its tentative conclusions are suggestive, paralleling as they do the explanations offered by British economic historians for the waning of Britain's industrial hegemony a century before.[21] They highlight the importance of America's size, both as a source of raw materials and as a market for finished products. In an age when political history is out of vogue, we are pushed toward an unfashionable conclusion: State structures were important.[22] Stated crudely, it mattered enormously for modern history that America was a *big* country.

Why was that the case? For many Americans this is a nonquestion. It is assumed to be a matter of "manifest destiny" that the Great Republic should extend "from sea to shining sea."[23] To a European this conclusion does not seem axiomatic; the idea of secession is not inconceivable. W. E. Gladstone, Britain's chancel-

20 Gavin Wright, "The Origins of American Industrial Success, 1879–1940," *American Economic Review* 80 (1990): 651–68. Compare Wright with David M. Potter, *People of Plenty: Economic Abundance and the American Character* (Chicago, 1954). Although outdated both in its use of the concept of "national character" and in its attempt to breathe new life into the Turner thesis, Potter's book nevertheless remains a suggestive and neglected examination of the role of natural resources in American development.

21 Britain did not lose "the industrial spirit" or somehow allow its erstwhile technological edge to become blunted. In fact, it is questionable that it ever possessed either of these. The British industrial revolution rested not on high capital investment, innovative technologies, or skilled workers but on the early and massive transfer of labor from agriculture to industry, concentrating on a few technologically simple industries in which Britain had resource advantage (notably those associated with water- and coal-power). See N. F. R. Crafts, *British Economic Growth during the Industrial Revolution* (Oxford, 1985). The importance of this for our understanding of the changing nature of Britain's international power is set out in David Reynolds, *Britannia Overruled: British Policy and World Power in the Twentieth Century* (New York, 1991), chap. 1.

22 As argued especially in Theda Skocpol, *States and Social Revolutions: A Comparative Analysis of France, Russia, and China* (New York, 1979); and Peter B. Evans, Dietrich Rueschemeyer, and Theda I. Skocpol, *Bringing the State Back In* (New York, 1985).

23 *New York Morning News,* 27 December 1848, extolled "the right of our manifest destiny to overspread and to possess the whole of the continent which Providence has given us for the development of the great experiment of Liberty and federated self-government entrusted to us." Albert K. Weinberg, *Manifest Destiny: A Study of Nationalist Expansionism in American History* (Baltimore, 1935), 145.

lor of the exchequer, spoke for many of his countrymen in October 1862 when, after Antietam, he claimed that "Jefferson Davis and other leaders of the South . . . have made a nation" and argued that "it is for the general interests of Nations that no State should swell to the dimensions of a Continent."[24] This speech was greatly resented in the North and in later life Gladstone made fulsome apology. But it reminds us of the spectacular unlikelihood of the American experiment, as it seemed to European contemporaries. And this sense of uniqueness may be recaptured anew today in the era of Soviet Dis-Union.

Historians of the American Revolution have rightly complained about the relative neglect of the diplomacy of the 1780s, a critical period not only internally but externally as the vulnerable new republic struggled to secure its international existence.[25] Others have bemoaned the "Great American Desert" in the historiography of U.S. foreign relations between 1815 and 1861.[26] Both of these lacunae surely point to a larger problem: the presumption that the United States was bound to become a world power and that what matters when studying its foreign relations is the period *after* it achieved that stature. But if manifest destiny is eliminated as an "unspoken assumption,"[27] then we can perhaps in retrospect see the whole period from independence to the Civil War as one in which the extent and unity of the United States constituted a critical issue not only for American politics but also for world history. What James Madison in the fourteenth *Federalist* called "the experiment of an extended republic" was truly audacious.[28] The geographical scope of the union was already vast in 1788; by 1850, after the annexation of Texas, the Oregon settlement, and the Mexican War of 1846–1848, it equaled the distance from the Pyr-

24 Gladstone speech at Newcastle, 7 October 1862, quoted in D. P. Crook, *The North, the South, and the Powers, 1861–1865* (New York, 1974), 227–28, 230.

25 See, for example, Frederick W. Marks III, "Power, Pride, and Purse: Diplomatic Origins of the Constitution," *Diplomatic History* 11 (Fall 1987): 316.

26 Kinley Brauer, "The Great American Desert Revisited: Recent Literature and Prospects for the Study of American Foreign Relations, 1815–61," *Diplomatic History* 13 (Summer 1989): 395–417.

27 James Joll, "1914: The Unspoken Assumptions," in *The Origins of the First World War: Great Power Rivalry and German War Aims,* ed. H. W. Koch (London, 1972), 307–28.

28 Max Beloff, ed., *The Federalist,* 2d ed. (Oxford, 1987), 65–66.

enees to the Urals and from Sweden to the Sahara. To many Europeans the breakup of this overgrown republican empire seemed inevitable. Apart from sheer size, the other reason for their incredulity was the lack of a recognizably European political system— a centralized, sovereign state. The unease of European conservatives about the subversive effects of American democracy ("when a country is so mob-governed as America there must be great dangers")[29] was not mere snobbery and status anxiety. It reflected a deeper constitutional skepticism that sovereignty could be lodged amorphously in "the people," rather than in a single person or at the very most a legislature, without creating anarchy. It seemed remarkable that society, in Alexis de Tocqueville's words, could act "by and for itself" without the existence of what Europeans would have considered an identifiable unitary state.[30] Incoherent mass political parties hardly seemed an adequate substitute. The growing movement for southern secession and the collapse of the second party system were therefore seen by many Europeans as presaging the breakup of a polity that was already too large and that had not developed a proper system of government.

It took America's most appalling war to hold the Union together: some 618,000 dead—50 percent more than World War II and, until Vietnam, about the same as all of the country's other wars combined. Overall, 8 percent of white males between the ages of thirteen and forty-three died; in the South, the death toll was 18 percent.[31] Appomattox ended secessionism for any realist, to adapt the words of Senator Arthur H. Vandenberg (R-MI). More positively, some historians also see the war as the crucible of a new Americanism, epitomized in Lincoln's growing use of "the nation" rather than "the Union" and reflected more generally by the "tran-

29   Charles Greville diary, 12 March 1841, quoted in Wilbur Devereux Jones, *The American Problem in British Diplomacy, 1841–1861* (London, 1974), 9.
30   Alexis de Tocqueville, *Democracy in America*, ed. J. P. Mayer (Garden City, NY, 1964), 60. Compare with Gordon S. Wood, *The Creation of the American Republic, 1776–1787* (New York, 1969), 382–83: "To someone steeped in British legal thought this explicit retention of legal sovereignty in the people was preposterous." The historical uniqueness of American state building is discussed most suggestively in Stephen Skowronek, *Building a New American State: The Expansion of National Administrative Capacities, 1877–1920* (New York, 1982).
31   Maris A. Vinovskis, ed., *Towards a Social History of the American Civil War: Exploratory Essays* (New York, 1990), 4–7.

sition of the United States to a singular noun"—the United States "is," not the United States "are."[32] Certainly many European commentators had no doubt after April 1865 that a historical Rubicon had been crossed. In an article published the following year, French political economist Michel Chevalier pointed to the "political colossus that has been created on the other side of the Atlantic." He warned of future transatlantic rivalry, even war, and predicted disastrous setbacks for the countries of Europe unless they forged a new unity.[33] By the 1880s, de Tocqueville's celebrated prophecy of fifty years before was becoming a commonplace—America and Russia were indeed looming as the two Great Powers of the future, the two "end points of the contemporary political magnet" that would "grow into mighty batteries," to quote the German writer J. H. Pulte, in an early use of the modern vocabulary of bipolarity.[34] While European federalists called for continental unity, the threats from America and Russia were used in Wilhelmine Germany to help justify 1890s *Weltpolitik* and wartime *Ostpolitik* and in Britain to buttress the case for imperial unity advanced by historian J. R. Seeley, politician Joseph Chamberlain, and others.[35]

Looking back on the late-nineteenth-century debate about incipient bipolarity, what stands out now is the fact that the Russian empire has finally crumbled while the American union lives on. The reasons for this are complex and numerous, not the least being

---

32   James M. McPherson, *Battle Cry of Freedom: The Civil War Era* (New York, 1990, paperback ed.), 859.

33   Michel Chevalier, "La guerre et la crise européenne" [The war and the European crisis], *Revue des deux mondes* 63 (1 June 1866): 784–85. Pierre Renouvin claimed that this was the first allusion to possible antagonism between the United States of America and a United States of Europe. P. Renouvin, *L'idée de fédération européenne dans la pensée politique du XIXe siècle* [The idea of European federation in the political thought of the nineteenth century] (Oxford, England, 1949), 23.

34   Quoted in P. F. H. Lauxtermann, *Constantin Frantz: Romantik und Realismus im Werk eines politischen Aussenseiters* [Constantin Frantz: Romanticism and Realism in the work of a political outsider] (Groningen, 1978), 67. Tocqueville had predicted that each of these "two great nations" seemed "called by some secret design of Providence one day to hold in its hands the destinies of half the world." See *Democracy in America*, 412–13.

35   This theme is examined in detail in Geoffrey Barraclough, "Europa, Amerika und Russland in Vorstellung und Denken des 19. Jahrhunderts" [Europe, America, and Russia in the imagination and thought of the nineteenth century], *Historische Zeitschrift* 203 (October 1966): 280–315.

that, relative to Russia, the United States *was* an "empire of liberty," with an ideology and a social structure that harnessed rather than suppressed the creative individuality of its citizenry (especially whites and males). What I wish to underline here, however, is simply the success of American federalism (for all its deficiencies, regularly pointed out across the Atlantic) in holding together a nation the size of a continent. So far, the American union has worked, whereas the Soviet Union did not. If we are interested in a more international history of the "American century," we need to stretch our minds not merely in space—to other countries and other languages—but also in time. For it may be that, in the long run, the most important fact of twentieth-century world history lies in the nineteenth century, in the failure of secession and the triumph of federal unionism. These developments secured a country the size of a continent, guaranteeing munificent resources and a vast internal market, which America's distinctive industrial revolution enabled it to exploit. These were the preconditions of international greatness in the twentieth century. Whether they will suffice for the twenty-first is a more open question.

22

A Usable Past for the Future

ROBERT JERVIS

To those living through it, each era seems unique. But I suspect that even later generations will share this perception of the 1990s. Rarely if ever has world politics been fundamentally reordered without a major war. Of course, in some sense we have witnessed a major war, and the Soviet Union lost it.[1] But the differences between a conflict that was prolonged yet bloodless—at least for the major protagonists—and a "normal" war are very great. This is even true for the victor. While the Soviet Union confronted the internal turmoil and revolution that often accompanies a military defeat, the United States, even with its triumph in the Gulf war, does not appear to have the strength, will, or vision to establish a "new world order."[2] The structure of power in the post-Cold War world also appears to be unique. Indeed, we cannot even characterize it in terms of the system's polarity, the concept of which political scientists are so enamored.[3] Is the system unipolar because the United States is so dominant, bipolar because nuclear weapons are still concentrated in two hands, tripolar because we can anticipate the emergence of a united Europe that will take its place alongside the two former superpowers, or multipolar be-

1 See John Mueller, "Quiet Cataclysm: Some Afterthoughts on World War III," in this volume.
2 For a good explication of what the administration appears to mean by this phrase see Stanley Sloan, "The US Role in a New World Order: Prospects for George Bush's Global Vision," Congressional Reference Service Report, 28 March 1991.
3 For an argument that we should pay less attention to polarity than to other measures of dispersion of power throughout the system see Edward Mansfield, "Measuring the International Distribution of Power," Paper prepared for the fifteenth World Congress of the International Political Science Association, 21–25 July 1991, Buenos Aires.

cause so many forms of power—especially economic power—are now widely dispersed?

The coming era also seems odd because it is hard to locate a main axis of conflict. In the past, the two leading states usually were adversaries because each constituted a potential if not actual menace to the other. But, for all of the discussion of figurative or even literal wars between the United States and Japan,[4] it is hard to see this as the most potent source of international violence. Perhaps the most obvious dividing line in world politics is between rich countries and poor ones. But a North-South conflict would be fundamentally different from what we have seen in the past, because it would involve a struggle between unequals, and, unlike instances of imperialism, it would be the poor states that were seeking change.

Most importantly, the post-Cold War situation is likely to be unique in the lack of armed conflict among the richest and most powerful states in the system—the "developed" countries of Western Europe, North America, and Japan. This topic is of course large as well as speculative, and only a telegraphic treatment is possible here.[5] One indication of the profound change is that although Great Britain's primary aim always was to prevent any power from dominating the continent of Europe, even those who opposed joining the European Community or who remain opposed to seeing it develop political sovereignty do not see it as a menace to Britain's life and liberty. The United States, too, fought to prevent the Germans from dominating Europe, but it continues to favor the integration of Europe even though Germany is its leader.

These dramatic breaks from the past and the general peacefulness of the West are to be explained by increases in the costs of war, decreases in its benefits, and, linked to this, changes in domestic regimes and values. Most obviously, the costs of war among developed states would be enormous. This would be true even if

4 For the latest example see George Friedman and Meredith LeBard, *The Coming War with Japan* (New York, 1990).
5 For more extensive treatments see Klaus Knorr, *On the Uses of Military Power in the Nuclear Age* (Princeton, 1966); John Mueller, *Retreat from Doomsday: The Obsolescence of War among Modern States* (New York, 1989); Richard Rosecrance, *The Rise of the Trading State* (New York, 1986); and Robert Jervis, "The Future of International Politics: Will it Resemble the Past?" *International Security* 16 (Winter 1991/92).

nuclear weapons did not exist.[6] But such weapons do exist, and by increasing the costs of war, they also increase the chances of peace.

Because of its extreme costs, only the strongest forces for war could produce such an outcome. Yet it is hard to conjure up any significant impulses toward armed conflict among the developed countries. The high level of economic interdependence among the developed states increases not only the costs of war, but the benefits of peace as well. The belief that one's economic well-being is linked to that of others is not sufficient to bring peace, however. Throughout history many values have been more important to people than wealth, and it is noteworthy that high levels of economic interdependence have not prevented civil wars. In international politics it is particularly true that wealth is not the primary national goal. While economic theory argues that the actor should care only about how an outcome affects him, in a world of anarchy actors who fear that they may have to fight need to worry about relative advantage as well as absolute gains.[7] Furthermore, states have reason to fear that if they become more dependent on others than others are on them, they will be vulnerable to pressure and blackmail, as the Balkan states discovered before World War II.[8]

Both the fear of dependence and the concern about relative gains are lessened when states expect to remain at peace with each other. Indeed, expectations of peaceful relations were a necessary condition for the formation of the European Common Market: The prospect of greater wealth would have come at an excessive price if violent conflict had been seen as a real possibility. (So it is not surprising that other regions have not imitated the European experience.) The other side of the coin is that when states fear each other, interdependence can increase conflict.[9]

6 This point is stressed in Mueller, *Retreat from Doomsday*.
7 See Waltz, *Theory of International Politics* (Reading, MA, 1979); Arthur Stein, "The Hegemon's Dilemma: Great Britain, the United States, and the International Economic Order," *International Organization* 38 (Spring 1984): 355–86; Joseph Grieco, "Anarchy and the Limits of Cooperation: A Realist Critique of the Newest Liberal Institutionalism," *International Organization* 42 (Summer 1988): 485–507.
8 Albert Hirschman, *National Power and the Structure of Foreign Trade*, expanded ed. (Berkeley, 1980).
9 Waltz, *Theory of International Politics*, 151–60.

There then is at least an element of circularity in the current situation: Interdependence has developed in part because of the expectations of peace, and the economic benefits of close economic relations in turn make peace more likely. Samuel Huntington argues that the answer to the question of why the United States is so concerned about the Japanese challenge is straightforward: "The United States is obsessed with Japan for the same reason that it was once obsessed with the Soviet Union. It sees that country as a major threat to its primacy in a crucial arena of power."[10] But it is far from clear that one state's economic progress constitutes a threat to another unless the two are likely to fight, the former's relative advantage eventually will diminish the other's wealth, or the former gains leverage it can use in important political disputes. The first condition does not hold and it is debatable whether either of the other two do. Rivalry without much chance of war is very different from rivalry conducted with an eye to future fighting.

To note that many wars have been fought not for wealth but in spite of expected economic losses raises the central question of what nations seek. The change in relations among the developed states is partly a result of a shift in basic outlook and values. As John Mueller has noted, war is no longer seen as good, or even as honorable, in anything less than desperate circumstances.[11] We may now be seeing, among developed states, the triumph of interests over passions, as Norman Angell and Joseph Schumpeter foresaw.[12] As the Gulf war reminds us, it is not as though developed states do not feel some sense of pride, or even self-identity, in asserting themselves abroad. But the impulse is more episodic than it once was, is not directed against other democracies, and is more often in the service of economic values than counterposed to them.

Related is the dampening of nationalism. The progress toward

10   Samuel Huntington, "America's Changing Strategic Interests," *Survival* 23 (January/February 1991): 8.
11   Mueller, *Retreat from Doomsday*. For a discussion of changes in values among Europeans on matters of domestic society and ways of life see Ronald Inglehart, *The Silent Revolution* (Princeton, 1977); and idem, *Culture Shift in Advanced Industrial Society* (Princeton, 1990).
12   Norman Angell, *The Great Illusion*, 4th ed. (New York, 1913); Joseph Schumpeter, "The Sociology of Imperialism," in his *Imperialism and Social Classes* (New York, 1951). The phrase is borrowed from Albert Hirschman, although the story Hirschman tells is much more complex than this: *The Passions and the Interests* (Princeton, 1977).

European unification is both made possible by and facilitates a weakening of the attachment to one's nation as a source of identity and personal satisfaction. Of course nationalism was discredited in some European states (but not Germany) after 1918, but this was because it had brought failure, not because being less nationalistic had produced success. The current success, furthermore, has become embodied in institutions that have become the focus of power and perhaps loyalty. There is then less danger that subsequent generations will return to the older outlook.

This change can also be seen in the absence of territorial disputes. Germans no longer seem to care that Alsace and Lorraine are French; the French, who permitted the Saar to return to Germany in a plebiscite, are not bothered by this loss, and indeed do not see it as a loss at all. The Germans did feel sufficient Germanness to seek the unification of their country, but the desire to regain the "lost territories" to the east seems extremely low. Furthermore, unification was not accomplished against the will of any other country and, unlike manifestations of a more disturbing nationalism, did not involve the assertion of the rightful domination of one country over another.

Equally important, the developed states are now liberal democratic and it appears that such regimes rarely, if ever, fight each other.[13] Again, values play a large role. In the absence of high conflicts that could not be ameliorated any other way, what would one democracy gain by conquering another? For example, the United States could conquer Canada, but why would it want to do so when much of what it would want to see there is already in place?

This does not mean that the future will lack international violence. Even if my analysis is correct, it is restricted to the developed states. Only those who see the Cold War as predominantly responsible for conflict in the Third World would expect strife there to drastically decrease. There are also many reasons for conflict and few unusual restraints in Eastern Europe and the former Soviet Union. Indeed, armed violence to the East is the only trigger I can imagine to warfare among the developed countries, although these linkages seem to be potentially controllable.

13 Michael Doyle, "Kant, Liberal Legacies and Foreign Affairs," Parts 1 and 2, *Philosophy and Public Affairs* 12 (Summer and Fall 1983): 205–35 and 323–53.

Implicit in some of the Bush administration's defense of its policy in the Persian Gulf is an argument that international politics in the Third World is likely to be quite peaceful: now that the United States and the United Nations have demonstrated their resolve by going to war, future challenges are not to be expected. This touching faith in the ease with which would-be aggressors are restrained by the unfortunate fates of others is unfounded. Even a fully rational challenger would not be likely to draw such wide-ranging inferences from this case. Because there were so many reasons for the United States and other countries to intervene—the blatant character of the aggression, the tyrannical nature of Iraq's regime, the previous adventures of Saddam Hussein, the importance of the geographic area, and the large number of countries that were menaced or offended by the aggression—others can reasonably believe that such a strong response would not be forthcoming in other cases. Furthermore, potential challengers rarely see their situations and the probable responses of others with great accuracy.

If my argument about the peaceful nature of relations among developed states is correct, however, there are questions about the utility of studying the past for predicting the future and guiding any country's policies. Of course, this is not to say that this has ever been the main purpose of studying history; most of us study the past for the intellectual and aesthetic pleasure of seeking to understand it. Furthermore, if we had ever been able to grasp the "laws" of international history, they might have no longer applied, as statesmen themselves would have understood the laws and altered their behavior, thus changing the pattern. But even putting this aside, generalizations that rested on the availability of force may no longer be valid.

This does not mean that there is no point in looking for a "usable past." Of course one should not do this to demonstrate that one's own policy preferences were once enacted or even that they can make earlier periods more intelligible.[14] While the latter motive can advance our understanding of the past, it does not speak to the concerns here. Instead, we need to seek episodes and patterns that may provide guidance for how international politics might

14 These seem to me to be the driving motives behind Barton Bernstein, ed., *Towards a New Past* (New York, 1967).

develop or for the choices various countries—particularly our own—
might face.

The paucity of incentives for armed conflict among the major
powers does not mean that cooperation is guaranteed. Conflicts of
interest and rivalries remain, as does the potential for suspicions
and misunderstandings. Even when countries agree on goals, they
often will disagree on the appropriate means and on the distribution of burdens. Politics often presents actors with problems of
collective or public goods.[15] That is, in many cases the good that
is desired (for example, a stable world, a healthy environment) is
public in the sense that all actors will gain from it and, indeed,
none can be denied the benefit. But the payments for public goods
come from individual actors—be they people or nations—and,
furthermore, it is usually the case that each actor's contribution is
relatively small and so will have only slight influence on whether
the collective effort will succeed. As a result, rational actors try to
avoid paying: If others pay and the goal is reached, they can be
"free riders" and get the benefits without paying the costs; if others do not pay, the goal will not be reached and any contribution
they might have made would be wasted. Conflict of interest is
structural. It does not grow out of concrete differences over territory, national ambitions, or the desire to exploit others.

In situations like this, cooperation is possible although not easy.[16]
It would be particularly useful to have a better understanding of
how states have managed in these circumstances. Of course, no
past situation matches the current one in all of its aspects, but the
obvious case that comes to mind is the Concert of Europe. Indeed,
some political scientists have urged that concertlike mechanisms
should now be established.[17] It appears to be the case that in much
of the nineteenth century, especially in the years immediately after the Napoleonic Wars, statesmen did not behave as standard
balance-of-power theory would lead us to expect. Rather, they were

---

15 The classic statement is Mancur Olson, Jr., *The Logic of Collective Action* (Cambridge, MA, 1965).

16 For political science research that explores this topic see Kenneth Oye, ed., *Cooperation under Anarchy* (Princeton, 1985) (also published as *World Politics* 38 [Oct 1985]).

17 Charles Kupchan and Clifford Kupchan, "Concerts, Collective Security, and the Future of Europe," *International Security* 16 (Summer 1991): 114–61; Gregory Gause,
"Post-War Gulf Security: Hegemony, Balance, or Concert?" (in possession of author).

more moderate in their demands and less cutthroat in their techniques. They sought stable cooperation and were willing to forego some of the possibilities for short-run advantage that presented themselves through others' temporary weakness or blunders in order to avoid endangering arrangements that were mutually beneficial over the long run. Fear and insecurity, although of course never absent, were similarly lessened because of the well-grounded expectation that others would reciprocate restraint because they too desired to avoid a full-fledged Hobbesian "state of war."

In broad outline, this behavior and the timing of the periods of concert and balance of power fit with the expectations generated by international politics theory.[18] But our knowledge of the concert is limited.[19] We know enough to realize that it would be a mistake to idealize it: Competition was not always subordinated to ideas of the common good; national interests were often defined narrowly; war was never out of sight; peace was often maintained at the expense of justice and the weaker powers. We also know enough to detect some features that, while apparently paradoxical, fit with our theories—for example, the concert was in part maintained by the fact that statesmen believed that it was fragile. If they thought that it could withstand major shocks, they would have felt freer to exploit others because they would not have feared that doing so would lead to a return to normal balance-of-power politics. But we need to know much more about how the system functioned, how statesmen calculated and saw the world, and how domestic politics and foreign policy related to each other. How were definitions of national interest formed? How well did the institutionalized mechanisms for cooperation work? How important was particularly skillful statesmanship?

A second and related area on which history could shed light is how international politics has been conducted when war is unthinkable, as may now be the case among the developed countries. Throughout most recorded history, it was conceivable that almost

18 Robert Jervis, "Security Regimes," *International Organization* 36 (Spring 1982): 357–58; idem, "From Balance to Concert," in Oye, ed., *Cooperation under Anarchy*, 58–79.
19 For an interesting analysis see Paul Schroeder, *The Transformation of European Politics, 1787–1848* (forthcoming).

any two states that had significant dealings with one another might come to blows. Karl Deutsch and his colleagues, however, noted the formation of what they called "pluralistic security communities,"[20] groupings of states that did not worry about fighting each other. Such a grouping may coalesce into a single country, a process perhaps under way in Europe today. But sometimes the units maintain their separate identities. The latter case is of concern here and needs much more attention. Of course, we have studies of relations among allies, books on the close relations between countries over extended periods of time (especially the Anglo-American relationship), and theoretically informed analyses of postwar relations among the developed states.[21] While useful, all of these are within the setting of the possibility of war between some of these states and others who lurk off stage. Indeed, in previous cases the danger of war with an outside power was a large part of the explanation for why war among other states was unthinkable.

But even if the past does not provide perfect analogies, we need to learn much more about how international politics is carried out when war is not available as the final arbiter of disputes. Conflicts and rivalries will not disappear; no world government is likely to arise to deal with them. States will need new approaches to conceptualize their interests, new tactics to further them, and unfamiliar mechanisms and processes to reconcile them with those of others. Frictions and disputes are likely to be considerable; indeed, the common expectation that they will not lead to fighting will remove some restraints on national vituperation. Conflict without war is, of course, a staple of alliance politics, but when it characterizes relations among all of the most powerful states in the system the shift from traditional international politics will be considerable. International politics will remain a self-help system, but many of the familiar patterns will be altered once armed conflict is not seen as a real possibility.

American values and traditions constitute the third area in which historical research could illuminate the future. If my analysis is

---

20 Karl Deutsch et al., *Political Community and the North Atlantic Area* (Princeton, 1957).
21 The main study in the last-named category is Robert Keohane and Joseph Nye, Jr., *Power and Interdependence* (Boston, 1977).

correct, the United States faces no compelling security challenges that need dominate its policy. During the Cold War, most Americans believed that the Soviet Union was a menace requiring some variant of containment,[22] and attitudes toward that country provided a clear axis of orientation for American policy. Now, however, the international environment is no longer a compelling one; there is much more room for freedom of choice. The United States could follow a path that minimizes its foreign military and political involvement. If it chooses to adopt an activist foreign policy, there are multiple values it could pursue: maintaining an "open" economic system of free trade; promoting human rights abroad; sponsoring and supporting democracies; minimizing the spread of nuclear weapons; developing a concert or even a collective security system. But not all of these goals can be pursued at once: There are conflicts among them and painful trade-offs will be necessary.

The Cold War submerged questions about the values the United States should seek. Neither the political nor the intellectual community is now well equipped to deal with them. Historical research could be of assistance by reexamining previous eras to study the choices that were made, the values that were sought, and the traditions that were developed. Changes in national moods or styles are particularly instructive,[23] because any effective policy will require public as well as elite support. While the population and domestic politics of the United States are of course very different from what they have been in the past, some characteristics of social structure, ethnicity, and outlook remain.[24] There are traditions in American foreign policy that may shed light on how the United States will—and perhaps should—behave in the future.

The gravamen of my comments is that the approach of classical realism will not be an adequate guide for the future of international politics or American foreign policy. Realist thought and practice depend on the possibility, if not the threat or actuality, of

22 For an analysis of American foreign policy in terms of two kinds of containment policies see John Lewis Gaddis, *Strategies of Containment* (New York, 1982).
23 See, for example, Robert Dallek, *The American Style of Foreign Policy* (New York, 1983).
24 Still very valuable is Louis Hartz, *The Liberal Tradition in America* (New York, 1955).

war. If it recedes far into the background among the developed countries, much new thinking will be required. Furthermore, realism never said a great deal about the role of domestic politics, a factor that was seen as an unhelpful complication in a world that was dangerous enough to suppress most domestically generated foolishness, at least over the long run. Of course, the foreign policies of many states were deeply marked by domestic politics during the Cold War, but with the decreased foreign threat, domestic impulses are likely to guide the fundamental choices states make.

In the Third World (to overgeneralize), mass movements, ideologies, ethnic loyalties, and religious beliefs are likely to play a larger role than realism accords to them. If the long-run consequences of the Gulf war turn out to be unfortunate from the American perspective, it will be for reasons that play little role in realism: the acceleration of anti-American and anti-Western feeling among mass opinion in the Middle East and perhaps throughout the Third World; domestic instability and the overthrow of moderate, pro-Western regimes; and increasing regional and North-South conflict. The United States intended Third World countries to be reassured by the Gulf war, to infer that America would come to their assistance were they to be victims of aggression. But it is not out of the question that instead the sight of white Christians destroying a Moslem Third World country will generate in other poor, nonwhite countries the feeling that non-Western lives are cheap (to the West, that is), that indigenous values and ways of life cannot thrive in a world dominated by the West, and that governments that cooperate with the imperialists are wicked. Obviously, no one can tell whether this will occur, although the expectation of such a reaction was a main reason why many Americans sought a negotiated resolution to the conflict. But what is important in this context is that these effects deal with mass opinion, not elites; religious and ethnic identifications, not traditional national interests; feelings and emotions, not subtle calculations. This is not the stuff of realism.

With a good deal of realism now inappropriate as explanation and prescription, the relevance of historical episodes and aspects of the past has changed. What was unusual previously may be more useful for us than much of what was standard. But, of course, both the future and a reexamination of the past always brings surprises: We will never have a full or definitive understanding of international history and, even if we did, it would not provide a sure guide to the future.

Selective Bibliography

Because the authors in this volume wrote general essays rather than scholarly articles, their contributions contain only occasional references to the literature on the Cold War. The essay that follows seeks to supplement those references for the benefit of the reader. It is by no means a definitive bibliography but rather a briefly annotated list of some of the best general studies of the Cold War, including key aspects of that struggle and different approaches to the topic.

There are innumerable surveys of the Cold War. For two excellent overviews that combine concise writing with a good synthesis of the current literature see Stephen E. Ambrose, *Rise to Globalism: American Foreign Policy since 1938*, 6th rev. ed. (New York: Penguin Books, 1991); and Walter LaFeber, *America, Russia, and the Cold War, 1945–1990*, 6th ed. (New York: McGraw-Hill, Inc., 1991). Other good general surveys include the early classic, Louis J. Halle, *The Cold War as History* (New York: HarperCollins Publishers, 1991); and Adam B. Ulam, *The Rivals: America and Russia since World War Two* (New York: Viking Press, 1971). Three more recent overviews are John Lewis Gaddis, *The Long Peace: Inquiries into the History of the Cold War* (New York: Oxford University Press, 1987); Ralph B. Levering, *The Cold War, 1945–1987*, 2d ed. (Arlington Heights: Harlan Davidson, 1988); and Linda R. Killen, *The Soviet Union and the United States: A New Look at the Cold War* (Boston: Twayne Publishers, 1989). For a good collection of essays dealing with economic policies during the Cold War see Peter J. Katzenstein, ed., *Between Power and Plenty: Foreign Economic Policies of Advanced Industrial States* (Madison: University of Wisconsin Press, 1978). On the last years of the Cold War see Raymond L. Garthoff, *Détente and Confrontation: American-Soviet Relations from Nixon to Reagan* (Washington: Brookings Institution, 1985). For two volumes that place the Cold War in the context of the larger international events since 1945

269

see Geir Lundestad, *East, West, North, South: Major Developments in International Politics, 1945–1986* (New York: Oxford University Press, 1986); and Peter Calvocoressi, *World Politics since 1945*, 6th ed. (London: Longman, 1991).

Historians have devised several new ways to conceptualize American foreign policy in the Cold War. In *Strategies of Containment: A Critical Appraisal of Postwar American National Security Policy* (New York: Oxford University Press, 1982), John Lewis Gaddis provides a "post-revisionist" model for understanding the different containment policies of successive American administrations. Melvyn P. Leffler provides a similar though more critical analysis in his recent book, *A Preponderance of Power: National Security, the Truman Administration, and the Cold War* (Stanford: Stanford University Press, 1992). Thomas J. McCormick, *America's Half-Century: United States Foreign Policy in the Cold War* (Baltimore: Johns Hopkins University Press, 1989), attempts to place American Cold War foreign policy within the framework of a larger world system. For the new corporatist approach to the study of Cold War foreign policy see Michael J. Hogan, *The Marshall Plan: America, Britain, and the Reconstruction of Western Europe, 1947–1952* (New York: Cambridge University Press, 1987), a detailed history of the Truman administration's geo-economic policy and the domestic context from which it emerged.

For surveys that focus on the Soviet side of the Cold War see Adam B. Ulam, *Expansion and Coexistence: Soviet Foreign Policy, 1917–1973*, 2d ed. (New York: Holt, Rinehart and Winston, 1974), which is still one of the best single volumes on Soviet policy. Ulam's early volume is complemented by his *Dangerous Relations: The Soviet Union and World Politics, 1970–1982* (New York: Oxford University Press, 1984), which covers Soviet policy to the end of the Brezhnev era. Another useful overview is Joseph L. Nogee and Robert H. Donaldson, *Soviet Foreign Policy since World War II* (New York: Pergamon Press, 1984). Michael MccGwire, *Perestroika and Soviet National Security* (Washington: Brookings Institution, 1991), analyzes the origins of the dramatic changes in Soviet policy initiated by Mikhail Gorbachev, especially the substantial reevaluation of Soviet national security policy and nuclear strategy. For additional accounts of the changes and reforms engineered in the last days of the Soviet Union see especially Ed A. Hewett and Victor H. Winston, eds., *Milestones in Glasnost and Perestroyka: Politics and People* (Washington: Brookings Institution, 1991); Ed A. Hewett and Victor H. Winston, eds., *Milestones in Glasnost and Perestroyka: The Economy* (Washington: Brookings Institution, 1991); and Geoffrey Hosking, *The*

Awakening of the Soviet Union (Cambridge: Harvard University Press, 1991).

For the origins of the Cold War the most concise general survey is Thomas G. Paterson, *On Every Front: The Making of the Cold War* (New York: Norton, 1979). John Lewis Gaddis, *The United States and the Origins of the Cold War, 1941–1947* (New York: Columbia University Press, 1972), offers a more detailed study of the events that precipitated the Cold War, as do new studies by Randall Woods and Howard Jones, *Dawning of the Cold War: The United States' Quest for Order* (Athens: University of Georgia Press, 1991); and Leffler, *A Preponderance of Power*. Daniel Yergin, *Shattered Peace: The Origins of the Cold War and the National Security State* (Boston: Houghton-Mifflin Company, 1978), is an extremely readable study of the men and ideas behind the Cold War. Fraser J. Harbutt, *The Iron Curtain: Churchill, America, and the Origins of the Cold War* (New York: Oxford University Press, 1986), gives a glimpse of the British role in the outbreak of the Cold War. Joyce and Gabriel Kolko, *The Limits of Power: The World and United States Foreign Policy, 1945–1954* (New York: Harper and Row, 1972), is a classic study of the origins of the Cold War from a New Left perspective. A far more conservative view can be found in Vojtech Mastny, *Russia's Road to the Cold War: Diplomacy, Warfare, and Politics of Communism, 1941–1945* (New York: Columbia University Press, 1979). William Taubman, *Stalin's American Policy: From Entente to Détente to Cold War* (New York: Norton, 1982), is one of the best available studies of the Soviet role in the coming of the Cold War.

For general studies of the policymakers who shaped the Cold War see Richard J. Barnet, *The Roots of War: The Men and Institutions behind U.S. Foreign Policy* (New York: Penguin Books, 1973); Lloyd C. Gardner, *Architects of Illusion: Men and Ideas in American Foreign Policy, 1941–1949* (Chicago: Quadrangle, 1970); and Richard K. Betts, *Soldiers, Statesmen, and Cold War Crises* (Cambridge: Harvard University Press, 1977). More recent and extensive is Walter Isaacson and Evan Thomas, *The Wise Men: Six Friends and the World They Made: Acheson, Bohlen, Harriman, Kennan, Lovett, McCloy* (New York: Simon and Schuster, 1988). For an interesting study of how policymakers have used history in making their decisions see Richard E. Neustadt and Ernest R. May, *Thinking in Time: The Uses of History for Decision-Makers* (New York: Free Press, 1988). Michael G. Fry has edited a volume of essays that also examines the way policymakers in both the White House and the Kremlin have used history. See *History: The White House and the Kremlin* (London: Pinter Publishers, 1991). For an interesting study of the impact of the Cold War on America's institutions and values see Rhodri Jeffreys-Jones, *The CIA & American Democracy* (New Haven: Yale University Press, 1989).

There are several excellent general studies of the various American administrations during the Cold War. A first-rate overview is Thomas G. Paterson, *Meeting the Communist Threat: Truman to Reagan* (New York: Oxford University Press, 1988). Useful surveys of the foreign policy of the Truman administration include William E. Pemberton, *Harry S. Truman: Fair Dealer and Cold Warrior* (Boston: Twayne Publishers, 1989); Robert J. Donovan, *The Tumultuous Years: The Presidency of Harry S. Truman, 1949–1953* (New York: Norton, 1982); and Robert James Maddox, *From War to Cold War: The Education of Harry S. Truman* (Boulder: Westview Press, 1988). For the Eisenhower administration three readable surveys are Stephen E. Ambrose, *Eisenhower*, vol. 2, *The President* (Norwalk: Eastern Press, 1987); Robert A. Divine, *Eisenhower and the Cold War* (New York: Oxford University Press, 1981); and H. W. Brands, Jr., *Cold Warriors: Eisenhower's Generation and American Foreign Policy* (New York: Columbia University Press, 1988). For essays that reassess Eisenhower's legacy see Richard A. Melanson and David Mayers, eds., *Reevaluating Eisenhower: American Foreign Policy in the 1950s* (Urbana: University of Illinois Press, 1987).

The literature is less developed on foreign policy during the Kennedy through Reagan administrations. A good place to begin is Thomas G. Paterson, ed., *Kennedy's Quest for Victory: American Foreign Policy, 1961–1963* (New York: Oxford University Press, 1989). Also on the Kennedy years see Richard J. Walton, *Cold War and Counterrevolution: The Foreign Policy of John F. Kennedy* (New York: Viking Press, 1972). Warren I. Cohen, *Dean Rusk* (Totowa: Cooper Square Publishers, 1980), bridges the Kennedy and Johnson years. For more on Johnson's foreign policy see Robert A. Divine, ed., *The Johnson Years*, vol. 1 (Lawrence: University Press of Kansas, 1986). George C. Herring, *America's Longest War: The United States and Vietnam, 1950–1975* (New York: Knopf, 1986), is the most concise and popular overview of the Vietnam years. For the Nixon-Kissinger years four books stand out: Seymour M. Hersh, *The Price of Power: Kissinger in the Nixon White House* (New York: Summit Books, 1983); Richard C. Thornton, *The Nixon-Kissinger Years: Reshaping America's Foreign Policy* (New York: Paragon Press, 1989); Tad Szulc, *The Illusion of Peace: Foreign Policy in the Nixon Years* (New York: Viking Press, 1978); and Robert D. Schulzinger, *Henry Kissinger: Doctor of Diplomacy* (New York: Columbia University Press, 1989). Gaddis Smith, *Morality, Reason, and Power: American Diplomacy in the*

Carter Years (New York: Hill and Wang, 1986), is a good overview of the Carter years. Also useful is Richard C. Thornton, *The Carter Years: Toward a New Global Order* (New York: Paragon House, 1991). Garthoff, *Détente and Confrontation,* is an excellent survey of U.S. policy in the 1970s and 1980s.

There are several good studies on nuclear strategy and the arms race. Among them are Gregg Herken, *The Winning Weapon: The Atomic Bomb and the Cold War, 1945–1950* (New York: Knopf, 1980); and Robert Jervis, *The Meaning of the Nuclear Revolution: Statecraft and the Prospect of Armageddon* (Ithaca: Cornell University Press, 1989). McGeorge Bundy, *Danger and Survival: Choices about the Bomb in the First Fifty Years* (New York: Vintage Books, 1990), is a massive but very readable study. Lawrence Freedman, *The Evolution of Nuclear Strategy,* 2d ed. (New York: St. Martin's Press, 1989), is an excellent history of American strategic thought and policy. Strobe Talbott, *Deadly Gambits. The Reagan Administration and the Stalemate in Nuclear Arms Control* (New York: Vintage Books, 1984), is a journalistic account of the arms negotiations of the Reagan years. Fred M. Kaplan, *The Wizards of Armageddon* (New York: Simon and Schuster, 1984), looks at the strategists behind the policymakers. Ronald Powaski, *March to Armageddon: The United States and the Nuclear Arms Race, 1939 to the Present* (New York: Oxford University Press, 1987), is another useful history of the arms race, while Walter A. McDougall, *The Heavens and the Earth: A Political History of the Space Age* (Norwalk: Eastern Press, 1991), is a prize-winning study of U.S. space policy.

There are a number of good regional studies that address the events of the Cold War in various parts of the world. For Europe see Anton W. DePorte, *Europe between the Superpowers: The Enduring Balance,* 2d ed. (New Haven: Yale University Press, 1986); and John W. Young, *The Cold War in Europe, 1945–1989: A Political History* (London: E. Arnold, 1991). Richard J. Barnet, *Intervention and Revolution: The United States in the Third World* (London: Paladin, 1972); and Gabriel Kolko, *Confronting the Third World. United States Foreign Policy, 1945–1980* (New York: Pantheon Books, 1988), are critical overviews of U.S. policy toward the Third World. Useful surveys of the Cold War in Asia include Akira Iriye, *The Cold War in Asia* (Englewood Cliffs: Prentice-Hall, 1974); and Russell D. Buhite, *Soviet-American Relations in Asia, 1945–1954* (Norman: University Press of America, 1989). Studies with a particular focus on East Asia include Robert M. Blum, *Drawing the Line: The Origins of American Containment Policy in East Asia* (New York: Norton, 1982); William W. Stueck, Jr., *The Road to Confrontation: American Policy toward China and Korea, 1947–1950* (Chapel Hill: University of North Carolina Press, 1981); and Gary R. Hess, *The United States' Emergence as a Southeast Asian Power, 1940–1950* (New York: Columbia University Press, 1987). Along with George Herring's book mentioned earlier, Neil Sheehan, *A Bright Shining Lie: John Paul Vann and America in Vietnam* (New York: Vintage Books, 1989), is a superb study of the Vietnam War.

The Cold War in the Middle East has generated a number of good books, including Seth P. Tillman, *The United States in the Middle East: Interests and Obstacles* (Bloomington: Indiana University Press, 1982); William Stivers, *America's Confrontation with Revolutionary Change in the Middle East, 1948–1983* (Hound Mills: Macmillan Press, 1986); and Bruce R. Kuniholm, *The Origins of the Cold War in the Near East: Great Power Conflict and Diplomacy in Iran, Turkey, and Greece* (Princeton: Princeton University Press, 1980). Thomas J. Noer, *Cold War and Black Liberation: The United States and White Rule in Africa, 1948–1968* (Columbia: University of Missouri Press, 1985), deals with U.S. policy toward Sub-Saharan Africa. Three of the best overviews of U.S. policy toward Latin America during the Cold War are Walter LaFeber, *Inevitable Revolutions: The United States and Central America* (New York: Norton, 1984); Stephen G. Rabe, *Eisenhower and Latin America: The Foreign Policy of Anti-Communism* (Chapel Hill: University of North Carolina Press, 1988); and Thomas M. Leonard, *Central America and the United States: The Search for Stability* (Athens: University of Georgia Press, 1991).

The fall of the Berlin Wall in 1989 and the ensuing revolutions in Eastern Europe and the Soviet Union clearly marked the passing of the Cold War. Books discussing the implications of the end of the Cold War are just beginning to appear and the selection is rather limited. Among the best studies published so far are John Lewis Gaddis, *The United States and the End of the Cold War: Implications, Reconsiderations, Provocations* (New York: Oxford University Press, 1992); and the collection of essays edited by Nicholas X. Rizopoulos, *Sea-Changes: American Foreign Policy in a World Transformed* (New York: Council on Foreign Relations Press, 1990). Two other collections are Robert Jervis and Seweryn Bialer, eds., *Soviet-American Relations after the Cold War* (Durham: Duke University Press, 1991); and David Armstrong and Erik Goldstein, eds., *The End of the Cold War* (London: Cass, 1990). For an analysis of the events of the 1980s that led to the end of the Cold War see Thomas W. Simons, Jr., *The End of the Cold War?* (New York: St. Martin's Press, 1990). John E. Mueller, *Retreat from Doomsday: The*

Obsolescence of Major War (New York: Basic Books, 1990), is also interesting. There are several studies that debate the cost of the Cold War to the United States. Among the best are Paul M. Kennedy, *The Rise and Fall of the Great Powers: Economic Change and Military Conflict from 1500 to 2000* (New York: Random House, 1987); David P. Calleo, *Beyond American Hegemony: The Future of the Western Alliance* (New York: Basic Books, 1987); and Joseph S. Nye, *Bound to Lead: The Changing Nature of American Power* (New York: Basic Books, 1991). For the end of the Cold War in Europe see Lawrence Freedman, ed., *Europe Transformed: Documents on the End of the Cold War* (New York: St. Martin's Press, 1990); and Bogdan Denitch, *The End of the Cold War: European Unity, Socialism, and the Shift in Global Power* (Minneapolis: University of Minnesota Press, 1990). Also worth perusing is Stuart Harris and James Cotton, eds., *The End of the Cold War in Northeast Asia* (Melbourne: Longman Cheshire, 1991).

Several journals have published roundtables and articles discussing the end of the Cold War. See the Winter and Spring 1992 issues of *Diplomatic History;* the November 1990 issue of *Diplomacy and Statecraft;* the Summer 1990 and Spring 1991 issues of *World Policy Journal;* the January–March 1991 issue of *The Political Quarterly;* and the Spring, Winter, and Summer 1991 issues of *The Washington Quarterly.*

Index